George Julian Harney
THE CHARTISTS WERE RIGHT

The Chartists Studies Series from The Merlin Press
Series Editor: Owen R. Ashton

EDITED BY
DAVID GOODWAY

George Julian Harney
THE CHARTISTS WERE RIGHT
Selections from the
Newcastle Weekly Chronicle, 1890-97

MERLIN PRESS

First published in 2014 by
The Merlin Press Ltd
99B Wallis Road
London
E9 5LN

www.merlinpress.co.uk

Reprinted in paperback 2015

Chartist Studies Series No. 12

© Introduction and notes, David Goodway, 2014

ISBN. 978-0-85036-717-1

Printed by Lightning Source

CONTENTS

SOME AUTOBIOGRAPHICAL FRAGMENTS

For

Catherine, the step-great-granddaughter of George Julian Harney

INTRODUCTION

Other than among students of Chartism the name of George Julian Harney is little recognised and there is even less appreciation of his achievements and political and intellectual stature. He is best known as the youngest member of the first Chartist Convention, admirer of the most radical figures of the French Revolution, and the advocate, in 1838-9, of extreme, physical-force Chartism. His interest to historians has tended to be as the leader, with Ernest Jones, of the Chartist left in the early 1850s, the friend of Marx and Engels, and the publisher of the first English translation of the *Communist Manifesto* in 1850. What tends, however, to be overlooked is his finest period, 1843-50, when he worked on the *Northern Star*: for five years he was an outstanding editor of a great newspaper. Almost everyone will be astonished to discover not only did he live until as late as 1897, but also that during the 1890s he was producing each week a vigorously polymathic, superbly written and politically challenging column for the *Newcastle Weekly Chronicle*, edited by W.E. Adams, another old Chartist and his younger admirer. It is a small selection of these columns that has been chosen to form this book, Harney's first.

***

George Julian Harney was a thoroughgoing Londoner. He was born on the Thames on a troop ship lying off Deptford, the son of George Harney (1784-1850), a man-of-war's man, on 17 February 1817. Of his mother nothing is known, not even her name. There were at least two other sons, one of whom was to drown in 1849. Brought up in poverty, Harney was educated at dame schools and by his own reading. He entered the Royal Naval School at Greenwich in 1828 to train as a merchant seaman; but the ill-health that dogged him throughout his life – he suffered from congenital quinsy and impaired hearing – kept him in the infirmary for much of the time and, after six months as a cabin-boy on voyages to Brazil and Lisbon, in 1831 he quit. His ambition was to become a compositor, but he had to settle for working as a London potboy.

He was to maintain that he had become a radical on the day of Queen

Caroline's funeral in August 1821. He was certainly among the crowd who attended in 1832 another funeral, that of Thomas Hardy, secretary of the London Corresponding Society in the 1790s; and it was through contact with an unidentified shoemaker that he joined the National Union of the Working Classes (NUWC) early in 1833 and got employed as shopboy by Henry Hetherington, then publishing the *Poor Man's Guardian* and spearheading the campaign against the newspaper tax, the 'War of the Unstamped'. Harney's education in what he was to describe as the 'radical school of the 'thirties' had begun.[1] It was he who, after seizure of Richard Carlile's stock for non-payment of church rates in October 1834, placed figures of a bishop and the devil in the shop window. As a vendor of the unstamped he served, during 1834-5, two short sentences in London prisons, Coldbath Fields and the Borough Compter, between the two becoming a NUWC class leader in Bermondsey. On his second release he was sent by B.D. Cousins to replace an imprisoned vendor in Derby and this assignment was to earn him in 1836 his longest term, 'a rough six months' in Derby Gaol.[2]

His major intellectual influence – his 'guide, philosopher, and friend'[3] – was the brilliant Irish social thinker, Bronterre O'Brien, editor of the *Poor Man's Guardian*, student of the French Revolution and shortly to become the 'Schoolmaster of Chartism'; yet whereas O'Brien was drawn to Robespierre Harney came to identify with Marat, frequently signing himself, throughout the Chartist years, as 'L'Ami du Peuple' or 'A Friend of the People'. Harney also learned from the group of old Spenceans in London, with some of whom, previously members of the now defunct NUWC, he was involved in forming in January 1836 a Paineite club, the East London Democratic Association. In August 1838 this was reorganised as simply the London Democratic Association (LDA) after the ultra-radicals had resigned from the London Working Men's Association (LWMA), following the rumpus occasioned by the revelation of Daniel O'Connell's hostility to trade unions.

The LDA's opposition resulted in its being entirely sidelined by the LWMA when the eight London delegates to the Chartist Convention were elected in September 1838; and Harney had to sit for Norwich, Derby and Newcastle. It was his opinion that 'as the Gallic Convention of 1793 required a jacobin club to look after it, so will the British Convention of 1839 require the watchful support of the Democratic Association';[4] but all efforts to

1 *Northern Star*, 22 December 1849, cited by A.R. Schoyen, *The Chartist Challenge: A Portrait of George Julian Harney* (London: Heinemann, 1958), p. 6.
2 *Westminster Gazette*, 17 August 1896.
3 *Operative*, 11 November 1838, cited by Schoyen, p. 12.
4 *Operative*, 9 December 1838.

swing the Convention behind physical force and immediate preparations to take power failed – whether by passing resolutions at open meetings, or by seeking to elect additional extremist delegates or to arouse the apathetic capital – and earned him censure within the Convention, hisses and groans outside, and the reputation among moral-force Chartists such as William Lovett and many twentieth-century historians as a mindless hothead. Not only did he wear the cap of liberty at public meetings, he also, notoriously, brandished a dagger.

In April-May 1839 Harney gained his first journalistic experience by co-editing a shrill weekly, the *London Democrat*. Of greatest significance among his activities of 1838-9, though, were his extensive travels outside the capital, especially in the north of England, during which this still very young man, recognised as one of the foremost spokesmen of physical-force Chartism, was enthusiastically received by the new movement's rank-and-file and permanently admitted to their hearts – something to be well attested by his *Newcastle Weekly Chronicle* readers.

In May 1839, shortly after the Convention had moved to Birmingham, a warrant was issued for his arrest for a seditious speech there, but he had already left for his power base on Tyneside and was apprehended in Bedlington in July. After several days in Warwick Gaol, he was bound over to the summer assizes and released on bail. Eventually, in April 1840, the case was dropped since his speech and those of two others had not been properly witnessed. Equally paradoxically, Harney failed to be implicated – indeed does not appear to have been involved in – the conspiratorial plans culminating in and following the Newport Rising of November 1839. While he continued to advocate physical force, he was, as he admitted at a Glasgow meeting in January, 'much wiser in the year 1840 than he had been at the commencement of 1839'.[5]

He first toured Scotland from 30 December 1839, coming back to England for his trial. After his acquittal he spent almost a year north of the border, travelling over two thousand miles and addressing hundreds of meetings, living on the collections taken and the sums paid by the *Northern Star* for his reports – and once again making numerous Chartist friends. In autumn 1840 he married Mary Cameron of Mauchline, Ayrshire, the daughter of a radical handloom weaver – Adam Cameron had been arrested in 1819 – and herself 'tall, beautiful, and of high spirit'.[6] It was a meeting of minds and an

---

5 *Scottish Patriot*, II, p. 73, cited by Schoyen, p. 97.
6 George Jacob Holyoake, *Sixty Years of an Agitator's Life* (1892; London: T. Fisher Unwin, 1906 edn), I, p. 106.

immensely happy union – she was 'a perfect wife of an agitator'[7] – although there were to be no children; and throughout his life Harney kept going back to Mauchline (the small town also had important associations with Robert Burns, whose poetry he greatly admired).

He returned to England in April 1841 and his position as a front-rank leader was confirmed by his appointment in August, after a visit to the imprisoned Feargus O'Connor, as the *Northern Star*'s correspondent for the major Chartist centre of Sheffield and, in effect, as full-time organiser for the city and its region. He was not a member of the Chartist Convention of 1842; but he did attend the conference of the Chartist Executive and delegates from the Manchester and West Riding that met in Manchester on 17 August, the anniversary of Peterloo, to unveil a statue to Henry 'Orator' Hunt and discuss organisational matters, and found himself in the midst of a great general strike movement. Harney caused a sensation when, in opposition to Thomas Cooper and Dr Peter Murray M'Douall, he supported the Rev William Hill's denunciation of the strike. Back in Sheffield he continued to speak out against strike action, yet in October he was arrested and charged with riot and conspiracy for his part in the Manchester conference. Standing trial at Lancaster in March and leading a collective defence with great ability, he was convicted on one count with 14 others, including O'Connor, but on appeal two months later the verdict was overturned.

When in July 1843 O'Connor dismissed Hill as editor of the *Northern Star*, replacing him with its printer and publisher, Joshua Hobson, Harney moved to Leeds to become sub-editor. Hobson increasingly allowed Harney a free hand and he was in practice editor well before his formal appointment as such in October 1845. These years, until 1850, were Harney's most influential. Throughout the 1840s Chartism cohered around the *Northern Star*, and under his editorship its unrivalled coverage of domestic working-class affairs was supplemented by an authoritative presentation of international radicalism and revolutionary movements, together with pronounced emphasis on literature. Harney himself was a bibliophile and voracious reader, particularly of poetry, above all Byron's. Although O'Connor was the *Northern Star*'s proprietor, he initially allowed complete editorial independence, Harney explaining in 1846: 'I must do O'C. the justice to say that he never interferes with what I write in the paper nor does he know what I write until he sees the paper'.[8]

7 Letter from George Jacob Holyoake, *Newcastle Weekly Chronicle* (hereafter *NWC*), 25 December 1897.
8 Frank Gees Black and Renee Métivier Black (eds), *The Harney Papers* (Assen: Van Gorcum, 1969), p. 241.

In the autumn of 1843 Friedrich Engels had visited Leeds, at the instance of the Manchester Chartist James Leach, to meet Harney at the office of the *Northern Star*. Harney and Engels became lifelong friends, Engels a writer for Harney's journals, and Harney, for the remainder of the 1840s, Marx and Engels's principal British contact (Harney and Marx first met as early as November 1847 in London). As Engels was to recall in 'On the History of the Communist League': 'We kept in touch with the revolutionary section of the English Chartists through Julian Harney, the editor of the movement's central organ, the *Northern Star*, to which I was a contributor'.[9] Engels considered that Harney should elbow the retrogressive O'Connor out of the Chartist leadership. We only possess Harney's reply, in an important letter of 1846, in which he not only indicates Engels's opinion of him but stresses O'Connor's considerable virtues, demonstrates his own powers of analysis and provides a revealing self-assessment:

I must next notice what you say about my '*leadership*'....You have thought proper in the letter I am now commenting on to credit me with all the revolutionary virtues. You say I am 'international', 'revolutionary', 'energetical', 'proletarian', 'more of a Frenchman than an Englishman', 'Atheistical, Republican and Communist'. I am too old a soldier to blush at this accumulation of virtues credited to my account, but supposing it to be even as you say, it does not follow that I am qualified for 'leadership'. A popular chief should be possessed of magnificent bodily appearance, an iron frame, eloquence, or at least a ready fluency of tongue. I have none of these. O'C. has them all – at least in degree. A popular leader should possess great animal courage, contempt of pain and death, and be not altogether ignorant of arms and military science. No chief or leader that has hitherto appeared in the English movement has these qualifications. We have never had a *Barbès*, for instance. In these qualifications I am decidedly deficient. I know nothing of arms, have no stomach for fighting, and would rather die after some other fashion than by bullet or rope. From a knowledge of myself and all the men who do live and figure in the Chartist movement, I am convinced that even in this respect, was O'C. thrown overboard, we might go further and fare worse.

Harney commented astutely that 'the very qualities you give me the credit of possessing, and which you emphatically sum up in the sentence, "You

9 Karl Marx and Frederick Engels, *Collected Works* (London: Lawrence & Wishart, 50 vols, 1975-2004), XXVI, p. 319.

are the *only* Englishman who is really free of *all* prejudices that distinguish the Englishman from the Continental man", are sufficient of themselves to prevent my being a leader': 'If I am "the *only* Englishman, &c", it follows that I would be a chief without an army, a leader without followers'.[10] Harney, a Londoner and indeed a proletarian, was then insufficiently English in outlook, whereas O'Connor, who belonged to the Irish gentry, exerted a mesmeric appeal on the English working class, many of whom were, of course, either Irish-born or of Irish origin.

Harney told Engels: 'To myself my proper position appears clear; I am a 'pioneer', the teacher of 'strange doctrines', the proclaimer of principles which startle the many, and are but timidly acknowledged even by the few; and the office of the pioneer is surely useful, and as surely not inglorious … I am but one of the humble workers in the great movement of progress, as such I desire to be considered'.[11] The 'strange doctrines' and 'principles' he proclaimed, Harney had confided two years previously to George Jacob Holyoake, a close friend from Sheffield days:[12]

The fact is that Owenism is by. It strikes me that we shall yet see a new party in this country combining the good of Socialism and Chartism. The latter *ism* cannot stay where it is, it must advance. Here is my idea of Chartism in the *Present* and the *Future*.

Political

Present	*Future*
The 6 Points	*Republicanism* including the 6 Points

Social

Present	*Future*
Protection to Labour Fair Days wage for Fair days work	*Communism* – Destruction of Landlordism and Profitism

---

10 Letter from Harney to Engels, 30 March 1846, in Black and Black, pp. 240-42.
11 *Ibid*, p. 242.
12 Letter from Harney to Holyoake, 22 April 1844, printed in Edward Royle (ed), *The Infidel Tradition: from Paine to Bradlaugh* (London and Basingstoke: Macmillan, 1976), p. 161.

(Anti) Theocratical

Present	*Future*
Anti-Church Statism	War with all Priesthoods
	and Priestcrafts

The *Northern Star* had been moved from Leeds to London in 1844 and Harney proceeded to build up during 1845-6 the Fraternal Democrats, a London society (but with country members) of Chartists and European exiles, principally French, German and Polish, and an obvious precursor to the First International of 1864. His new revolutionary internationalism exercised a much broader appeal, attracting key Chartist militants (for example Philip M'Grath, President of the National Charter Association, and the new recruit Ernest Jones), than had the sterile Jacobinism of 1838-9. The new tendency reached a wider public in the expression of support for Poland following the insurrection of 1846. The Fraternal Democrats and London Chartists together convened a great meeting in March, with even O'Connor speaking, and at which the Democratic Committee for Poland's Regeneration, in effect a sub-committee of the Fraternal Democrats, was launched.[13]

Harney's concern with foreign affairs led him, incensed by British intervention in Portugal, to contest Tiverton, Palmerston's seat, in the general election of 1847. It was his position that: 'The people are beginning to realise that foreign as well as domestic questions do affect them, that a blow struck at liberty on the Tagus is an injury to the friends of freedom on the Thames'.[14] On the hustings he dissected in a two-hour speech the policy of the Foreign Secretary; and Palmerston responded, in a manner 'fit for the explanation of a minister to his sovereign', with what was judged the 'most lengthy and plain-spoken account of his stewardship ever given to the British public'.[15] On a show of hands the crowd of 3,000 overwhelmingly defeated Palmerston, but since few if any would have been electors Harney declined to go to the poll. Under a democratic franchise it would have been Harney, not Palmerston, at the Foreign Office.

In March 1848, following the successful revolution the previous month in France, Harney, M'Grath and Jones were appointed at 'the largest indoor meeting ever seen in London' to visit Paris to deliver a congratulatory

13 The minute-book of the Democratic Committee for Poland's Regeneration is in the editor's possession.
14 *Northern Star*, 9 June 1847.
15 Cited by Schoyen, p. 151.

address.[16] Back in England, Harney was elected delegate for Nottingham in the new National Convention; but otherwise, during the third and final upsurge of Chartism, nowhere stronger than in London, he maintained a low profile publicly. Despite his support for the National Assembly of May (and much improved organisation) he was not a member, faced with an ultimatum concerning the editorship of the *Northern Star* by O'Connor, who was unhappy with what he viewed as disproportionate coverage of the European revolutions. In addition, the events of 1848, both at home and abroad, convinced Harney that Chartism's advocacy of political democracy must now be supplemented by a social programme; and he was instrumental, with Ernest Jones after the latter's release from prison in July 1850, in moving the Chartist left to a socialist position. By April 1851 a Chartist Convention had adopted a ten point programme that included land nationalisation.

From June 1849 Harney edited his own *Democratic Review of British and Foreign Politics, Literature and History*, alongside the *Northern Star*, until the inevitable break with O'Connor came in May 1850. He worked out three months' notice, continuing to run the *Democratic Review* up to September; but he had immediately, from June, begun to publish the *Red Republican*, in which the *Communist Manifesto* was to appear in Helen Macfarlane's translation, the first in English: 'A frightful hobgoblin stalks throughout Europe. We are haunted by a ghost, the ghost of Communism'.[17]

Yet it was just at this point that relations between Harney and Marx and Engels deteriorated. Whereas in domestic politics Harney instinctively adhered (and in practice also until 1854) to the imperatives of an independent working-class politics, with respect to the European exiles he maintained a generously inclusive eclecticism, printing extensively in the *Democratic Review* and *Red Republican* (which became the *Friend of the People* in December 1850) contributions by Mazzini, Ledru-Rollin and Louis Blanc. At the very end of his life, learning of the death of Emmanuel Arago, son of the astronomer François Arago, who had been a leading figure during the Second French Republic, Harney recalled meeting him when an exile in London, commenting:

> ... he commands my respect as one of the noble band of 'Republicans of the eve' called into prominence by the bouleversement of 1848. It is the way of some of our 'progressive' people to stigmatise such men as

16 *Reynolds's Political Instructor*, 20 April 1850.
17 *Red Republican*, 9 November 1850. Further portions appeared on 16, 23 and 30 November.

'Bourgeois Revolutionists'. I stay not to enquire whether they were of the aristocratic [*sic*], bourgeoisie, or the proletariat. Enough for me that they were men of earnest convictions, which they maintained through every kind of adversity, including bonds, exile, and to death. Fifty years ago I believed in their sincerity, and I believe so still. Homage to their illustrious memories – from Lamennais to Schoelcher, from François to Emmanuel Arago![18]

This attitude infuriated Marx and Engels, who in their correspondence bitched about Mary Harney and designated her husband 'Citizen Hip Hip Hurrah', finally breaking contact in March 1851.

The breach, which lasted some years, contributed to the fratricidal rivalry that ballooned in 1851-2 between Harney and his former friend and assistant editor on the *Northern Star*, Ernest Jones. Jones became a devout disciple of Marx and rejected Harney's pragmatic approach towards trade unionism and the co-operative movement. The proposed launch of a new weekly newspaper jointly edited by the two men came to nothing, Jones going ahead with his own *Notes to the People* in May 1851. Harney was obliged to suspend the *Friend of the People* in July as the gravely diminished movement was unable to sustain two such similar journals. A second series was absorbed in the *Northern Star* when it was acquired by Harney in April 1852, but by the end of the year the resulting *Star of Freedom* had folded, succumbing to the relative success of Jones's *People's Paper*.

In the general election of July 1852 Harney was persuaded to go to the hustings at Bradford, but suffered the disgrace of coming last on the show of hands – the contrast between his intervention at Wakefield in the West Riding election of 1841 and, especially, at Tavistock in 1847 indicating that mass support for Chartism had evaporated. In January 1853 came his final effort with a Chartist publication, the weekly *Vanguard*; its failure after only seven issues coincided with his devastation at the death on 11 February of Mary Cameron Harney at the age of 35 from, it would appear, cancer.[19] In December he was obliged to relocate to Newcastle and compromise humiliatingly by assisting the middle-class Republican Joseph Cowen with

18 *NWC*, 5 December 1896. For a discussion of the *Democratic Review* and *Red Republican*, see Joan Allen, ' "The Teacher of Strange Doctrines": George Julian Harney and the *Democratic Review*', *Labour History Review*, LXXVIII (2013).

19 Harney was to commiserate in 1878 with Engels on his loss of Lizzie Burns, observing: 'You may remember that my first wife died of the same cruel disease...she lingered many years' (Black and Black, p. 283). Burns was afflicted with 'an aggressive tumour of the bladder', according to Engels's most recent biographer: Tristram Hunt, *The Frock-Coated Communist: The Revolutionary Life of Friedrich Engels* (London: Allen Lane, 2009), p. 270.

his *Northern Tribune* from January 1854 until its termination in March 1855.

Always an ardent, unremitting Russophobe, Harney hailed the outbreak of the Crimean War with enthusiasm; but, although he had considerable admiration for the deliriously Turcophile David Urquhart – 'a man of genius....for his hostility to Russia, for his valiant warfare against that perfidious and truculent Power, I honour him[20] – he and Cowen fought successfully to gain total (yet temporary) control of the local Urquhartite organisation, the Tyneside Foreign Affairs Committee. So it was that in October 1855, following the expulsion of Victor Hugo and other French political refugees from Jersey (to Guernsey and London), Harney was deputed by the Committee to investigate the situation and, aged 38, he left Britain and working-class politics.[21] Hugo's daughter Adèle, while complaining that Harney only spoke English, approved that '*sa figure expressive et intelligente qu'orne une longue barbe et ses manières vives sont toutes françaises*' ('his expressive and intelligent face which sets off a long beard and his lively ways are entirely French').[22] One of his recurrent severe illnesses then laid him low for several weeks and, on his recovery, he settled in the Channel Islands, having accepted the editorship of the twice-weekly *Jersey Independent*, which he was to use to campaign against feudal survivals. Here in 1859 he married the widow of a prosperous St Helier draper, Marie Métivier (née Le Sueur), who had been born in 1829 and whose family was sufficiently grand for her to have received piano lessons in Paris from Chopin. With his second marriage Harney acquired a six-year-old stepson, James Métivier, a strong bond developing between the two males.

In 1862 Harney was sacked by his proprietor for inflexible support of the Union in the American Civil War; and the following year he emigrated to the United States, his family joining him later. On Harney's departure from the Channel Islands Hugo, who had remained in Guernsey, presented him with a photographic portrait, inscribed '*A l'éloquent et vaillant écrivain Julian Harney*' ('To the eloquent and courageous writer Julian Harney').[23] In Boston he edited briefly his final newspaper, the abolitionist *Commonwealth*,

20 David Goodway, 'The Métivier Collection and the Books of George Julian Harney', *Bulletin of the Society for the Study of Labour History*, no. 49 (Autumn 1984), p. 58; and also Margaret Hambrick, *A Chartist's Library* (London and New York, 1986), pp. 247-8.
21 A poster advertising a Newcastle meeting for 12 November, protesting against the expulsions, is reproduced in Bernard Porter, *The Refugee Question in Mid-Victorian Politics* (Cambridge: Cambridge University Press, 1979), p. 166.
22 Frances Vernor Guille and Jean-Marc Hovasse (eds), *Le Journal d'Adèle Hugo*, IV (Paris and Caen: Lettres Moderne Minard, 2002), p. 412.
23 In the possession of Mrs Catherine Black Cohen.

after the departure of its founding editor, Moncure Conway, for England. The remainder of his working life was then spent in the Secretary's Office in the Massachusetts State House as clerk in charge of public documents (or librarian, as a well-informed obituary put it). On a photograph of 1884 he wrote a line from Byron's *The Prophecy of Dante*: 'They made an Exile, not a slave of me'.[24]

He did not forget Britain. While in Jersey he had been on the council of the Northern Reform Union. During his American years he was a member of both the Reform League and the First International, and visited his home country in 1878 and 1884-6. He also became a frequent contributor to the *Newcastle Weekly Chronicle*, owned by Joseph Cowen and edited from 1864 by Harney's disciple W.E. Adams, under whose direction it became a most impressive radical paper.[25] In 1876 he brought out a privately-printed pamphlet, his only free-standing publication, *The Anti-Turkish Crusade: A Review of a Recent Agitation, with Reflections on the Eastern Question*, in reply to Gladstone's *The Bulgarian Horrors and the Question of the East* of earlier in the year. While he had originally respected Gladstone, the implicit turn towards a pro-Russian foreign policy initiated what was to become a rancorous loathing of the 'Grand Old Mountebank', an antipathy amply sampled below together with his analysis of Victorian foreign affairs. Also, whereas Harney had in 1843 been the first English Chartist to join the Repeal Association in Sheffield, regarding Ireland as the 'Poland of the West', he came to oppose vehemently Irish Home Rule for various reasons, pre-eminently his rationalist antagonism towards Catholic 'priestcraft' and Gladstone's identification with the issue. It needs to be appreciated that old Chartists tended to be independently-minded individualists; and while Thomas Cooper became an enthusiastic Liberal, on the issue of Home Rule he too was a virulent rejectionist.[26]

Harney returned permanently to England in 1888 by himself, living initially in Enfield. 'Madame' Harney continued in Cambridge, Mass, where she ran a very successful language school, although visiting her husband most years. During the summer of 1890 he moved to 2 Clarence Villas, St

24 *Ibid.* The photograph is reproduced on the cover of this book.
25 For Adams, see W.E. Adams, *Memoirs of a Social Atom* (London: Hutchinson, 2 vols, 1903); Owen R. Ashton, *W.E. Adams: Chartist, Radical and Journalist (1832-1906): 'An Honour to the Fourth Estate'* (Whitley Bay: Bewick Press, 1991). Harney's articles on the States are discussed in Owen R. Ashton and Joan Hugman, 'Letters from America: George Julian Harney, Boston, USA, and Newcastle upon Tyne, 1863-1888', *Proceedings of the Massachusetts Historical Society*, CVII (1995).
26 See Stephen Roberts, *The Chartist Prisoners: The Radical Lives of Thomas Cooper (1805-1892) and Arthur O'Neill (1819-1896)* (Bern and Oxford: Peter Lang, 2008), pp. 151-2.

Mary's Grove, Richmond, Surrey. He was increasingly an arthritic cripple, confined to just one room, and it was there that the overwhelming bulk of his *Newcastle Weekly Chronicle* columns were written. The last surviving member of the 1839 Convention, nursed for five months by his wife, Harney died on 9 December 1897 and was buried in Richmond Cemetery, where his monument commemorates him as 'THE LAST OF THE CHARTIST LEADERS'.

***

Harney's first weekly column, most appropriately, given his longstanding concern with the country, on 'The Latest Russian Atrocity' appeared on 11 January 1890; his last, discussing Madame Blavatsky and Annie Besant and which had to be dictated, on 27 November 1897, a fortnight before his death. (Both are reprinted below.) In between, for almost eight years he had written an article each week – unless on holiday or too ill to do so – for the income, little as it was, was a necessity. The 336 columns run in total to around 850,000 words, only 70,000 of which have been selected for this volume.

His range was very considerable. His informed engagement with contemporary politics was unfailing. There are recollections of the radicalism of the third quarter of the nineteenth century. Yet he also wrote on history – of all periods and all nations – and literature, particularly poetry, his first love. His historical and literary columns are almost always book reviews. Although he despised fiction, there are also many reviews of novels, but usually of new editions of the eighteenth-century writers he admired, notably Defoe and Fielding. Under the heading of 'The Roll-Call' he wrote obituaries of deceased comrades, often little-known or unknown friends, but also the important Chartists, Thomas Cooper and Samuel Kydd, as well as Engels.[27] At the core of the sprawling piece on Cooper is a finely judged assessment, warm but critical. Charles Bradlaugh, although certainly a radical, was excluded from 'The Roll-Call' – 'his energies ... did not attract my sympathies' – but Harney did write a probing obituary (included here under 'Other Radical Personalities').

Of the Chartist leaders there are repeated affectionate references to Feargus O'Connor, William Lovett, John Frost, Dr John Taylor and Ernest Jones, as well as Cooper and Kydd. Also much esteemed are Richard Oastler and, markedly, the Rev Joseph Rayner Stephens.[28] Bronterre O'Brien, in contrast,

27 For Kydd, see Stephen Roberts, *Radical Politicians and Poets in Early Victorian Britain: The Voices of Six Chartist Leaders* (Lampeter: Edwin Mellen Press, 1993), chap. 6.
28 For these two mavericks see, especially, Cecil Driver, *Tory Radical: The Life of Richard Oastler* (New York: Oxford University Press, 1946), and also John A. Hargreaves and E.A.

is scarcely mentioned and this neglect cannot be unintentional. The reader is likely to learn much previously unknown: that the Chartists proposed that the House of Commons should be reduced to 300 members (a reform which continues, in the twenty-first century, to be much overdue); that all the members of the First Convention wore top hats, with the exception of the 'eccentric' Dr Taylor who sported a slouch hat; that none of the reports of the debates in the 1839 Convention are reliable, not even the *Northern Star*'s; that Harney published translations in the *Jersey Independent* by a local schoolmaster, later to become well-known as James Thomson (BV), author of *The City of Dreadful Night*; that at the time of Ernest Jones's death he and Harney were in amicable correspondence.

It has to be asked why none of these absorbing articles have previously been reprinted. Two explanations seem probable. First, in the course of a long column Harney characteristically slides between his various interests. This is definitely not the rambling of an old man, for he always returns to the main theme, deftly resuming his argument. And, his asides – or intermissions – should be seen, not as going off at a tangent, but as decorations or enrichments. So his reflections on Chartist imprisonment are buried in a review of a biography of Leigh Hunt, the Romantic poet and friend of Shelley and Byron. His account of entering Scotland on New Year's Eve 1839 as a Chartist propagandist is to be found within a masterly appreciation of Robert Burns. The editor finds all this exhilarating, but other readers may react very differently. The traditional partners of history and literature have long since been uncoupled and we are now living in an age of increasingly narrow specialism in which interests, let alone expertise, spanning disciplinary boundaries are becoming rare.

The second explanation will be more troubling, even decisive, for radical readers. The Jacobin of 1838-9, the friend of Engels in the 1840s, had by the 1890s – although still an intimate of the Marx-Engels circle – become a conservative and reactionary. Holyoake was to recall that on reading *The Anti-Turkish Crusade* he complained to Harney that

'it read like the production of a full-blown Tory'. He resented the imputation – when all the time it was true. He had cast off his Liberal garments, and was naked, and ashamed. Afterwards he cast off the shame.

Hilary Haigh (eds), *Slavery in Yorkshire: Richard Oastler and the Campaign against Child Labour in the Industrial Revolution* (Huddersfield: University of Huddersfield Press, 2012); as well as Michael S. Edwards, *Purge This Realm: A Life of Joseph Rayner Stephens* (London: Epworth Press, 1994).

Harney's admirable biographer, A.R. Schoyen, denies this, but although an accusation of 'full-blown Toryism' is exaggerated – and Harney had never been a 'Liberal' – there is no doubt that during his residence in the USA he came to expound a whole raft of Conservative beliefs.[29]

We have already seen that Harney grew to detest Gladstone – and this dislike and distrust he extended to the entire Gladstonian Liberal Party – and that he became a vehement opponent of Home Rule for Ireland to which Gladstone committed the Liberals in 1885-6. But Harney went significantly farther than this, judging Salisbury's administration of 1886-92 as the best within his memory, emphasising, in 'The Conflict', that he was able to 'look back over sixty years of intelligent interest in political questions and public affairs …' In contrast, he rightly condemned the brutal treatment Chartist prisoners had experienced under Whig administrations; and denounced that of 1831-5 as 'hard and cruel' – with its ideological onslaught on the poor unparalleled until the actions of the Conservative/LibDem coalition of 2010.

He loathed the aggressive capitalism, materialism and racism of the post-bellum USA. His observation of the operation of its politics eroded his faith in the beneficial effects of extending the suffrage for he could see how the enfranchised masses were manipulated by the party apparatus ('the Caucus' is his bogey term). In 1885 he observed to Engels:

I am glad you … can yet feel some confidence in and hope of the English working classes. I daresay I too might have retained my "youthful illusions", not much impaired, if I had remained in England. But the long banishment of thirty years – including the Jersey sojourn – has made a difference …. Any way a man in continual pain is apt to take a depressed view of 'things' and of men.[30]

(Engels's comment to Laura Lafargue, Marx's daughter, was that Harney had emigrated to Boston, 'only to find there, in an exaggerated form and ruling supreme, those very things and qualities which he hated most in England …. All he has learnt in America is British chauvinism!')[31] While on his visit to Britain, Harney also had written to an unknown correspondent:

29 George Jacob Holyoake, *Bygones Worth Remembering* (London: T. Fisher Unwin, 2 vols, 1905), I, pp. 111-12; Schoyen, p. 269.
30 Black and Black, p. 303.
31 Letter of 13 December 1886, Marx and Engels, XLVII, p. 538.

I suppose you are still a young man and so have more sanguine views than I have as to what 'is sure to occur when the masses receive the Franchise' ... I have lived in 'the States' twenty-one years and after that experience I am sceptical.

Besides, here, even now, I see the working people voters and non-voters eager to have Lords, called 'Liberal', and 'men of property', for their leaders and law-makers. The 'Caucus', too, is not a favourable element in calculations as to the results of extended franchise. I have seen more than enough of that in America.[32]

So, as working-class representatives began to be elected to the Commons, he criticised their subservience to the middle-class politicians and the interests of the Liberal Party. The first socialists took their seats in 1892 and he predicted they would continue the dependence. Although he admired John Burns and Tom Mann, he did not care for Keir Hardie. When the Independent Labour Party adopted a socialist programme he scorned the party, in 'The New Crusade: A Prelude to ...?', for its religiosity and socialism for its impracticability. Of the young socialists he was closest to H.H. Champion, distrusted by others for his Tory leanings and whom Harney praises in 'Two Periodicals': they shared a vehement dislike for the Liberals and concurred on the need for genuinely independent working-class organisation.

Back in 1844 Harney had told Holyoake how he wanted Chartism to advance and was advocating Communism, Republicanism and Secularism ('War with all Priesthoods and Priestcrafts'). By the nineties he had ceased to be any kind of socialist, although believing in the nationalisation of certain industries, including the mines and railways. While he had saluted 'the great revolt' of the London Dock Strike in 1889 – 'Not since the high and palmy days of Chartism have I witnessed any movement corresponding in importance and interest ...'[33] – he was antipathetic to the selfishness of skilled workers, criticising the coal disputes of the following decade for the miners' lack of concern for fellow proletarians. Republicanism had been replaced by a respect for and kindly tolerance of the monarchy. He extolled patriotism, the Empire and national security. He even lamented the death of Gordon at Khartoum. Only the Secularism continued intact, actually expressed with biting militancy. This latter provides a clue as to how Harney had not entirely transmogrified into a crusty old reactionary,

32 Letter of 5 September 1884, in the possession of the editor.
33 Quoted in Eric J. Hobsbawm (ed.), *Labour's Turning Point ... 1880-1900* (London: Lawrence & Wishart, 1948), p. 85.

but that the *Newcastle Weekly Chronicle* columnist in fundamental ways remains the young Chartist. He proclaims in his articles on the Anti-Corn Law League and free trade: 'The Chartists were right'. For him Chartism and the Chartists, exemplifying a fully independent working-class politics, were the benchmark against which all later movements were measured – and found wanting. We need to take seriously what he said about being educated in the 'radical school of the 'thirties'. It was then that he was absorbed into the London infidel tradition through his contact with the likes of Richard Carlile, Henry Hetherington, James Watson and the old Spenceans. He repeatedly recalls the 'War of the Unstamped' and his three spells of imprisonment as one of its vendors. Much of his curmudgeonliness at end of the century relates to fears that both the liberty of the press and freedom of thought were being curtailed, not by legal challenge but through disregard and conformism – and his disappointment at the lack of intellectualism displayed by the late-Victorian press.

There is also continuity in his views on imperialism. In 1894 he recollected his speech at the Tiverton election half-a-century earlier: 'Strongly condemning the conduct of the British Government in India and Afghanistan he yet took care to dissociate himself from the Manchester School of "Little Englanders" of that day ... protesting against any separation, but urging that colonies and dependencies should be held to the mother country by links of justice, and then the world might see the whole "floating down the stream of Time, one happy, one free, one triumphal British nation"'.[34] In the *Red Republican* he seemed to be arguing for a social imperialism:

> The integrity of the British empire must be maintained; but the advantages of that empire must be no longer monopolised by privileged usurpers, and Moloch-like mammonites. It is high time the proletarians of Great Britain and Ireland came into possession of their rightful heritage.[35]

In contrast, ever the contrarian, Harney was to denounce the New Imperialism and the 'exploitation of the African Continent': 'The pretence of spreading civilisation is a lie to mask the inhuman greed of the so-called "civilisers"'.[36]

The Chartists revered above all others two radical writers and thinkers:

34 F.J. Snell, *Palmerston's Borough: A Budget of Electioneering Anecdotes, Jokes, Squibs, and Speeches* (London: Horace Marshall, 1894), p. 86.
35 *Red Republican*, 31 August 1850.
36 *NWC*, 27 June 1896.

Tom Paine and William Cobbett. By the 1890s Paine has dropped from Harney's world view, presumably too much associated with the American Revolution and Constitution – and, by extension, probably the despised South American republics. Cobbett, in contrast, is incessantly mentioned and with enormous approbation, second only in Harney's pantheon to Byron, 'pre-eminently, the poet of Revolution ... still more essentially the Poet of Freedom'. On a wall of his room hung, framed together, a letter of Cobbett's and his portrait, both given to Harney by Cobbett's daughter Eleanor.[37] Cobbett can be reasonably categorised as a 'Tory Radical' and this seems to be what Harney himself had evolved into. His approbation of Oastler and Stephens is a pointer to this. He had come to believe in tradition, continuity and reform only if it were organic.[38]

Some of Harney's *Weekly Chronicle* readers were, as was to be expected, infuriated by his opinions, especially his anti-Gladstonianism. When in 1893 he rejoiced in the defeat of the Second Home Rule Bill, joining William Cobbett in rejoicing, 'Thank God there is a House of Lords!', an adversary signing himself 'Bungaree Bill' retorted:

> Just fifty years ago, while he still 'gloried in the name of Chartist', and still believed (I am quoting his own words) that the 'remedy for the present evils will be found in investing the people with their rights', he stood in the Court House at Lancaster and said: 'Does not the present state of things proclaim trumpet-tongued that the privileged classes of society have abused the powers they have exercised? that they are neither fit to govern the nation at large, nor themselves as a class, for in working the misery of millions they are certainly conspiring their own ruin?'[39]

But Harney was not, of course, now supporting the peers as a class; he simply exulted in the provision of a bicameral legislature. And in his offending column he had stressed: 'Not Irish Home Rule, not the Newcastle Programme – not all the items of which will fill a hungry stomach or give work to the unemployed – but the Condition of England Question, which

---

37 In the possession of Mrs Catherine Black Cohen.
38 There are obvious similarities between Harney's Tory Radicalism and the patriotic, imperial socialism at the end of the nineteenth and beginning of the twentieth centuries of, most notably, H.M. Hyndman and Robert Blatchford. And for a helpful treatment of working-class Conservatism and the involvement of former Chartists, particularly in Lancashire, see Neville Kirk, *Change, Continuity and Class: Labour in British Society, 1850-1920* (Manchester and New York: Manchester University Press, 1998), esp pp. 95-107. Even allowing for these important currents, though, Harney's personal intellectual and political trajectory from the 1830s and 1840s to the 1870s, 1880s and 1890s is astonishing.
39 *NWC*, 23 September 1893.

still calls for solution, should engage the attention and earnest endeavour of those who make the law-makers'.[40] 'The Condition of England Question'! With this Harney reverts indubitably to the 1830s – and the 1840s when he had run a regular feature in the *Northern Star* under this title. (He thought well of Thomas Carlyle, who had coined the term in 1839, although it was John Ruskin whom he perceptively considered 'one of the greatest of Englishmen'.)[41]

***

To mark Harney's eightieth birthday in February 1897 a testimonial amounting to a handsome £200 was collected. The committee included not only Cowen and Adams but also the Lib-Lab Thomas Burt (the miner who in 1874 had been one of the first two working-class MPs), the veteran secularist publisher Edward Truelove and the London bookseller and publisher Bertram Dobell, while the subscribers ranged, extraordinarily, from Joseph Chamberlain, the current Colonial Secretary, and the armaments manufacturer, Lord Armstrong, by way of the trade unionist Robert Applegarth, Liberal Clubs in Leeds as well as the Bury Social Democratic Federation, to Marx's daughters Eleanor and Laura (and their respective partners, Edward Aveling and Paul Lafargue). What other Victorian could command the respect, the admiration, and the affection of such a diversity of persons and organisations?

By a unique combination of circumstances – his remarkable longevity, his outstanding leadership built on the trust of the Chartist rank-and-file, his originality, his access as a journalist to the influential printed word, and an internationalism extended by his sojourn based, in Massachusetts, at the heart of a seat of global power – Harney's career and indeed legacy epitomised, in a fast-changing and increasingly interconnected world, the challenging assertion that 'The Chartists were right'.

While the intention has been to include all the Chartist plums in the present selection, an equally interesting second volume might be drawn from Harney's *Weekly Chronicle* columns. Another exciting book could probably be made from his contributions to the paper from 1864 through to 1889. And what about his Chartist journalism, for the both *Northern Star* and his own periodicals? It is hoped that this small book will inspire such others. This great spirit, this great British radical, even if ultimately a Tory Radical, deserves no less.

---

40 *NWC*, 16 September 1893. For the Newcastle Programme, see n220 below.
41 *NWC*, 10 April 1897.

THE ROLL-CALL

Thomas Cooper

Thomas Cooper dead! What a world of associations that sad announcement summons from the records of the stormy past! For a moment I imagine myself back to the days of 1841. Chartism had experienced some sore rebuffs: the attempted National Holiday of 1839 had proved a fiasco; the Convention, torn by factions and dwindling to a mere remnant, had passed away; Frost and his associates, barely escaping death on the scaffold, were undergoing the pains of penal servitude in Australia; O'Connor, O'Brien, Vincent, Lovett, and Collins, and many more of the leaders, had experienced the discomforts of varied terms of imprisonment; the ranks had been scattered, and a large number of the most earnest of the rank and file had sought refuge from disappointment in emigration. But new converts were still being made, and new leaders were coming forward to fill the places of those who had fallen or deserted, or to co-operate and work with those who, despite persecution, were still faithful, and whose zeal had been intensified by the experience of personal suffering added to their settled conclusion that the Charter must be struggled for and won as the only sure means of rescuing the masses from the Slough of Despond, and aiding their march to the Promised Land of Liberty, Prosperity, and Social Regeneration. It was that moment that Thomas Cooper appeared in our midst with potent pen and still more potent voice to help in realising the prophecy of Thomas Muir:[1] 'It is a good cause; it shall yet prevail; it shall finally triumph'.

Thomas Cooper was thoroughly English: his father, a descendant from Yorkshire Quakers, his mother, a native of Lincolnshire, a descendant of small farmers and carriers. He was born in the Midland town of Leicester on 20 March 1805. His father was a dyer, apparently of unsettled habits, perhaps driven by circumstances to woo Fortune in different localities – always in vain. This parental wandering took Thomas, when only twelve months of age, to the fine old city of Exeter. By a sad fatality Thomas Cooper's father, who had been rendered fatherless when he was a boy, was himself called away when Thomas was but four years old. His mother soon left 'grand old Exeter', and returned to her native Gainsborough. There she took up the business of a dyer, the art and mystery of which she had learned from her husband. John Wesley was a brand plucked from the burning. Thomas Cooper was a waif saved from drowning, for in Exeter, when he was two

---

1 One of the Scottish Jacobins – or 'Martyrs' – and sentenced in 1793 to 14 years' transportation. He escaped from Australia, dying in France in 1799, aged 33.

years old, he fell into the Leate, a small tributary of the Exe, and, when rescued, was supposed to be dead but by medical skill was restored to life. At Gainsborough he experienced a much more painful misfortune: smallpox, so severe that he was blind for 19 days, and the bones came through his skin at the knees, hips, and elbows. The anti-vaccinators of Leicester know nothing these days of what smallpox was like in Thomas Cooper's childhood. Measles and scarlet fever quickly followed, and the little sufferer was brought to death's door. The time when he been saluted as 'a pretty boy' was gone, never to return. The scars of the fell disease remained upon his visage for life.

Thomas Cooper's mother was an admirable woman, an unceasing toiler, and resolutely intent on procuring for her son the best education within their very humble means. When he was fifteen, Thomas was seized with that sea fever which takes possession of so many English boys. He must be a sailor! After much worrying of his almost broken-hearted mother, she gave her reluctant consent. He went to Hull, and was taken on board a brig as a cabin-boy. He was soon disillusioned. The swearing brutality of the skipper quickly effected a reaction in the boy's mind, and after nine days he obtained leave to return home, much to the delight of his weeping mother – weeping for joy at the truant's return.

Subsequently, Thomas Cooper took to shoemaking, and was enrolled under the banner of St Crispin. That, too, was a disappointment to his mother, but she consoled herself with the prophetic reflection: 'The Lord's will be done! I don't think he intends thee to spend thy life at shoemaking …. He'll bring it all right in time'.

Of course, having tasted of the fruit of the tree of knowledge, which, though it is not the tree of life, does impart a delight to life which no poverty, no suffering can altogether neutralise, Cooper must needs persist in his pursuit of knowledge under difficulties; and these difficulties were of the severest or, including the want of proper nourishment, even of the poorest, coarsest kind. Not regularly apprenticed, Cooper, as long as he was a shoemaker, never earned more than 10s weekly. Yet in his Autobiography[2] he says: 'What glorious years were those years of self-denial and earnest mental toil from the age of nearly 19 to nearly three-and-twenty that I sat and worked in that corner of my poor mother's lowly home!'

It would take half a column to repeat merely the names of the books Thomas Cooper read and studied before he was 25 years of age. Of course, poetry was for him an irrepressible fascination. It is with strong sympathy I read in the Autobiography that in his thirteenth year there fell into his hands

2 *The Life of Thomas Cooper: Written by Himself* (1872).

one of the cantos of *Childe Harold* and the drama of *Manfred*. He adds: 'I wanted more poetry to read from that time, but could get hold of none that thrilled through my nature like Byron's'. But he did hesitate to enter on the thornier paths of learning: mathematics and the study of languages, attaining a proficiency of much value to him in after years. He left his bed at three or four o'clock in the morning to pursue his studies until seven. But he overtaxed his body, if not his mental powers. He tells us that he not unfrequently swooned away when trying to take a cup of oatmeal gruel at the end of his day's labour. Finally, he was utterly prostrated for nine weeks, and, perforce, had to give up his studies for a time.

Well-advised by kind friends, he renounced shoemaking and proceeded to turn his hard-won acquirements to account by opening a school. His school was successful. But, after some time, he tired of a work he did not find congenial. Towards 1830 he became a local preacher among the Wesleyans. That experience would prepare him for his future success as a lecturer. In 1833 Thomas Cooper left Gainsborough, and took charge of a school in Lincoln. In 1834, he married, and his mother came to live with the wedded pair. Subsequently she returned to Gainsborough, where she died at the age of 71. Some unjust treatment led to Cooper renouncing his connection with the Wesleyan Methodists. Soon afterwards he entered upon an engagement as local reporter, or contributor, to a very old weekly newspaper, the *Lincoln, Rutland, and Stamford Mercury*.

On 1 June 1839, Thomas Cooper left Stamford, whither he had removed from Lincoln, to seek his fortunes in London. The first Chartist Convention was in session, but the part he was to take in politics had not then been revealed to the future Chartist lecturer. He experienced the usual trials of unknown, friendless votaries of literature in the great metropolis, and was obliged to sell his books for bread. At length he had the good fortune to be engaged by Mr Macgowan, printer, Great Windmill Street, at a salary of three pounds per week as editor of the *Kentish Mercury*. That was in March 1840, and until November Mr Cooper was a resident of pleasant Greenwich. I may remark that when the *Northern Star* was removed from Leeds to London, it came to be printed at Macgowan's. It sounds comical enough that the *Kentish Mercury*, now, I believe, a well-established journal, was printed in Great Windmill Street, London! Its editing by Thomas Cooper was not of long duration. The views of the proprietor and the editor clashed, and he gave notice to leave. Almost immediately afterwards his services were sought as reporter and contributor to the *Leicester Mercury*. He had left Leicester when a year old, and now returned to the place of his nativity at the age of 35. There he found, as far as Chartism was concerned, his 'destiny'.

He was sent to a Chartist meeting to supply a short account of a Chartist lecture by John Mason, 'a Birmingham shoemaker' – so described in the Autobiography but there may be still living in the neighbourhood of the *Newcastle Chronicle* office some half-dozen, or more, who remember that John Mason, shoemaker, was of Newcastle-upon-Tyne before he went to Birmingham. Soon came to Cooper revelations of the misery of the framework knitters or 'stockingers', and soon thereafter he began to make his reporting and paragraph-writing subordinate to his sympathy with the Chartists, an offence not to be tolerated in the office of the *Leicester Mercury*, so the reporter had to look elsewhere. The result was the unprofitable editorship of a weekly penny Chartist paper – the *Midland Counties Illuminator*. For the next few years, Thomas Cooper's biography is part and parcel of the history of Chartism.

With his natural talents and acquired knowledge, it cannot be doubted that, had he merely sought to live by his pen, his first difficulties in journalism surmounted, he would have rapidly achieved a good paying position in connection with the press. But Thomas Cooper was a born crusader, and valued journalism only as a means – one of the means – to enlighten the ignorant, to impart hope to the despairing, and to stimulate the unrepresented toilers to struggle for emancipation.

Flinging aside the reporter's notebook, and mounting the platform of popular agitation, he found in his tongue's eloquence a more aggressive power of warfare than journalism could supply. He at once became the leader of the Leicester Chartists. But for a time his influence was limited to that town and the not distant town of Nottingham.

It is just fifty years ago this month since the great and mysterious 'turn-out' of the mill hands in Lancashire, part of the West Riding of Yorkshire, and part of Cheshire, took place. There was at the same time a strike of coalminers in the Potteries and South Staffordshire. Without any foreknowledge of these events, a Chartist Conference had been convened to meet in Manchester on 16 August. To that convention Thomas Cooper had been elected a delegate. He had planned his route to go through the Potteries to Manchester. At Hanley he delivered some stirring speeches, and these were followed by scenes of violence and incendiarism occasioning his arrest; but, there being no definite charge against him, he was set at liberty, went to the conference, returned to Leicester, and was again arrested. He was put on his trial for arson, utterly without foundation, and acquitted. He was next charged with sedition and conspiracy, traversed to the next assizes, was tried and found guilty, and finally sentenced to two years' imprisonment.

On each trial he made a lengthy and brilliant defence. His prison treatment, and that of his fellow victims, Richards and Capper, was barbarous in the extreme. No books; no liberty to write a letter, not even to his wife. Such treatment was the rule. Most of the imprisoned Chartists suffered in silence; Cooper however rebelled. The course he took was justified by the result. Anyway, it was his nature to act as he did. His highly-strung nervous organisation impelled him to that action which nearly threw the dismayed chaplain into fits, and with beneficial effect of compelling attention to his well-founded complaints, and bringing about a very material amelioration of his treatment.[3]

Of his 'Prison Rhyme' – *The Purgatory of Suicides* – and other literary productions, I have not the space to speak. His most valuable work is his Autobiography, for its lessons to those who aim at something nobler than 'beer and skittles' in the conduct of life, and who cannot fail to find encouragement in the record of Cooper's perseverance. Not to all men is possible such an indomitable course of struggle as that of the ill-paid shoemaker, schoolmaster, writer, and lecturer; but the very aim to rival Cooper's struggles cannot fail to greatly benefit those who may fall short of his attainments. As I have said, the most stirring years of his life belong to the History of Chartism, and the story cannot be repeated within this circumscribed space. By many still living his remarkable powers as a lecturer on historical subjects are still remembered. Of his brief connection with Douglas Jerrold's newspaper, of his own ventures in the *Plain Speaker*, *Cooper's Journal*, etc, I can only make mention; as also of the 'Christian Evidence' lectures and sermons of his later years.[4] Until within the last ten years of his life, he never seemed to tire. Excepting about two months in the year, he, for a number of years, travelled and 'talked' (as he phrased it), lecturing every six days out of seven, and often preaching twice on the Sunday. He, surely, has earned his rest.

His qualities were commanding, but he had the defect of his qualities – more than one. I am satisfied that no man can succeed in public life without a goodly spice of egotism in his composition. That quality may be, and, perhaps, nine times out of ten, as history attests, is abused, employed to promote personal ambition or the obtainment of wealth; but, the quality is necessary, indispensable. A man without egotism, or with but a poor development, may be a good man, a true patriot, but as a public man he will

3 He banged at the governor's door, haranguing him and gaolers; broke windows; grabbed and shouted at the chaplain during a service; and insisted on a petition being delivered to Thomas Slingsby Duncombe, in effect a Chartist MP.
4 Christian Evidence aimed to provide a rational defence of the Christian faith against secularist objection.

not be successful in any sense, and, therefore, cannot be counted on to much advance a cause, however righteous and desirable for mankind's welfare. Nevertheless, egotism is a dangerous, though necessary, gift; especially when egotism meets egotism in conflict. It was the nature of Thomas Cooper to take to the advocacy of a new cause, and to fraternise with new associates, in a spirit of boundless enthusiasm; but it was also in his nature to find out the imperfectability of supposed ideals, and then to be as fierce in hostility as he had previously been fervent in admiration. It is said, 'Once a captain, always a captain'; it is much more true that 'Once a schoolmaster, always a schoolmaster'; and grown men, also having their egotisms, are apt to resent the ferule of the pedagogue. Frankly, it was not always easy to 'get on' with Thomas Cooper. I might recall, I think, more than one 'squall' with our deceased friend. But Thomas had a warm heart. He could be bitter enough when carried away by passion; but he could be as warm in reconciliation as he had been hot in hostility. A few years ago, I called on him at his home in Lincoln. Naturally, at first he did not recognise me, though my voice struck him as from a far-off time. His sight had dimmed and deafness had increased, but on repeating my name he flung his arms around me, combining French fervour with English sincerity. Thomas Cooper was not well fitted to be the leader of a party, of a league, union, association. He was most useful, and caused and experienced least friction, when standing alone. And he only is the free man who stands alone.

His mental changes from Wesleyanism to – well, I had best say – Strauss-ism,[5] and from ultra-scepticism to evangelist Christianity, were startling. But he was always sincere – I may say, with no injustice, intolerantly sincere. Could he have lived to the age of Methusaleh, and in the course of years have become Moslem, and at the end of another term Buddhist, and finally have veered round again to Christianity, or to d'Holbach's *Système de la Nature*, and I could have witnessed such changes, I must have held Thomas Cooper to be, in every instance, equally sincere: for his renunciations and adoptions would have been without the ulterior aim of acquiring power, place, or pay. I suspect my old comrade was a disappointed man. First, disappointed in the political conduct of the enfranchised working men – a disappointment I, too, fully share. When he printed in his Chartist Song Book[6]

> ... Earth has no beauty to see
> Like the broad beaming brow of a Nation when free,

5 David Strauss (1808-74) was a German theologian and a leading figure in Biblical criticism and the historical examination of Jesus, whose divinity he denied. George Eliot was the translator of his *Life of Jesus* (1846).
6 Might this be the *Shaksperean Chartist Hymn Book* which Cooper edited and published in Leicester c.1842 (but of no copy is known to be extant)?

he had no anticipation that working-class voters would become the creatures of party election agents. In another matter, he was disappointed. He must have felt that his 'Christian Evidence' lectures had, in the main, failed to produce any general or lasting effect.

I have said Thomas Cooper was warm-hearted. He was a free giver. He had that quality which is pronounced the noblest attribute of a rich man, but which, indulged in by a poor man, is counted as little short of a crime. When I tried to raise a subscription for the late John West,[7] a miserable amount of under £35 was the result. Of that amount there were two sums of £5 each. One was from 'An Old Chartist' – Thomas Cooper. He requested I would conceal his name for reasons not to be made public. I dare say many could testify to his generosity and large-hearted sympathy.

It was but very shortly before his death that the name of Thomas Cooper came again before the public in connection with a grant of £200 from the public funds. His death came so soon after the announcement of the gift that it may doubted whether he received the money; he certainly could not have 'enjoyed' it. The grant was made on the application of Mr Mundella, the member for Brightside, Sheffield, one of Thomas Cooper's earliest political converts when he was leading the Leicester Chartists. It was to the credit of Mr Mundella to make the application; it was to the honour of Mr Balfour[8] that he made the grant; its acceptance was no discredit to Thomas Cooper. So small a largess from the national funds had been more than earned.

There have been many press notices of his death, of which I have seen but two or three. *The Times* gave an extended biographical sketch and a very good and kindly editorial, containing one mistake. There was nothing more socialistic about Feargus O'Connor's Land Scheme than there is about the Small Holdings Act.[9] Cooper opposed O'Connor's scheme because, as he urged, it had nothing to do with the movement for the Charter, which it was likely to injure. He was right.

Thomas Cooper was of medium height, apparently well-formed, and, despite his early and many years' privations, possessed of considerable muscular strength. He favoured the Roundheads, but his hair was rather of the Cavalier cut. His face was pitted and discoloured by the smallpox, which was unthought of under the magic of his smile – never wanting in female society.

I never heard Thomas Cooper in debate, and cannot recall that I ever

7 A Chartist from Stockport and a great friend of Harney, who mentions him frequently in his columns.

8 A.J. Balfour, the Conservative politician, who had become First Lord of the Treasury in 1891.

9 A Conservative measure of 1892.

heard one of his set lectures; but in his Chartist harangues he was a very effective speaker, at once impassioned and satirical. He had a fine voice both for speaking and singing, as I remember him in Paradise Square, Sheffield, about fifty years ago, in the course of his speech leading in the Chartist song:

The Lion of Freedom[10] has come from his den;
We'll rally around him again and again.

Alas! For the instability of hero-worship, and the instability of political friendship! The time came when the Lion of Freedom was in conflict with the singer, who was by no means lamb-like in dealing with the lion.

'We're wearing awa''– passing away like bubbles on the stream of time. Of the prominent men of the Chartist time, I can name only two: Mr Samuel Kydd, barrister-at-law, I think a little my junior; and Mr W.J. Linton, the famous artist, poet, and essayist, some four years my senior, and who, I believe, is so hale and hearty that he promises to be 'the last of the Mohicans'. If I have sometimes omitted to speak of Mr Linton as a surviving Chartist leader, it is because I have always regarded him as much more than a Chartist, a friend and sympathiser, but whose aim soared beyond the 'six points'. Mr Linton, however, is no more ashamed of being classed as a Chartist than I am. It is a satisfaction to know that the friends who remain, like the friend who has departed, are not the dupes of the prevailing delusion, but are sternly devoted to the country's safety, unity, and high standing among the nations of the earth. Thomas Cooper fought the good fight, and, repudiating the blandishments of prostituted rhetoric, refusing to minister to any man's inordinate vanity or to further his unscrupulous ambition, remained steadfast in his allegiance to the country, in devotion to his native land. Honoured be the name and memory of Thomas Cooper. 'After life's fitful fever, he sleeps well'.[11]

23 July 1892

Samuel Kydd

Had I known what I came to know a few hours after sending my last letter to the *Weekly Chronicle*, its theme would not have been 'Scotch Humour'. The paragraph in the 'Gossip's Bowl'[12] (7 January) has made known the fact of the death of Mr Samuel Kydd, barrister-at-law, an old-time Chartist leader, whose answer to the Roll-Call should have something more than the notice of a line or two in this journal.

10 Feargus O'Connor.
11 Shakespeare, *Macbeth*, Act 3, Scene ii.
12 A column signed by 'Robin Goodfellow', the pseudonym of W.E. Adams.

Although in friendship with Mr Kydd over fifty years, my knowledge was not intimate; partly owing to my long exile from England and residence in the States, and partly, perhaps chiefly, owing to what I must term my deceased friend's Scotch reticence – a good quality, but, like some others, liable to be carried to excess. I class it as a good quality, for it is in my estimation one of the secrets of Caledonian success. It is good especially because it nourishes self-respect. Is a Scotsman, at the outset of his career, bent upon fighting the battle of life, with a foregone conclusion to win, hampered by poverty, he keeps the knowledge of that disagreeable fact as much as possible to himself; and so fosters his self-respect and baffles 'the proud man's contumely'.[13] As his acquisitions, whether of skill, or capital, or both, increase he keeps a close grip upon those acquisitions, and is not to be detected in what the Americans term 'giving himself away'. His foothold is as firm as Ailsa Craig; every step he advances is a positive gain, once achieved, never lost. But the typical Scotsman, though he overcomes obstacles, tramples upon impediments, defies temptations, and never lets go his grip upon anything gained, is, after all, not exactly the embodiment of perfection, and his reticence, carried to excess, may at least deprive his friends of the means of doing justice to his memory.

Samuel McGowan Kydd, to give the full name, was a native of Arbroath, Forfarshire, sixteen miles north-east of Dundee. I remember having been there once, and still have a hazy recollection of the sad and solemn ruins of the once splendid abbey of Aberbrothwick. Curious that Dr Johnson, writing the account of his visit to the Hebrides, 120 years ago, and giving an account of his journey from England along the Eastern Shore of Scotland, does nothing more than mention Dundee, evidently of but small account in his day, merely remarking – 'We stopped awhile at Dundee, where I remember nothing remarkable, and, mounting our chaise again, came about the close of the day to Aberbrothwick'. He was struck by the magnificence of the ruins, but says nothing about the modern town, its manufactures, trade, and people.

I had always supposed Mr Kydd to be slightly my junior, but, born on 22 February1815, he was all but five days my senior by two years. Of his parents, his schooling, his early life, I know nothing. I have understood that in his youth and young manhood he was a member of the gentle craft presided over by those saints to whom Harry the King referred on the morning of Agincourt, and which has on its roll of honour many famous names, including the ill-fated Admiral Sir Cloudesley Shovel, first shoemaker

13 Shakespeare, *Hamlet,* 3, i.

and then common seaman;[14] Gifford, the Editor of the *Quarterly Review*; Bloomfield, the poet; our own Thomas Cooper; and Thomas Edwards, of Banff, the eminent naturalist. More illustrious names might be cited, but enough of good company for Samuel Kydd, whose first printed letter I am told was addressed from 'a cordwainer's bench'.

I have seen it stated that Mr Kydd came to London as early as 1834. I think that is an error. If he did, it was not immediately he took any leading part in politics. From 1833 to 1838 I was in the habit of attending most political meetings of pre-Chartist days, held in the Crown and Anchor,[15] of old-time political celebrity, and elsewhere; but I have no recollection of my deceased friend's participation in any of those meetings. My impression is that he did not cross the Border until some time in 1842.

Robin Goodfellow's note in the 'Gossip's Bowl' last Saturday would seem to imply that Mr Kydd was a member of the first Chartist Convention. Had he been, that would have brought him to London in 1839. But he was not a member. Mr Richard Moore passed away some ten or more years ago, since which time I have been, so far as I know, the sole survivor of the Convention, unless Mr Hugh Williams, of Newport, or Pontypool, is still living. No one has responded to my inquiries respecting that gentleman in a recent issue of the *Weekly Chronicle*.[16]

I am not sure as to my first meeting with Mr Kydd, but think it was early in 1840, in Glasgow, when, as I fancy, I met him in the company of Thomas Gillespie, John Adams, Con. Murray, John Colquhoun, and other 'advanced' Chartists.[17] In 1842, Mr Kydd was sent by the Glasgow Chartists to the Sturge Conference at Birmingham, where he voted with William Lovett, Humffreys Parry, Feargus O'Connor, and the majority, for the retention of the People's Charter and the rejection of the Complete Suffrage project. This introduced him to a wide circle of delegates and local leaders, and he soon took rank as an effective Chartist lecturer. He was also a member of certain of the Chartist Conventions and delegate meetings between 1840 and 1848, and, I think, served on the Chartist Executive. It would take a considerable time ransacking old *Northern Stars* to get at particulars. In the conflict of opinion

14 Shovel (or Shovell) (1650-1707) drowned when his ship and three others were wrecked off the Isles of Scilly. It was one of the greatest maritime disasters in British history.
15 A tavern in the Strand.
16 Hugh Williams, actually a Carmarthen solicitor in 1839, had died in 1874. It is most surprising that no *Weekly Chronicle* reader had been able to volunteer this information.
17 These militants were strongly opposed to the Chartist Church grouping, some of whom were shortly to migrate to the Complete Suffrage Union of Joseph Sturge. They wanted the focus to be entirely on the Charter, not on diversions such as the Churches or repeal of the Corn Laws. Harney misremembers the first name of Adams, which was 'James'. (Information of Hamish Fraser, author of *Chartism in Scotland* (Merlin Press, 2010).)

between the Chartists and the Anti-Corn-Law Leaguers, Mr Kydd took a prominent part. Of Mr Kydd's style of speaking I prefer to say but a word or two. I cannot recall that I ever heard him delivering a set lecture, and I never heard him at the bar. His ordinary speeches were marked by thought, research, vigour, and fluency. Any difficulties that might have arisen from his national accent were overcome by his clear enunciation, though I have heard him when excited give to a volubility somewhat marring the otherwise good effect of his address. He was not wanting in Scotch sarcasm when occasion warranted, and, altogether, he was one of the most effective of the Chartist speakers. In private life he was a pleasant companion, ready to give and take a jest .... At the General Election in 1847, a number of the leading Chartists appeared on the hustings to vindicate the principles of Chartism in presence of audiences a large proportion of whom never attended ordinary Chartist meetings, to wit – the squirearchy and farmers, manufacturers and shopkeepers. Once duly moved and seconded, the candidates had free speech, and they made good use of their opportunity. In every instance the voiceless multitude held up their hands for the Chartist candidate, who in most cases then retired from a hopeless contest. Mr Kydd contested the Greenwich seat. His opponents were – Admiral Dundas and Mr Barnard, Whigs, and Alderman Salomans, Liberal. The two first had a very poor show of hands, the third a larger number; for Mr Kydd every hand seemed to be upraised; but he did not go to the poll. Dundas and Barnard were elected.

Though advocating the Charter, Mr Kydd kept social questions well in view, and strongly denounced the then New Poor Law. He very early shared in the Factory agitation for the Ten Hours Bill. In that connection he acquired the friendship of the late Earl of Shaftesbury and other distinguished men, and more especially that of the late Richard Oastler, the dauntless champion of the factory children and factory workers generally. When the stress of the fight was over and the victory won, Mr Kydd set himself to recording the history of the struggle, which in due course (1857) appeared in two handsome volumes under the title of *The History of the Factory Movement from the Year 1802 to the Enactment of the Ten Hours Bill in 1847*, the two volumes comprising upwards of 650 pages. The work is inscribed in a manly dedication to Lord Faversham. Mr Kydd made one mistake, that of bringing out his work under the nom-de-plume of 'Alfred', when 'by Samuel Kydd' would have been the proper name for his title-pages. Apart from the merits of Mr Kydd's writing, the value of the volumes as the record of one of the most important movements in the social history of England cannot be gainsaid, and working men should see that the volumes are in the catalogue of every Public Library. I assume that they are yet to be obtained from the publishers, Simpkin, Marshall, and Co, or through the dealers in second-hand books.

A little over four years ago Mr Kydd published a thin octavo volume on *The Growth of Public Opinion* (Elliot Stock, 1888), which was duly noticed at the time in these columns.

In addition to the factory workers, the grievances of classes largely attracted Mr Kydd's attention, and, if memory serves, he was a very ardent worker in the cause of the miners, principally, I think, of Lancashire, Yorkshire, and the Midlands. 'But', as Robin Goodfellow said last week, 'old servants and old services are soon forgotten'.

Previous to the commencement of *Reynolds's Newspaper*, the projector of that journal issued *Reynolds's Political Instructor*, a sort of pilot balloon to the intended newspaper. I believe there is some of Mr Kydd's writing in that publication, and among the portraits of leading Chartists and other public characters was one of Mr Kydd, with a slight biographical sketch .... On the appearance of *Reynolds's Newspaper*, Mr Kydd commenced a series of letters therein above the signature of 'Gracchus'. I believe that signature is still continued, but many years have passed since it represented the thought, criticism, and counsel of Mr Kydd. He wrote for other London papers ...

What special circumstance induced Mr Kydd to turn to the study of the law I do not know; I was not in England at the time; nor have I knowledge of his career from the time he assumed the barrister's wig and gown. The mourning card I received describes him as of Gray's Inn, but he had his chambers in the Middle Temple. I suppose he studied in and is on the roll of the long-robed fraternity of that ancient temple of Themis, Gray's Inn. Although but little conversant of Mr Kydd's forensic career, I think it right to pay tribute to that strength of character which enable him at a mature age to turn with success to the study of law. His previous career, both as workman and agitator, was by no means a good preparation for burning the midnight oil over *Coke upon Littleton*, or the dreadful toil of courting familiarity with the *Statutes at Large*. That he won the respect of at least some who might have been expected to look askance at the ci-devant Chartist lecturer is sufficiently attested by an incident mentioned by a member of the Cobbett family, that when Mr James Cobbett came to London from Manchester he always called on Mr Kydd in the Temple. A few years ago Mr Kydd gave up his chambers, and retired to his home at Sutton, Surrey, which, indeed, had been his home for some five-and-twenty years. About the end of last autumn the death of a brother – unconnected with political life, but remarkable as a man of travel and enterprise – obliged

Mr Kydd to make several journeys into Warwickshire for the settlement of his brother's affairs. On his last journey he suffered greatly from cold, and, arrived at the station nearest to his destination, he had still some miles to proceed in no better conveyance than an open cart. The consequence was something worse than that fertile cause of death, 'a chill' – he was frozen. With difficulty he got through his business and returned home, with his death doom upon him. He was very ill, but would not allow a doctor to be called in until two days before his death. He had resisted taking to his bed, but after the doctor's visit, consented. His wife and maid-servant were in the act of taking him to his chamber, when, before the bed could be reached, he fell from their kindly hold. With great difficulty he was placed on the bed, and the doctor was at once re-summoned, but too late to be of any use. After saying a few words to his wife, Mr Kydd passed quietly away. He leaves a widow to lament loss, but no children, so much the better. 'What from this barren thing do we weep?' Some fleeting joys, that 'come like truth and disappear like dreams' – with a terrible balance on the other side, of sorrow and suffering, disappointment and disease – culminating in the mystery of dissolution. Men are such fools as to rejoice when a child is born; they should weep, for birth foredooms all the ills of life – death included.

I knew nothing of Mr Kydd's illness, and, strange to say, I had no word of his death, which occurred on 21 December, until late on the evening of 3 January. Hence the delay in making any obituary announcement. It is ended. The curtain has fallen. Samuel Kydd has joined the great majority. He has but preceded the writer and all who read these remarks. Scorning to be party's tool, or the courtier of one or of the many, he stood upright and remained free and independent to the end.

Princes and lords are but the breath of kings;
'An honest man's the noblest work of God'.[18]

14 January 1893

Abel Heywood

In the *Newcastle Daily Chronicle* of 8 August appeared a brief but interesting article under the heading of 'An Old Newsagent' making reference to the death of Mr Thomas France, which event occurred on 31 July. The article in the *Chronicle* stated that the deceased was a Lancashire man who fifty years ago came to Newcastle to assist in his uncle's business of newsagent in the Side. The article made reference to the War of the Unstamped, and the part

18 Burns, 'The Cotter's Saturday Night'.

taken therein by the elder France; complimentary allusion was also made to Alderman Abel Heywood, of Manchester, one of the early 'victims' to the Unstamped War. A slight error in the article led to a brief letter on my part, in which, referring to the gentleman just named, I said, 'It is pleasant to know that our friend Alderman Heywood still survives, "full of years and honours" – as regards the latter "he won them well, and may he wear them long" '.[19]

My letter appeared in *Daily Chronicle* of 11 August. A week and a day more and 'finis' was written at the foot of the scroll recording Alderman Heywood's career. My wish that he might continue to wear his honours long was superfluous: he had worn them long. Dying at the age of 83 it could not be said that the shaft had been broken midway, or that he had been prematurely gathered to his fathers, or that longer life would have materially added to the municipal honours conferred upon him by his fellow citizens during the long term of well-nigh sixty years.

I had no intimate knowledge of Mr Heywood. He was of interest to me principally because of his connection with the Unstamped in the remote days of 1830-36, and the almost as remote days of the early years of Chartism – when William Lovett gave Parliamentary form to the 'Six Points', Feargus O'Connor thundered from many a platform, and John Frost stood in peril of his life for devotion to popular cause manifested 'not wisely, but too well'.[20] As a bookseller or newsagent, Mr Heywood, who came to be the proprietor of a very large business, began in a very small way, and it was in his earliest days as a newspaper dealer that he came into conflict with the law as it then stood. He was accused of selling the *Poor Man's Guardian*, an unstamped, and, therefore, as the prosecution averred, an illegal publication. I have before me the *Poor Man's Guardian* of 17 March 1832, giving a brief report of the case .... In one corner was a burlesque imitation of the Government stamp, enclosing a representation of an old-fashioned hand-press, with the motto, 'Knowledge is Power', printed in black instead of red. The price of the *Guardian* was one penny. On Tuesday, 8 March, Mr Abel Heywood, bookseller, Oldham Street, appeared before Mr Foster and Mr Brierly, the magistrates at the New Bailey, to answer six summonses for selling the *Poor Man's Guardian*. Mr Casson appeared as attorney for the Stamp Office, and Mr E. Owen for the defendant. The information had been laid by Mr Alfred Ford, distributor of stamps for the Manchester district. Didsbury, an informer employed by the Commissioner of Stamps, London, proved having purchased six copies of the *Poor Man's Guardian* from

19 Byron, *Don Juan*, Canto 1, Stanza civ.
20 Shakespeare, *Othello*, 5, ii.

Abel Heywood, the defendant. The magistrates held the case proved, but pretended to let the defendant off easily by inflicting only the lowest penalty of £5 on each information, and the costs! The costs were modified from £3 8s to £3 on each of the informations, making, according to the *Guardian*'s report, a sum total of £48. But Mr Heywood, at the banquet given to him in the Manchester Town Hall, September 1888, stated that he was fined £54. It is very probable that *Guardian*'s report was not exactly accurate. Curiously enough, it omits mention of the sentence of four months' imprisonment on Mr Heywood's refusal to pay the fines. The laying of six informations, when one would have sufficed to obtain a conviction, showed the mean vindictiveness of the Stamp Office in seeking to inflict as much pecuniary injury as possible upon the defendant. The five Stamp Commissioners were, at the same time, dividing among themselves £7,748 of public money derived from the Taxes on Knowledge.[21] Well, in the long run the Stamp Commissioners, with the Government at their back, were – horse, foot, and artillery – put to the rout and compelled to surrender: first one surrender, then another, until at last the Press became entirely free.[22] In the case of Haslam's Letter to the Bishop of Exeter[23] he bore the brunt of Government prosecution, though he escaped the penalties which he might have had to suffer but for the protective shield of public opinion signally manifested on his behalf.

Alderman Heywood's connection with Chartism was mostly restricted to the sale of the *Northern Star*. It was said that in 1839 twenty thousand copies passed through his hands weekly. Only a portion would be sold at the retail price (4½d) in Manchester; a large number would be passed to sub-agents in Manchester and Salford, and a greater number to all the outlying towns and villages in Lancashire, West Yorkshire and Cheshire. It is probable that Mr Heywood's large agency for the *Star*, necessarily involving much labour and trouble, was not all profit. Among the multitude of sub-agents the majority were poor and struggling men, and it is likely that many defaulters contributed to take a good deal of gilt from the gingerbread which otherwise might and ought to have accrued to Mr Heywood.

Though sympathising with the advocates of Radical Parliamentary Reform, Mr Heywood in his early years belonged to the Owenite Socialists rather than to the Chartists. But he was always courteous, and I dare say not infrequently helpful, to men with whose political principles he agreed,

21 The chief was the newspaper tax, but there were also taxes on pamphlets and almanacs, a tax on newspaper advertisements, and an excise duty on paper.
22 The newspaper tax was reduced from 4d to 1d in 1836, but not abolished until 1855. The final Tax on Knowledge was the paper duty, repealed by Gladstone in his 1861 budget.
23 Charles Junius Haslam was an Owenite active in Manchester.

though he had declined to endorse their too sanguine expectations and too indiscreet enthusiasm in the stormy times of 1838-48.

Of his municipal career it is not for me to speak, beyond the mention that he was regarded as the Father of the Manchester Corporation. He was twice Mayor – 1862 and 1876; and in 1891 he was made an honorary freeman of Manchester, a distinction which has been granted to only four other men.

Mr Heywood leaves two sons: G.W. Heywood, County Court judge, Manchester; and Abel Heywood, who conducts the publishing business in Oldham Street. He was twice married. I have reason to believe that his first wife was a brave helpmate in his young and struggling days; and his second a lady of large and liberal views, to whom Manchester is indebted for the striking statue of Cromwell at the entrance of Victoria Street. Would that I, or some one, could Don Juanise[24] that statue to step from its pedestal and give us the great Oliver's views on 'the Bill for the better Government of Ireland'!

So passes Abel Heywood from this life. 'Full of years and honours', he has had, like humbler men, to answer to the roll-call. Unlike Henry Hetherington, James Watson, and other fighters in the Unstamped War, Alderman Heywood's name is not 'writ in water',[25] but is likely to endure longer than brass or marble, associated with the history of the city to the good government of which he by his untiring labours so largely contributed.

26 August 1893

John Bedford Leno

The obituary of this year will be memorable, including many great names, of whom I will name but some half-dozen: Earl Grey, John Anthony Froude, John Walter (of *The Times*), Oliver Wendell Holmes, the Comte de Paris, and Alexander III. Of these, the happiest in life was, doubtless, the American author. In the case of the 'Autocrat of the Breakfast Table', life was almost all sunshine. He was hardly more respected and beloved in his own country, in the 'Hub of the Universe', and his native Cambridge, than he was in the land of his forefathers – wherever his books were known. Every reader became at once his admirer, and, had it been his lot to have represented the States at the Court of St James's, his popularity would at least have rivalled that of his great compatriot, literary compeer, and personal friend,

24 At the conclusion of Mozart's *Don Giovanni* the statue of the Commendatore comes to life.
25 Keats's gravestone in Rome bears the words: 'Here lies One Whose Name was writ in Water'.

James Russell Lowell. In the plaudits Oliver Wendell Holmes spontaneously elicited was no jarring note; the genial character of the man and the author evoked harmonious and unanimous applause. The historian[26] whom strove to rehabilitate Henry VIII, and told elaborately the story of 'the spacious times of great Elizabeth', was honoured by the majority of those who could estimate his great powers as a vivid delineator of perhaps the most important as well as the most picturesque period of English history. But he had fierce and not too scrupulous critics to contend with; and though a man may bear with outward equanimity criticism which wounds and is intended to wound, it is impossible to suppose him sharing in that enjoyment of life which marked the career of the American author. Of Earl Grey and the Comte de Paris I will not speak; the demise of the principal proprietor of *The Times* will, doubtless, be the subject of fitting editorial comment; and of Alexander III, by far and away the least to be envied of the eminent above-named, I have said quantum suff. in another column. I turn to the name of a much humbler man than any of those named, but whose departure from this life should not miss record in the columns of the *Newcastle Weekly Chronicle.*

On Saturday, 3 November, I received the barest possible notice of the death of John Bedford Leno, at Uxbridge, on Wednesday, 31 October. It must be five years since I met Mr Leno, when he visited me at Enfield. At that time he still lived in London; but, shortly afterwards, increasing infirmities drove him to leave the haunts of old Drury and to return to his native place, Uxbridge, Middlesex, where he passed his last days in the company of family-friends. When he was at Enfield, I saw he was 'breaking-up'. For a year or two I continued to hear from him, occasionally; and for the last few years – four or five at least – I have sent him the *Weekly Chronicle* regularly. He ceased, however, to be able to write, and my own miserable infirmities prevented visiting him at Uxbridge, though always intended and hoped for. I received a letter from Mr James Leno, only about a week before the end, in which, speaking of his brother, he said: 'He is much about the same, being confined to his room. He wishes to be remembered to you', et cetera. I little thought the end was so near.

The funeral took place at Uxbridge Cemetery yesterday (Sunday), and I much regretted my enforced absence. I have waited until the latest possible moment for some account of the last sad offices, but nothing has come to hand. I have consulted the most likely newspapers – one morning and four evening; they are all silent.

John Bedford Leno was born in Uxbridge on 29 June 1826. After passing

26 Froude.

some time as a rural postboy, he entered a printing office, and, though not immediately, became an apprentice to learn the typographic art. Very early politics engaged his attention, in part owing to intimacy with two young men – Kinsbury, a free trader, and Farrell, a Chartist. After some hesitation, Leno adopted Chartism as his political creed, and soon afterwards opened a branch of the National Charter Association in Uxbridge. His apprenticeship ended, he passed some time as a wanderer, 'on tramp', seeking employment, which he only occasionally found and for short terms. Ultimately he returned to Uxbridge, and there made the acquaintance of Mr Gerald Massey. Very soon the two young enthusiasts, with but little assistance and a capital of 15s produced No. 1 of *The Spirit of Freedom*, a publication breathing the very spirit of militant Chartism. It continued for twelve months, though published under difficulties. His next essay was in London in a co-operative printing office, where the work was not always certain, and the pay even less so. Leno became contributor to the *Christian Socialist* and a very active worker in the Chartist movement until its collapse in the early fifties. Subsequently he came associated with Edmond Beales, Odger, and Howell, the last still to the fore and MP. With noted foreign revolutionists he also had amicable relations, including Alexander Herzen and Karl Marx.[27] He always managed to have a small printing office of his own, but never made a fortune by 'the art preservative of all arts'.[28] He also for some years was a trader in second-hand books in Booksellers Row, where I found him on coming from America in 1878. Within a few years subsequently, the loss of his wife and eldest son evidently told injuriously upon his health, and no doubt went far to make him prematurely aged. The story of his life, more fully told, will be found prefixed to the last issue of poetry, *The Aftermath*, published in 1892 by Reeves and Turner, 196, Strand.

Mr Leno was better known as a poet than a political leader to the generation which has arisen within the last twenty years. A minor poet, it must be said; but his lyrics have received the warm commendation of such authorities as the *Athenæum* and a number of the London and country weeklies. The titles of his poetical works are *Drury Lane Lyrics, Kimburton, The Last Idler*, and *The Aftermath*. Their merits would well entitle them to appear in a collected and uniform edition if any publisher would venture upon the work. In *Drury Lane Lyrics* and *Kimburton*, there are excellent specimens of his muse, such as 'The Song of the Spade', 'The Old and New Parson', with many more that could be worthily named, did space and time permit.

27 Leno had been a member of the general council of the First International.
28 A traditional way of referring to printing.

How few now survive of the men who entered the movement when John Bedford Leno and Gerald Massey enlisted under the Chartist banner, and fewer still – how very few! – who assisted at the inception of the People's Charter of 1837. But be there no lament. 'Nothing is here for tears, nothing to wail'.[29] John Bedford Leno as honestly as enthusiastically threw himself into the struggle for Freedom and Right, and Pope and Burns have placed the honest man upon a pedestal from which no hostility, no detraction can dislodge him.

10 November 1894

Frederick Engels

Never did it flash upon my mind that under the above well-known headline[30] I might have to inscribe the name of Frederick Engels. True, I knew him to be no longer young, nor free from infirmities; but, considering his bodily vigour – at least until a year ago – and still more marked mental power, the idea of death in connection with his personality never occurred to me. I did not know, until the very day I am writing these words, of distressing and (as the event has proved) fatal maladies besieging his house of life for some months past – once more attesting that

> Death is here, death is there,
> Death is busy everywhere.
> First our pleasures die, and then
> Our hopes, and then our fears, and when
> These are dead Earth claims its due:
> Dust to dust, and we die too.

In one respect Shelley's lines[31] fail to apply to Frederick Engels. His hopes never died. He classed himself as a pessimist, but he was far from being a disciple of Schopenhauer. To the last he remained singularly hopeful of the best results destined to spring from this country's conflicts and struggles. He may have been right, he may have been wrong; but his optimistic anticipations inspired a joyous participation in the activities of younger men. Per contra: the same cause spurred him on to undertake tasks beyond his bodily strength, though quite within the compass of his intellectual powers.

29 Milton, *Samson Agonistes*.
30 'The Roll-Call'.
31 From 'Death'.

I had known him, he had been my friend and occasional correspondent, over half-a-century. It was in 1843 that he came over from Bradford to Leeds, and enquired for me at the *Northern Star* office. On responding to his enquiry, I found a tall, handsome young man, with a countenance of almost boyish youthfulness, whose English, in spite of his German birth and education, was even then remarkable for its accuracy. He told me he was a constant reader of the *Northern Star*, and took a keen interest in the Chartist movement. Thus began our friendship fifty and two years ago.

Frederick Engels first saw the light on 28 November 1820, and thus at the time of his death was well advanced in his 75th year. He was born in the manufacturing town of Barmen, near Elberfeldt, Rhenish Prussia. Barmen is a name not familiar to newspaper readers in general, but quite familiar to our textile manufacturers as a competitor of Manchester, and more specifically, Coventry. Probably at the birth of Frederick Engels the population would have been considerably under 30,000. It must now be from 110,000 to 115,000, constituting one of the busiest hives of varied industry to be found on the surface of the globe.

In that industrial centre Frederick Engels's father was a manufacturer, energetic and thriving. Of the education of the deceased I have no particulars, but he must have been a rapid learner; and, thanks to a splendid memory, all that he gained he retained. I believe he did his term of service in the Prussian ranks, and that experience did not increase his admiration of the Prussian military system or the Prussian Government. He must have engaged early in business, for at the age of 22 he was sent by his father's firm to Manchester, where he remained two years. Over and above attending to his father's interests as a cotton-spinner, Frederick Engels made a personal and searching investigation into the condition of the factory hands and the working people generally, one result of which was his book on *The Condition of the Working Classes in England*, a work throwing a lurid light upon the causes which imparted so much bitterness to the Chartist movement and easily accounted for the frantic responses to the wrath-provoking speeches and sermons of the Methodist preacher broke loose – the Rev J. Rayner Stephens. Frederick Engels went back to Germany in 1844, returning by way of Paris, where he for the first time met Karl Marx – to whom he attached himself with a devotion which never changed, or in the slightest degree cooled, to the last hour of his life. Four years subsequently came the crash of the Paris Revolution, quickly followed by the European bouleversement, in which most of the thrones were shaken to their foundations, and the King of Prussia had to make his humble obeisance to his insurgent Berliners, and the Machiavellian Metternich had to seek safety for his carcase through hasty and undignified flight from Vienna. In the course of the turmoil of these years Marx and Engels made themselves a power in Rhenish Prussia – feared and hated – through the formidable instrumentality of their *New Rhenish Gazette*. But the reaction triumphed, the *Gazette* was suppressed, and Marx and Engels had to leave Cologne and betake themselves elsewhere. Many a gallant spirit and noble heart sank, fallen on the battlefield, immolated on the scaffold, consigned to years of misery in fortress-prisons, or driven into exile to linger out bitter years of disappointment and penury. Karl Marx and Frederick Engels, sometimes together, at others apart, mistrusting merely political revolutions even when achieving a measure of success, set themselves to the further study of social questions, with such results as the International Working Men's Association, Marx's famous book *Das Kapital*, the rapid growth and now formidable strength of the German Socialist party, and that International Socialism on the Continent which 'with fear of change perplexes monarchs'[32] and even Society at large.

In 1850 Frederick Engels returned to business in Manchester, and in 1864 was made a partner in the firm; but in 1869 he retired from business on such an arrangement as assured him a sufficient competence to enable him to give his time to study and authorship in collaboration with his friend. On the death of Karl Marx in 1883, he naturally became his friend's literary executor; and under his editorship, and mainly by his labour, the second and third volumes of Marx's great work were published in English. I believe there have been Russian and other translations. The fourth and concluding volume, in English, has not yet appeared. Of original work besides the book above mentioned, Frederick Engels wrote on *The Origin of the Family*, and *Socialism, Scientific and Utopian* – works I have not seen. I had the idea he had written, or was writing, a Life of Karl Marx, but am told that is a mistake. I had hoped he had left some memoirs or notes of his own life; but I hear such is not the case. When urged to write memoirs of himself, he would reply, 'What the world is entitled to know of me is contained in my books; the rest must be considered private'. The story of his life told by himself would have been highly interesting. In this country he had known intimately leading Owenites, Chartists, and trade unionists, and on the Continent a large number of public characters and revolutionary celebrities.

His knowledge of European languages placed almost innumerable sources of information at his command, and gave him an authority which no one-tongue man can ever claim. He is said to have been the master of ten languages! O cruel Fate! why must we lose such men? With all his knowledge of tongues he was not a public speaker. It was the same with Karl Marx. Of

32 Milton, *Paradise Lost*, Book 1.

course with minds so richly stored as theirs they could easily have given speech-utterance to their profound, far-reaching and overflowing thoughts. But they seemed to share Mazzini's dislike of platform oratory, shrinking from the notoriety so much desired by lesser men.

He had become the Nestor of International Socialism. Not more natural was it for Titus to succeed Vespasian than for Frederick Engels to take the place of his revered friend when Karl Marx had passed away. He was the trusted counsellor whose advice no one dared to gainsay. Probably the private history of German Socialism could tell how much the party is indebted to his wise counsels in smoothing acerbities, preventing friction, mildly chastening ill-regulated ambition, and promoting the union of all for each and each for all. The author of *Das Kapital* was supremely fortunate in having so devoted a friend. The friendship of the two was something far away from the common. If not positively unique, we must go back to ancient friends to find a parallel. Either would have emulated Damon's offered sacrifice for his friend Pythias. In their public work, as champions of their ideas, they were like 'the Great Twin Brethren who fought so well for Rome'.[33]

For many years Frederick Engels's residence was at 122, Regent's Park Road, nearly opposite to one of the gate entrances to Primrose Hill. Within the last twelve months, or something over, he had removed to 41, Regent's Park Road, and there the illness began which, no doubt, sapped away his life – that cruel disease, cancer of the throat. The immediate cause of death is ascribed to an attack of pneumonia. 'Now I must sleep', said Byron, and closing his eyes, he entered upon his long sleep. And so with Frederick Engels; he had fallen into a blissful slumber, and in that state peaceably and painlessly passed away.

I must leave to the editor to give an account of the funeral, including the names of the more prominent mourners. Besides strong Socialist delegations from Germany, France, etc, some members of the deceased's family were present, and must have been impressed by the signal marks of respect paid to the honoured dead. The remains were disposed of by cremation at Woking. It was well. It is a pleasing reflection that the horrors of the grave and mortality's corruption cannot be associated with our remembrance of Frederick Engels. In the case of his remains, 'ashes to ashes, dust to dust', has no double or imperfect meaning.

In person, Frederick Engels would have been remarkable amidst ten thousand. Slender and tall, he must have stood 5ft 11in or 6ft. Of late years

33 Thomas Babington Macaulay, *Lays of Ancient Rome.* 'The Great Twin Brethren' are Castor and Pollux intervening at the Battle of Lake Regillus.

his height was somewhat detracted from by a stoop, not arising, I fancy, from age, but from almost incessant stooping over the writing-desk. He was near-sighted, and that materially tended to increase the habitual stoop. His eyes were blue, his hair brown, his complexion somewhat florid. He had been the victim of a growing deafness for some years, and that was some obstacle to his conversational powers. Like, I believe, most short-sighted people, he wrote a very 'small hand'; but his calligraphy was very neat and clear. His letters were marvels of information, and he wrote an immense number in spite of his long hours of original composition or given to the work of translation. He attended most of the eight hours demonstrations[34] in Hyde Park, but I doubt if 16 hours covered his average day's work when he was at his best. For many years he 'burnt the midnight oil' until 2am. Of late years, I believe, under medical advice, that error was abated, it may be suspected, too late. But he was one of those men with whom it is useless to argue on such a question, their fixed conviction being 'better to wear out than rust out'. They must work or die. That is a failing that leans to virtue's side. But this man so given over to toil of mind and body could always find or make time to answer the claims of friendship, to listen to the stories of the aggrieved, and to express his sympathy in corresponding action. With all his knowledge and all his influence, there was nothing of the 'stuck up', or 'standoffishness' about him. He was just as modest and ready for self-effacement at the age of 72 as I had found him at the age of 22 when he called at the *Northern Star* office. Not only his intimate friends, but dependents, servants, children, all loved him –

Of manners gentle, of affections mild;
In wit a man, simplicity a child.[35]

Although Karl Marx was his great friend, his heart was large enough for other friendships, and his kindness was unfailing. He was largely given to hospitality, but the principal charm at his hospitable board was his own 'table talk', the 'good Rhine wine'[36] of his felicitous conversation and genial wit. He was himself laughter-loving, and his laughing was contagious. A joy-inspirer, he made all around him share his happy mood of mind. One remarkable trait of his personal appearance I had nearly forgotten, and must insert here. Of course he could not prevent, nor did he seek to avert the natural ravages of accumulating years. But, looking at him, you could not suppose he had ever been middle-aged. He had passed from the first to

34 The eight hours movement originated in 1886 with the publication of Tom Mann's pamphlet, *What a Compulsory Eight-Hour Working Day Means to the Workers.*
35 Alexander Pope, 'Epitaph on Gay'.
36 From a popular song, 'The Good Rhine Wine'.

the third stage of life, without passing through the second. I speak of him as he continued until about a year ago; I had not seen him since. You could see the young man, almost the boyish youth, beneath the (hardly visible) lineaments of riper years. In that respect, he more than any other man I ever knew, resembled Ralph Waldo Emerson, whose almost boyish face I have seen many times in Boston when the great essayist and poet had become, in years, 'an old man'.

Enough! No more. I must conclude these few words of esteem, regard, and affection:

> Friend of my earlier days;
> None knew thee but to love thee,
> Nor named thee but to praise.[37]

17 August 1895

OTHER RADICAL PERSONALITIES

Karl Marx

Review of *Revolution and Counter-Revolution in Germany: Or Germany in 1848*, edited by Eleanor Marx Aveling[38]

In spite of the bitter disappointment experienced by the hopeful believers in human progress at the latter end of 1848 and in the course of 1849, it was worth while living in those years. The events of the two or three preceding years, especially 1847, had created the expectancy of great changes in Europe, at least among those who desired such changes. For the rest they had no idea that they were on the edge of a volcano, nor that the thin crust on which they trod might at any moment break beneath their feet and possibly engulph them in the revolutionary lava. Only a week or two before the outbreak in Paris, the *Spectator* was commenting on the general dullness and uninteresting character of European politics: when, lo! as if from the stroke of an enchanter's wand, apathy gave place to excitement, confidence to fear, and languid hope assumed the character of burning enthusiasm.

37 Fitz-Greene Halleck, 'On the Death of Joseph Rodman Drake'. Halleck (1790–1867) was a US poet highly regarded and much read in his day.

38 The original articles had been published in 1851-2 under the sole name of Marx, although essentially written by Engels, a fact unknown to Eleanor Marx when she published the collection as a work of her father's. Harney reviewed a copy inscribed: 'George Julian Harney / from his old friends' Karl & Jenny Marx's daughter / Eleanor Marx Aveling / August 1896'.

Paris rose, and the monarchy of July fell. Vienna, Berlin, Milan, followed suit; in fact, all Continental Europe was in a blaze. The granting of liberal constitutions, the flight of kings, or their submissive appearance with tears in their eyes, and penitential attitude, before their triumphantly rebellious, half-contemptuous, but too generously-confiding people – these were events of almost daily occurrence for a time. All things seemed possible, all visions but portents of coming realities:

> Ancient and holy rebel, Freedom, dear!
> Arm'd with fetters our forefathers wore;
> Triumphant! bids Equality appear;
> And she, O! Man, descends from Heaven once more,

as someone has 'Englished' Béranger.[39] But these effulgent hopes were soon overclouded: 'They came like Truth, and disappeared like dreams'.[40] In this volume we have to meet its author, not as the prophet of International Socialism, the Moses of Collectivism, but the recorder of revolutionary events in which he had participated. A prefatory note by the editor gives a brief sketch of her father in the early days of his exile, when, with his wife and three young children, he was living in Dean Street, Soho, and writing the letters to the *New York Tribune* which constitute the chapters of this volume. Privation, anxiety, sickness and death, shared, or were visitants to, the exile's rooms. But no pen inferior to the inspired stylus of Lamennais[41] could do justice to the theme of exile; its privations, humiliations, its sorrows, and sometimes, black despair, when a grave among strangers in a strange land became the exile's last and best refuge.

The letters of Karl Marx to the *New York Tribune* do not profess to review the history of Europe in revolution – 1848-1849; they are mainly devoted, as the title of the book indicates, to the revolution and counter-revolution in Germany. It is easy, as the Scotch say, 'to be wise ahint the han' ',[42] and the imbecilities of the Frankfurt Diet, and the halting weaknesses of the various revolutionary administrations for a brief term invested with power, are mercilessly laid bare under the Marxian scalpel; and, of course, the bourgeoisie are held accountable for the complete and ruinous failure

39 Pierre-Jean de Béranger (1780-1857), an enormously popular French poet, Bonapartist, and a great favourite with Harney.
40 Byron, *Childe Harold's Pilgrimage*, 4, vii.
41 Hugues-Félicité Robert de Lamennais (1782-1854), the French Catholic priest and thinker who was excommunicated, becoming increasingly liberal and progressive and sitting as a deputy in the Constituent Assembly of 1848. He was briefly in exile, 1815-16.
42 'To be wise behind the hand.'

which befell, not only Germany, but Continental Europe in general. It might be asked: Would the result have widely and more happily differed had the bourgeoisie been thrust aside and the proletariat conducted the revolution? Some of us have a good recollection of the ideal working man, with a less agreeable knowledge of the real working man. Be it understood the ideal working man was not a myth. He was to be found on the barricades and in the fortress-prison, slain, or dying in exile; he was to be found even among our humbler Chartists, attested by self-sacrifice quite unappreciated by his successors. But the ideal working man was far from constituting the majority, else there would have been no counter-revolution. Twenty years after the complete suppression of the revolution, the proletariat of Paris had their opportunity. Was the Commune other than a ghastly failure? I do not speak of its suppression under superior force; I refer to its conduct day by day – its acts inspired by hesitation and inconsistency and attended by suspicion and terror. Dr Marx himself laments, in more than one place, the ignorance and unfitness of the working classes in 1848-49 to take themselves the stern duties which the circumstances of the time required. But enough! Looking for brief and suitable extracts from these letters, I select from the author's vivid account of the storming and betrayal of Vienna. It should be premised that the Viennese had generously and gallantly risen against the armed forces of the government about to be employed to crush the Hungarians. The immediate object of the rising had been achieved. The Emperor and Court fled to Olmütz, but, gathering courage, a vast army was collected outside the insurgent capital under the command of the truculent Windischgrätz, reinforced by the brutal savage Jellachich[43] and his Croats – the perpetrators of atrocities rivalling, if not exceeding, those which in after years were so cleverly engineered by Mr Gladstone to effect his return to power, but which failed to elicit any expression of his sentiments in 1848-9. The forces for the defence of the city were utterly inadequate. The provisional government hesitated and omitted to call in the Hungarian army encamped but a few leagues from the city. For a short term, the Polish General Bem was in command, but he gave up the task overwhelmed as he was by distrust ....

In the following extract the writer severely censures the Hungarians for not taking the initiative in making the defence of Vienna their own battleground. I think his strictures perfectly justified and that the Hungarians made a most lamentable mistake ....

43 Josip Jelačić (1801-59), military commander, who was successful in tying Croatian nationalism to the Habsburg cause in 1848. He has remained a great Croat hero, contemporary Zagreb's central square bearing his name and a triumphal equestrian statue.

... I must try to find room for Dr Marx's notice of one of the noblest martyrs of the Revolution – Robert Blum ....

It only remains for me to very heartily recommend this volume as a valuable contribution to the history of Revolutionary Europe in 1848; and as a welcome souvenir of the extraordinary man, its author. To many the name of Karl Marx as the author of *Das Kapital*, the prophet pioneer of Militant Socialism, is a name of terror; but those who knew him personally can entertain only pleasant recollections of one of the most warm-hearted, genial, and attractive of men.

26 September 1896

Arthur O'Neill

In my letter on the death of Thomas Cooper, speaking of the very few surviving Chartist leaders, I made mention of Mr W.J. Linton and Mr Samuel Kydd.[44] Another survivor should have been named – the Rev Arthur O'Neill, of Birmingham. The omission brought me the following note from Mr William B. Smith, of Birmingham: 'In your notice of Thomas Cooper's death, published in the *Newcastle Chronicle*, you forget to mention the name of Rev Arthur O'Neill as one of the remaining Chartists who suffered imprisonment about the year 1841-2. Arthur O'Neill, who at that time resided in Birmingham, was sentenced to twelve months' imprisonment in Stafford Jail, and was confined in Stafford at the same time as Thomas Cooper served his imprisonment. Mr O'Neill is still residing in Birmingham, and delivered an address at Thomas Cooper's funeral'.

I remember Mr O'Neill in the stormy days of early Chartism. Originally, I think, of West Kilbride, Ayrshire, he early adopted and advocated the principles of the People's Charter. Passing on a lecturing tour into England in 1840 or 1841, he was attracted to Birmingham, where as a 'Christian Chartist' he joined and was appointed pastor of a little chapel in Newhall Street. I believe he had not been trained for the ministry, but had taken part in the Chartist Church movement, which for a time attracted attention in the West of Scotland and some places in the North of England. The recently started 'People's Church' in Manchester and elsewhere is in spirit a revival of the 'Chartist Church', again illustrating the affirmation of the author of Ecclesiastes: 'There is no new thing under the sun'. Mr O'Neill and his congregation subsequently joined the Baptists, and took possession of Zion Chapel, originally belonging to the Swedenborgians, from whom it had

44 'The Roll-Call: Thomas Cooper' above.

been purchased by the Baptists in 1814.

At the outset of his ministerial career, Mr O'Neill continued to give his services to the cause he had early embraced. The agitation of 1842, which brought Thomas Cooper to trouble, had a similar result in the case of Mr O'Neill. For a speech at Cradley, branded as seditious, he was arrested with much parade of soldiery and yeomanry, and treated with the usual inhumanity at that time, while under arrest and remand. Tried in 1843 at Stafford, he defended himself with marked ability, but, of course, was found guilty and sentenced to one year's imprisonment without hard labour. He appears to have been better treated than Thomas Cooper was at the start, and until the elder of the two had given the luckless governor and much-scared chaplain a foretaste of *The Purgatory of Suicides*. Indeed, Mr O'Neill has described his twelve months' durance vile as 'more like a home and a study than a prison, every officer being kind and courteous'.

Since that time, Mr O'Neill's labours, ministerial and other, have been mostly restricted to Birmingham and the neighbourhood. About seven or eight years ago, he resigned his pastorate, with a provision, I believe, for his declining years. It must be, I think, 52 years since I met Mr O'Neill. He is now, I suppose, about 73 years of age, and time must have brought some change in the good looks I remember. I believe he still preaches and lectures occasionally, and quite recently addressed an open-air meeting of 2,000 at Cradley, where he was arrested in 1842. The Rev Arthur O'Neill has my sincere good wishes. I read in a Birmingham paper that 'in politics he is a staunch Gladstonian and Home Ruler'.

6 August 1892

The Deaths of Ernest Jones and Henry George

My friend Mr Stroud was with me on Sunday, and, in the course of conversation, he spoke of the excitement in New York. Mention was made by one of the persons present of the name of Mr Henry George. 'He is dead', said Mr Stroud, with startling effect. I had not seen a Saturday daily paper – the *Newcastle Daily Chronicle* not arriving until late in the evening on that day, and it had not been opened.

I find a striking similarity between the deaths of Mr George and of our eloquent Chartist advocate, Ernest Jones. At the time of the latter's death,[45] I was living at Roxbury, Massachusetts, and was in the habit, when arriving at the Boston Terminus of the Providence Railway, of buying the *Boston*

45 On 26 January 1869.

Advertiser from the station stand. Before I could pick the paper, my eye fell upon the paragraph announcing the death of Ernest Jones. It seemed inconceivable. I had had a few lines from him two or three days previously, telling me that he would send me a full letter as soon as the electoral struggle was over. It will be remembered that he was a candidate for the representation of Manchester, and had been passing through a preliminary contest to determine whether he or the 'Liberal' candidate should be the standard bearer of the United Reform Party.[46] Everything was promising well for the selection of Mr Jones and his ultimate election. He had been speaking at meeting after meeting; sometimes, I believe, two or three times in a day. In his case the end came more rapidly than in that of Mr George. He had arrived home, but before he could reach his bed, he fell upon his wife's shoulder, and, after a few brief pangs, expired: thus happily escaping months or years of pain. But his death was a great loss and a blow to the Manchester Radical Reformers and old Chartists, from which they never recovered.

Mr George, after speaking at four or five meetings, and returning to his hotel apparently none the worse, appears to have died early the ensuing morning, after two hours of unconsciousness.

There is nothing wonderful in such deaths – the wonder is they do not happen more frequently. Impassioned appeals, unceasing excitement, may be borne with at least for a time while men are under forty. But the Fate 'with the abhorred shears' is apt not to allow the like immunity to men of more advanced years.[47]

Mr Henry George was an extraordinary man. But of his career and his written works I say nothing. I once met him at Cambridge, Massachusetts. The portrait given in the *Daily Chronicle*, and which doubtless will appear in the *Weekly*, seems to me excellent. I told him he would not succeed in his crusade.[48] He answered cheerfully: 'Probably not, but when the torch falls from my hands, it will be taken up by another, and so on, until success is assured'. A pleasing and consoling thought often indulged in by unsuccessful reformers, but not often realised.

Mr George was the Working Men's Candidate, fighting alike against the Republican party, too generally corrupt, and the baneful domination of Tammany Hall.[49] Of his chances, had he lived, I cannot speak. Probably,

46 The coalition of disparate elements that was fast becoming the Liberal Party.
47 The Fate is Atropos; the quotation from Milton, *Lycidas*. Jones had died at the age of 50; George was 58.
48 For the 'single-tax' (a tax on the unearned increment of land value).
49 The nickname for the seat of the Democratic Party's political machine in New York City and a byword for corruption and graft. For Harney the physical location of 'the Caucus'.

they were satisfactory to him, and he may have anticipated occupying the Mayoral chair of the Greater New York. Alas! for the vanity of human wishes!

Whether any substitute for Mr George, equally sufficient, can be found by the 'Working Men' is very doubtful. Probably the best next thing that can happen for New York will be the election of the Republican candidate, Mr Seth Low.[50] I had some small knowledge of his father 34 years ago, an eminent ship-owner and merchant, who had suffered considerably from the depredations of the *Alabama*.[51] But he never lost his goodwill towards England. The son is a rich man, and has been a munificent benefactor to New York and I should say is possibly the best candidate the Republicans could have selected.

The loss of Mr George is much to be regretted. He was not only an able, but, I believe, an honest and earnest man. But the curtain has fallen!

6 November 1897

Charles Bradlaugh

How indescribable and inexplicable the mysteries of life: birth, growth, adolescence, maturity, and, then, alas! decay; how awful and inscrutable the mystery of death! Strangely constituted must be that man who can mock at death or find matter for a jest in the associations of dissolution. Whether the departed was believer or unbeliever, and no matter to which category surviving friends belong, Death comes a shock which no fond imaginings of priestly speculation can prevent, no sophisms of philosophical teaching can mitigate. The deceased was, and is not: there is the one unquestionable fact, not to be set aside by preacher or rhetorician. The world was too small for Alexander's ambition in life but a little urn sufficed to hold his ashes in death. The strong as well as the weak must succumb, and this seems passing strange. Universal and certain, Death fails to attract attention to the ordinary cases occurring around us day by day. But the death of a public man whose individuality had strongly impressed his contemporaries, challenges and enforces attention; we feel as if a light had been unexpectedly extinguished, and that 'Black Sunday' of our lives had suddenly descended upon us.

I had but little personal knowledge of the late Mr Charles Bradlaugh; and

50 He was unsuccessful in 1897, but became mayor of New York in 1901. He was one of the leading municipal reformers of the Progressive Era.
51 The British-built Confederate vessel which sank much Northern shipping. See also n185.

the propagandism to which he mainly devoted his energies – for some years under the nom de guerre of 'Iconoclast' – did not attract my sympathies. I thought his energies in a great measure misdirected. His capacity, his courage, his fluent eloquence, his doggedness of purpose, his ability to transform defeat into the means of achieving victory, showed him to be possessed of unusual qualities.

Men who differed widely from many of the views held and championed by Charles Bradlaugh, sympathised with his efforts to break down the barriers that hindered men of his way of thinking from fully participating in the rights and franchises of their fellow citizens. There may be political reasons for opposing the aggressions or intrigues of a political religion, as Milton believed and Cromwell enforced. But Agnostics or other Freethinkers are certainly not a danger to the State, and have the fullest right to share with Christians and Jews in the guardianship and administration of the Commonwealth. So, too, will Moslems, Buddhists, Parsees, and the believers in Brahma and Vishnu, should representatives of those faraway subjects of the British Crown present themselves, as in the days to come they may, before the Speaker to inscribe their names on the Parliamentary roll. The admission of Charles Bradlaugh to a seat in the House was the crowning victory of Good Sense over Prejudice and of Justice over Intolerance. With that victory the name of the deceased member for Northampton is inseparably connected. Had he lived, it is probable that a few years would have seen him something more than what is called 'a private member'. That he would have retained his old popularity is doubtful. He was already at feud with the Socialists and New Trades Unionists,[52] and the two combined present the appearance of a growing power. His Malthusianism would have made him obnoxious to our old Chartists who had listened to the noble-hearted Richard Oastler, and been inspired to frenzied enthusiasm by the Vesuvian eloquence of Joseph Rayner Stephens. The cause of Republicanism was certainly not advanced by connecting it with Malthusianism and Atheism. The deceased has been likened by newspaper writers to William Cobbett. But the only likeness I see is in the dogged perseverance of both. There would have been fierce war between them had they been contemporaries.

It is curious that the act of reparation which the House of Commons performed in abrogating the resolution of 1880 denying the elected of Northampton both affirmation and oath – a preposterous resolution – was voted almost simultaneously with his death. Voted on the Tuesday evening, it is true, and the last breath of the sufferer was not aspirated until Friday

52 The New Unionists. Harney invariably calls trade unions 'trades unions' even when only a single occupation – or trade – was organised.

morning; but it has been stated that he was too ill, or unconscious, to permit of the decision of the House being made known to him. 'They run!' was the cheering cry that recalled light to closing eyes of Wolfe dying on the plains of Abraham, for it announced that, after a gallant struggle, the French had scattered before the British charge; and in the gory cockpit of the *Victory*, the ringing cheers of his sailors, as ship after ship of the enemy 'struck',[53] brought joy to the heart of Nelson, though in the throes of death; and it seems hard to deny that a similar consolation, unstained by blood, was denied to the late member for Northampton.

Charles Bradlaugh's stalwart strength, both of body and mind, made the spectacle of that mortal helplessness [which] must come to us all the more pathetic. Strange that the big and powerful man who was but yesterday (so to speak) so pronounced, so prominent, with probabilities before him of attaining to more than even dreams of ambition may have suggested in his earlier years, should now be nothing – nothing but a name! 'We are such stuff as dreams are made of, and our little life is rounded with a sleep'.[54]

7 February 1891

Edward Aveling – and the Northampton By-Election

The Northampton election will be over before this letter can appear in print; but I may offer a few words on a matter of public interest, quite independent of who may be elected or which party may triumph. As politically the late member[55] was a Gladstonian, it may be presumed that the Gladstonian candidate will most likely be returned. There was a third candidate; at least Dr Aveling would have been a third candidate but for the iniquitous law which demands that £100 'guarantee money' for the expenses of the election be lodged in the hands of the returning officer. Had Dr Aveling found that £100, and gone to the poll, elected or not elected, he would have been mulcted[56] in a further and larger amount. Not being in a position to advance the £100, his nomination was refused.

I have some slight knowledge of Dr Aveling. I fancy we are not of the same opinion on more than one point; but I must acknowledge my belief that he would make his mark in Parliament. He is young, ardent, able, a man of untiring activity, who looks as if he never rested or slept. I never heard him speak, but as he speaks frequently, he is probably a good debater.

53 Surrendered.
54 Shakespeare, *The Tempest*, 4, i.
55 Bradlaugh.
56 Swindled.

He certainly has the courage, I may, without offence, say the audacity of his opinions. Let him or any other man be excluded from Parliament on principle, if his principles or opinions are deemed by the electors injurious or unsound; but not because he cannot find £100 toward expenses which ought no more to be charged to his account than should be the salary of the Town Clerk of Northampton. Such a charge is mere robbery, whether the person mulcted is poor or rich. Northampton desires representation in Parliament. Very well: let Northampton pay the expenses of the election. Every charge in connection with that election should be paid out of the rates.

Of what use the abolition of the property qualification if the working man, or the poor man, is told he must find £100 down, with the prospect of some hundreds more to pay! The pretended free election, with all its ballot paraphernalia, is a fraud. More on this theme – the present mode of conducting elections – on another occasion. Meanwhile, let the injustice, the legalised wrong done at Northampton, be kept steadily in view. I think the Parliamentary system an intolerable humbug; but as long as it lasts, I say, as the Cornish pastor said to his congregation of wreckers: 'Let us all start fair!'

14 February 1891

Madame Blavatsky – and Annie Besant

That portion of the earth's surface termed the United States is very largely a land of cranks. If any one has a new quack medicine, a new quack government, or a new quack social system to introduce into the world, the States constitute his 'happy hunting ground', and of course, in such experiments, Boston is the 'hub' of the universe. Amongst the 'lions' on view in Boston is a Mr J.M. Wade, who dabbles in Spiritualistic literature, and keeps up personal intercourse with great departed. At a recent spiritual séance he 'had a long talk with James Freeman Clarke,[57] Michael Faraday, and many of the most notable men who have lived in the past ages'. But more important still – one of his familiar spirits promised to assist him to write out, at her dictation, the Memoirs of Madame Blavatsky since her death. He was to get a new Yost typewriter (a capital advertisement for the Yost), and place it in a cabinet with some folio paper. Nothing like a 'cabinet' in these matters! That was all! The memoirs came typewritten on the paper out of the cabinet: what more could be desired! They have been

---

57 James Freeman Clarke (1810-88) was a progressive US theologian and writer.

duly printed – at Mr Wade's expense, of course.

Helena Petrovna (Madame Blavatsky) had a curious life of adventure. She was born at Ekaterinoslov, in the South of Russia. She was of German descent, and she says, 'I was called within my earliest recollection Mlle Hahn, or von Hahn, or de Hahn'. 'When she was taken to be baptised, the sponsors were just in the act of renouncing the Evil One and his deeds, when a little relative, a child, toying with her lighted taper, in a moment of forgetfulness set fire to the long flowing robes of the priest, resulting in the burning of the old priest and several persons'. On her seventh birthday, she says she 'was found in company with a tall man of dark skin and with a long dark beard'. 'This', she informs us, 'was my first meeting with the abstract form of my Master'. HBP, or her personator, goes on: 'At this interview with my "Master", he gave me an amulet and some fine grass, which, when turned, gave me power over the elementary life, and made the Roussalka, domovoys, gnomes, sylphs, and undines obey and protect me'. We are suddenly jumped from this Mabatmic, or Satanic, visit to an uncertified statement of her marriage 'on 7 July 1848 to General Nicephore Blavatsky, who was Vice-Governor of the province of Erivan, Caucasus. Soon after we find her in Paris, London, and elsewhere. One incident in Mexico is worth recording in her own words: 'There it was that I saw a Jesus on the outside of one chapel, dressed in green tights, and a wild bull in full pursuit, thus mixing the pastime in the thoughts of the people with their idea of an immortal life and their redeemer'. She turned up in India just before the Mutiny. She says: 'I had changed my name so many times that I really did not remember but vaguely who I was. I had been male and female alternately, as it suited my purposes and surroundings.' As to India, many suspected her of being a Russian spy, though a spy, if even in appearance feminine, should have some charm of look or manner. A portrait of her appeared in her friend Stead's paper, and, judging from it, she must have been 'in the flesh', about the ugliest specimen of the petticoated sex. According to her own story, she married Mr Bethinelli in America, the record being in the registers of Philadelphia. But she declared herself 'sexless'. She married Nicephore Blavatsky because it was revealed to her that 'you find in the name Blavatsky the key to your incarnate existence at this era'; and she married Mr Bethinelli to 'avoid his astral companionship, which he had promised if I failed to connect myself with him by this act'.

This farrago of 'rubbidge'[58] makes no revelation of Madame's doings since 'she turned up her toes to the daisies', and so her pretended Memoirs are published under false pretences. Any one who professes to take

58 A jocular term, unfortunately much relished by Harney, for 'rubbish'.

them seriously must belong to one or two sets whose names need not be particularised. I quote what is said (in the article under notice) respecting one of the best known of Madame's disciples.

As most of the readers of the *Weekly Chronicle* are aware, Mrs Annie Besant[59] has become one of the most shining lights of what she calls 'Theosophy': by many regarded as the English successor of Madame Blavatsky, who, however, appears not to be very proud of the performances of her follower, judging of the way in which she speaks of that lady in these memoirs:

As to Mrs Besant, these Posthumous Memoirs say her deception of the public, however unintentional, under the Machiavellian influence of William Q. Judge, is most mischievous, resulting in her failure in the trust imposed (sic) by me in her, and before the public partially undoing the good work by losing the good opinion of capabilities as a trained oculist, well fitted to observe phenomena. How anyone who stood so close to me as did Besant could be fooled by these flimsy communications, I cannot conceive. I certainly thought and believed that I left in the possession of Besant and the household the secret of my return as a metaphysical fact in metempsychosis, and to be led by the nose and fooled before the public as to the most signal of our powers, in the messages of the Mahatmas, is a crowning disgrace, and one which the Masters will not easily pass by. She can never regain the confidence of the public in this work, and no matter what the desire the Masters might have to give something to the world as to their intentions, they could not possibly do it through the organism of Mrs Annie Besant, for it would only bring her into greater ridicule, and the public would not believe her credulity or even honesty after her fall.

Further on, she thus apostrophises the erratic lady: 'Poor Annie'. After the above outbreak, it is needless to add anything, save Hamlet's counsel: 'Go to a nunnery, go!', though perhaps one reflection may be pardoned. Ladies and gentlemen, who throw off the yoke of superstition, renounce all religions, and abjure all priests and priestcraft, will do well to pause before taking to the press and the platform for the ventilation of their opinions. Their opinions simply concern themselves; but their propagandism cannot fail to concern other people. I have seen 'great leaders' go about denouncing all religions, but subsequently giving their adhesion to the most bare-faced charlatanry and imposture under the name of some new religion. Their adherence to the heresies, and then to the new orthodoxies, may be quite

59 Besant, once Bradlaugh's helpmate and intimate, was a Fabian socialist and proponent of trade unionism before being drawn to theosophy.

sincere at both ends, but their 'Jump-Jim-Crowisms'[60] may not be so easy to their followers.

To conclude. As to the great Theosophist, Wade, I fear he is too hopelessly submerged in the miry waters of credulity to save him from wreck and ruin. But I will remind my Boston readers that they have excellent institutions for feeble-minded youths and mature imbecility – including one of the best lunatic asylums at Waverley, where the wavering may find rest and refreshment of the mind as in the institution formerly at Somerville.

27 November 1897

THE 1830s AND 1840s

The Society for the Diffusion of Useful Knowledge

If memory serves it was in the year 1827 or '28 (I think '27) that Henry, subsequently created Lord Brougham (Baron Brougham and Vaux), with a number of kindred spirits, the most active and efficient being Charles Knight, the author and publisher, founded the Society for the Diffusion of Useful Knowledge. Of the publications issued under the patronage or the encouragement afforded by the said society, the two best remembered were the *Penny Magazine* and the *Penny Cyclopædia* – so called because issued in penny weekly numbers – a monumental work rather 'sniffed at' by 'respectable people' on account of its plebeian 'penny' title. It may still be picked up complete in a number of volumes for a few shillings at the second-hand booksellers; and though many of its articles are now necessarily not up-to-date, three-fourths of the contents of the *Penny Cyclopædia* are still of excellent value for reference. The labours of the Society for the Diffusion of Useful Knowledge were not too favourably viewed by others than the 'respectables'. The political upheaval stimulated by the 'three glorious days' of 1830[61] called into existence the Unstamped Press – beginning with Carpenter's *Political Letters* and Hetherington's *Poor Man's Guardian*. The conductors of the Unstamped, repeating and enlarging on the iniquities set forth in the *Black Book* (1821, and subsequent editions), were contemptuous in their reference to such knowledge as that provided by the *Penny Magazine*, with its pictures of old abbeys, birds, beasts, reptiles, etc, affirming that the

60 'Jump Jim Crow' is a song and dance imitating African-Americans; 'to jump Jim Crow' is to act like a stereotyped stage caricature of a black person. Harney is using 'Jump-Jim-Crowisms' to cover the exaggerated dance movements and contorted physical movements of blackface performers.
61 The July Revolution of 1830, overthrowing the Bourbon monarchy in France.

true useful knowledge was to expose the evils brought upon the country by oligarchical government, and to promote the guidance of the people to claim their rights with the necessary instruction to perform their duties as men and citizens. From their point of view the Unstamped writers were correct. Still it would have been better if they had admitted that all learning is not limited to the political questions of the day, and that (Pope's dictum notwithstanding) even 'a little knowledge' concerning things in general is far preferable to none. Included in the Society's publications was a cheap, well-written history of Greece, well calculated to impart political knowledge of much interest and value. According to Richard Cobden, a single day's number of *The Times* is of more value to us moderns than the work of Thucydides in its entirety. My humble opinion differs very much from that of the great Free Trader: in my view Thucydides' History is worth infinitely more than a copy of *The Times*, or of all the big (and little) London papers put together.

The Society for the Diffusion of Useful Knowledge was hardly a success, though the publication of the *Penny Magazine* continued for over a dozen years. Since the disappearance of the society, there has been no similar organisation set up. The Cobden Club's numerous publications are all restricted to one theme, for, whatever the text, the sermon is devoted to the defence or furtherance of Free Trade. There are now other politico-literary societies, for example, the Humanitarian League,[62] with a long list of publications, some of which will have notice in this column when I can find opportunity. The Fabians have issued a large number of Socialistic pamphlets and tracts; and, per contra, there is the newer organisation of the Liberty and Property Defence League,[63] also prolific in its countermining publications.

But as far as I am aware there is no society or other organisation taking for its mission the diffusion of Knowledge on British historical subjects, for which there is sore need. I am aware that many valuable historical works come from the British press, not the least valuable being those epitomes of history, and those narratives of special periods, such as the Wars of the Roses and the decline of Feudalism, the Great Civil War, the rise of modern industrial England, etc, mainly printed for school-use and the reading of

62 Launched in 1891 by the socialist and vegetarian Henry Salt and, opposed to avoidable suffering inflicted on any sentient being, it seeking to end corporal and capital punishment, hunting and vivisection.

63 Founded in 1882 by Lord Wemyss (also known as Lord Elcho), a Conservative politician, for the support of *laissez-faire* trade and attracting those alarmed by socialism and trade unionism as well as many liberals and philosophical individualists. Wemyss was a generous contributor to Harney's testimonial in 1897.

young people wanting means and time to purchase and study the larger works. Still it is lamentable to have to acknowledge the great majority's ignorance of their country's history, of the measures of right and justice wrung from oppressive rulers, and of the noble services of the men who gained those victories, daring dungeons and death. Of the tens of thousands of cyclists who swarm on our roads, of the twenty or forty thousands gathered to witness some football match between two rival counties, how many, with their ugly scull-caps and short pipes, care or know aught of the men – the great and the humble – who built up this England of ours? Patriotism has become a by-word, by knaves and fools made synonymous with 'Jingoism', whilst whole pages of the newspapers are given up to 'the Pastimes of the People'. If there are any who would set their hands to the good work of attempting to efface the present shame, I can offer them a noble example and model in the acts and deeds of the Old South,[64] Boston, United States of North America [two volumes of whose leaflets Harney continues by reviewing].

30 June 1896

"TO STOP THE DUKE, GO FOR GOLD"

In the section of Mr Holyoake's Autobiography[65] in the *Weekly Chronicle*, 5 July, there are some statements concerning Francis Place, including a reference to a famous poster or placard said to have had considerable moral effect in driving the Duke of Wellington from power at the climax of the Reform Bill agitation. Well acquainted with the placard, I was surprised to read Mr Holyoake's account of the authorship, which I had always understood was the work, not of Francis Place, but of John Brooks,[66] of Oxford Street.

When I was a lad and going, helter-skelter, into all kinds of heterodoxy, I often flattened my nose against a window of a shop in Oxford Street, nearly opposite Rathbone Place, looking wistfully at certain books. There were two windows, with a door between. It was the shop of John Brooks, stationer. The window westward was filled with account-books, writing-paper, and the miscellaneous articles of a stationer's business; the other, eastward, with similar contents, and, in addition, some handsomely-printed volumes, a series of which were named *The Reformer's Library*, and included Paine's

---

64 This had no connection whatsoever with the Southern, former slave States.
65 Published by George Jacob Holyoake in 1892 as the book, *Sixty Years of an Agitator's Life.*
66 Radical bookseller and a publisher of Shelley.

Rights of Man, Common Sense, Crisis, etc, Bolingbroke's *Patriot King* – with notes having reference to William the Fourth and the politics of 1831-32. One of the volumes was a masterly recital and exposure of the crimes of the Papacy, the Inquisition, etc. These volumes had choice steel engraved frontispieces, including excellent portraits of Paine and Washington. There was also, not in the same series, a handsome edition of Shelley's *Queen Mab.* Mr Brooks's business was that of stationer; he was not an extensive publisher; but the few books he did issue were all that he did issue were all that could be desired.

I flattened nose against the window, but could not enter the shop to buy, for a sufficient reason. Some years later I obtained the books. A copy of the *Queen Mab* was given to me by Mr Brooks.

Soon after I went to the Isle of Jersey, in 1855, I became aware of the fact that Mr Brooks had retired from the Oxford Street business, and was living in the island. Indeed, familiar with the Chartist reputation of my name, he sought me, and we remained fast friends during my stay in Jersey, some eight years.

I very distinctly remember Mr Brooks telling me that in the feverish height of the Reform Bill agitation it struck him to print a poster *similar* to the one described by Mr Holyoake. Having prepared the forme for the press, he was attending, on the platform, a public meeting of the Political Union. In the course of the proceedings Mrs Brooks was seen forcing her way as best she could through the wedged mass of the meeting. With difficulty she reached near enough to her husband to hand to him a roll of paper. Unrolling it, Mr Brooks exhibited the poster, literally wet from the press, inscribed: 'To stop the Duke, go for Gold!' It is superfluous to add that the poster excited the most frantic enthusiasm. My friend prided himself on that feat, of which he was fond of speaking to all who cared to listen.

Mr Brooks not only told me of the poster; he gave me two or three copies. They are (with most of my books) in America. But I have before me another copy procured by a grandson of John Brooks – Mr Alfred Brooks, son of the late Vincent Brooks, of Lincoln's Inn Fields, from his uncle, Mr Frederick Brooks, still living in the Isle of Jersey. Let it be understood I do not dispute Mr Holyoake's statement. Francis Place may have done all that Mr Holyoake has stated. There may have been *two similar* placards, whether issued pari passu, or that one preceded the other by a few hours; on these points I cannot speak with authority.

Mr Holyoake's wording of the poster differs from that issued by John Brooks. Mr Holyoake says 'there but two lines only': 'Stop the Duke – Run for Gold'. The wording of the poster before me is in four lines:

> TO STOP THE
>
> # DUKE
>
> GO FOR
>
> # GOLD.

Thomas Doubleday, in his *Life of Sir Robert Peel*, says that the placard 'To stop the Duke, go for Gold', was

> the device of four gentlemen, two of whom were elected members of the reformed Parliament. Each put down £20, and the sum thus clubbed was expended in printing thousands of these terrible missives, which were eagerly circulated and very speedily seen upon every wall in London. The effect is hardly to be described. *It was electric.*

The four gentlemen, two of whom became members of Parliament, are not referred to by Mr Holyoake; nor can I recall that John Brooks made mention of such to me. I believe my old friend was not a practical printer – that is, he had not a printing office of his own, although the books he issued bear his 'imprint'. He may have employed a printer 'in a court in Holborn', which would have been no bar to Mrs Brooks, who shared her husband's enthusiasm, being in attendance, and carrying the poster wet from the press to the Political Union meeting. Anyway, John Brooks assumed the responsibility. What Francis Place may have done stealthily, as described by Mr Holyoake, John Brooks did openly. In the left corner of the poster before me are these words in the usual small type: 'J. Brooks, Printer, Oxford Street, London'.

I by no means wish to deprive Francis Place of any of his 'laurels'; but I must, as a matter of justice and fair play, put forward the claim of John Brooks for his share of such credit as may be due to him for his patriotic, prompt, and fearless action in the stirring times of 1832.

16 August 1890

Holyoake amended his text thus:

Two years later the Duke of Wellington was driven from power a second time. One morning when the citizens of London appeared in the streets they found placards on the walls in large letters bearing two lines only: 'Stop the Duke – Go for Gold'.

How came these placards there? What printer had the temerity to print them? ... It was Francis Place who devised the scheme – which certainly he carried out.

He knew a printer in a court in Holborn who could be trusted. One Saturday afternoon when the men had left he went in to the master, examined his stock of paper, and finding it sufficient, he went out and brought in beer and food sufficient for two days, flour, a billsticker's flat can and a brush. They then locked the doors, and he and Place worked all night and the greater part of the Sunday, Place and he pulling alternately at the hand press. They made paste, and a bag which hold the placards concealed under a loose overcoat, and on midnight of Sunday, Place went out and put up the placards himself, sticking them up in the most convenient places he came to. At certain points, he passed his friend, the printer, who had a supply of placards, which he put quickly into Place's bag, who then went on with his bill-sticking until daylight – when they went back and distributed the type. So, when the men returned to work on Monday morning, no one but Place and the printer knew how London had been placarded ...

Debate has risen as to whether the words of the placard were 'Run for Gold' or 'Go for Gold'. The evidence is in favour of 'Go'. The competent testimony of Mr Collet admits that Place devised the placard. On hearing Joseph Parkes[67] read a copy of a proposed wall-bill, Place stopped him and wrote instead a placard of one line 'To stop the Duke – Go for Gold'....Mr [G.J.] Harney relates that he saw a placard at St Hiliers [sic] which bore the words 'J. Brooks, Printer, Oxford Street, London', probably a reproduction of Place's placard, as £80 was subscribed to multiply them. Mr Brooks claimed to have been the originator of the bill. Doubleday, in his *Life of Sir Robert Peel*, says

The placard was the device of four gentlemen, who each put down £20 that thousands might be printed of the terrible missives. The effect was hardly to be described. It was electric.

Miss Helena Cobbett, the last surviving daughter of William Cobbett, writes to Mr Harney that 'Her Father in the [*Political*] *Register* ... mentioned the placard at the time of its appearance, and that her brother James had added

67 Birmingham lawyer and Radical. He acted as intermediary in November 1831 between the Whig government and the Birmingham Political Union, convincing the latter to abandon reorganisation on a semi-military basis. He was the grandfather of the writer Hilaire Belloc.

to it a note, saying, "The placard was suggested by Mr John Fielden[68] to Mr T. Attwood,[69] Mr J. Parkes, and others"'. Mr Samuel Kydd sends an extract from Alison's *History of Europe*, which supplies a name for the placard which explains its efficiency.

Then were seen the *infernal* placards in the streets of London. 'To Stop the Duke – Go for Gold!' and with such success was the suggestion adopted, that in three days no less than £1,800,000 was drawn out of the Bank of England in specie ...

The Duke resigned his first Premiership 16 November 1830, and returned to office 9 May 1832, and resigned on the 18th. The public agitations of which the placard was but a symbol, limited the Duke's second reign to nine days.

George Jacob Holyoake, *Sixty Years of an Agitator's Life* (1892; London: T. Fisher Unwin, 1906 edn), I, pp. 219-21)

The Sacred Month

TO THE EDITOR OF THE *DAILY CHRONICLE.*

The *Daily Chronicle* of 1 March contains a column with the heading – 'The Proposed National Coal Stoppage.[70] A Parallel Movement Fifty Years Ago. The Chartists and the Sacred Month'. In that article I am made to 'loom large' as an advocate of the Sacred Month, only one other member of the Convention, Mr Lowery,[71] being mentioned. I suppose I carry off 'the honours (?) of publicity' in your columns because I am the only member of the Convention now living – one of the disadvantages of living too long.

---

68 Wealthy cotton spinner from Todmorden, Yorkshire, who was close to Cobbett and later to both Owenism and Chartism.
69 Thomas Attwood, Birmingham banker and principal leader of the Birmingham Political Union.
70 During 1888-9 the formation of the Miners' Federation of Great Britain had brought together most of the county associations, although Durham and Northumberland were among those which remained outside. Early in 1892 the Durham coal-owners demanded a ten per cent reduction in wages. In consequence the Federation held a week's 'holiday' from 12 March 'for the sole purpose of clearing the markets from surplus coal'. On the same day a lock-out began in Durham, lasting for 12 weeks and with the miners obliged to accept the reduction. Durham affiliated to the Federation in June and Northumberland soon after...
71 A tailor, lamed by rheumatic illness, and delegate for Newcastle and Northumberland. He later became a temperance lecturer.

I must correct an error or two before speaking of my own doings (sayings included, for 'words are things'). *Richardson's Local Historian's Table Book* is quoted from as the authority for most of the statements in the article. I suspect the *Table Book* is like most other local 'annals', not altogether trustworthy, because such annals are usually – probably always – made up from newspaper reports or paragraphs vitiated by the prejudices and hostile feelings prevalent at the time of the original publication. The author of the *Table Book* says that the Northern Political Union in the preceding November 'pitched upon Mr George Julian Harney as their delegate to the National Convention'. Mr Richardson seems not to have known even the proper title of the Convention, which was 'The General Convention of the Industrious Classes'. He makes it appear that I was *the* delegate, whereas I was but one of three. So far from being 'pitched upon' – does that mean drawing lots? – the delegates were elected at a large open-air meeting in 'the Forth', on Christmas Day, 1838, which meeting was attended by deputations, in some instances processions, from the district on both sides of the Tyne. The other two delegates were Robert Lowery and Dr Taylor.[72] Mr Lowery enjoyed local influence I never possessed; and Dr Taylor was famed for rhetorical powers and volcanic eloquence such as I could never pretend to. Both these delegates were in favour of the Sacred Month.

A portion of a speech imputed to me is given: it is not said where taken from; perhaps from the *Table Book*, though it would appear therein only at second-hand. I may say truly there is no reliable report existing of the speeches made in the Convention. Even the *Northern Star* reports are wretched and unreliable. I *may* have made *some such* speech. It is very likely I did. I waive the question of accuracy, and at once say that, if I uttered the words imputed to me, they constituted a very foolish speech. No doubt I spoke as I believed. But alas! belief founded upon the enthusiasm of 22 has to be revised at the sober age of 75. Doubtless there was 'spirit' enough among those with whom I mingled; but my horizon was too contracted. 'A run upon the Banks of the Tyne'! Our poor fellows, as a rule, had nothing in the banks, save a few who may have had some pounds in savings banks. I could not have been perpetrating a joke at so serious a time; though 'a run on *the banks* of the Tyne' is suggestive of one. Besides, excepting along a portion of Quayside, there was no room for 'a run'; certainly not on the Gateshead side – at least prior to the great fire and disastrous explosion on 6 October 1854. It is of no use further dwelling on this matter. I don't admit

---

72 The Byronic and mysterious surgeon from Ayr who was delegate for not only Newcastle but also Carlisle, Renfrewsire, Wigtown, Alva and Tillicoultry. He died in 1842 at the age of 37.

that, to my knowledge, the speech as given was really uttered word for word; but as I cannot disprove it, and admit that I may have so spoken, I have only to add that a political enemy or unfriendly critic, reading that speech, cannot more strongly condemn it than I do.

I must add a few words on the origin of the Sacred Month.

Half a year before the Convention met, the idea had been started, not by 'extremists', but by 'moderate men' – by members of the council of the Birmingham Political Union, from whom came the delegates who early deserted the Convention. It was also advocated in the *True Scotsman* (the moderate 'moral-force' organ) – I am not sure if by the editor, Fraser,[73] but certainly by Dr Taylor in Fraser's paper – until the two quarrelled over 'moral *versus* physical force'. After the rejection of the national petition, and the refusal by an immense majority of the Commons to hear the petitioners (by counsel or delegates) at the bar of Parliament, the question of 'ulterior measures' came up. The draft of those measures was prepared by William Lovett, the secretary, who has the credit of having been one of the most moderate and conservative members of the Convention. The ulterior measures included the Sacred Month. I have a sincere respect for the memory of Mr Lovett, as I have for that of Robert Lowery. Somehow Mr Lowery, too, acquired a character for reasonableness and moderation, and yet according to your article the Convention had accepted the motion of Mr Lowery that the Sacred Month should commence on 17 August, 'when the corn is ripe and the potatoes in a position to be dug'. Whether Mr Lowery uttered those words I do not know. At any rate he was unquestionably an advocate of the Sacred Month as long as there was any hope of seeing it carried out.

It was a vain hope. As vain as the hope that the people would abstain from the use of as many taxable articles of consumption – such as beer, spirits, tea, coffee, etc – as could possibly be dispensed with.

The compiler of the article draws a fanciful parallel between the Chartist attempt and the organised stoppage of the coal mines to commence on the 12th inst. There is but small likeness. There may be a sort of parallel, but parallel lines never meet, and, beyond a contemplated cessation from labour, there is no likeness between the two. The Miners' Federation, as I understand, propose to throw all the pits in the country idle to reduce the output and so maintain the current rate of wages. They have a right to protect themselves by all fair and honourable means. But what they aim at is a particular class benefit, at, probably, a fearful cost to others. Ironworks, chemical works, mills, factories, workshops closed, or brought to 'short time',

73 John Fraser (1794-1879), former schoolteacher and bookseller.

an immediate rise in the price of coal, inflicting suffering upon thousands of their own class; and the cessation from work prolonged, producing a coal famine. On the other hand the Chartists, of all shades and sections, sought nothing for themselves alone, nothing at the expense of others. The benefit they sought was to be shared by all. If the people at large engaged in the then prolonged cessation from labour, the act would be voluntary; there was not, there could not be, any such coercion as trades unionists can and do exercise. That the coal stoppage will be national I do not believe; but that so far as it extends it will inflict loss and injury upon multitudes I cannot doubt. Whether the result will justify the Miners' Federation we must wait to see. The Chartists indulged in a splendid dream; their enthusiasm got the better of their judgment, they were the victims of their own illusions, and suffered accordingly. For my own part, personally, I have some things to regret; but I have no reason to be ashamed of subscribing myself An Old Chartist – and yours, etc, GEORGE JULIAN HARNEY

12 March 1892

Feargus O'Connor and a Self-Portrait

The scene is a somewhat isolated Scottish village, in the extreme south-west of Scotland, famous as Annandale, and situated about midway between Lockerbie and the Solway Firth, standing in a hollow, almost surrounded by a pleasant amphitheatre of wooded slopes; the village mainly one long, wide street, the houses of a white and bright aspect; a stream, or burn, running through the centre, here and there crossed by bridges or covered ways, the burn joining another water at the 'toon-fut',[74] which in its turn unites with Annan Water, at some short distance. The inhabitants, at the least the working population at the time I have in view, mostly hand-loom weavers, keen and very pronounced politicians. Several inns, not then shorn of their glory by the railway invasion. One especially noticeable as the post-house, or favoured hostelry, where the Glasgow mail-coach changes horses. Time: – over fifty years ago. There is public excitement: the weavers having word that there will arrive on the Glasgow coach a public character whose name, for blessing or for banning, is in the mouths of all men; and, lo! the looms are deserted, and men of all crafts and callings, and almost as many women, gather together in excited expectancy – some, a mere minority, inspired by no friendly curiosity; the great majority by the wildest enthusiasm. The coach arrives, and 'There he is!' is the cry. As the coach halts, a traveller,

74 Foot of town.

stalwart, large-limbed, fair, freckled, auburn-haired (his enemies called him 'red-headed'), in the very prime of his life, of a commanding presence and gifted with a sonorous voice, with graceful bows and smiles, makes his acknowledgments. Responding to the cheers of the weavers, he exhorts them to 'stand by the Charter, and no surrender!' Then the coach is borne onward to its destination; the parting cheers of the weavers ringing sweet music in the ears of Feargus O'Connor. In the crowd a small boy, partaking, as boys are apt to do, of the surrounding excitement; he is not altogether ignorant of the meaning of the oration, for his father is a reader of the *Northern Star.*

On another occasion a repetition of the excitement. A Chartist gathering in the open air, even a procession to welcome an English Chartist, member of the then recent Convention, a young man of three-and-twenty, of slight make, with a stoop unusual in one of his age, of ruddy complexion, blue-grey eyes, and dark brown hair. It is perhaps fortunate that in all probability no record of his speech remains; for, otherwise, it might have been that the writer of these remarks would have had to criticise some of the sentences which elicited the wildest cheers! The small boy, now aged 11, is one of the audience. The speaker knows not, probably sees not, the boy; but the boy never forgets the speaker. Time flies. Seas between the two had roared; yet at one time they were both standing on the same continent, three thousand miles from North as from South Britain. 51 years had passed, when favourable notice of a book written by the erstwhile 'boy' brought the two once more 'en rapport', and the beginning of a pleasant epistolary connection, doomed to be quickly, abruptly, lamentably snapped and broken by the merciless hand of Death ....

20 February 1892

On 30 January 1892 Harney had written:
Closer to me comes the startling announcement of the death of a new-found friend: the Rev James Milligan, DD, native of Ecclefecchan, and pastor of the United Reform Church, Houghton-le-Spring.[75] I cannot remember that I had ever seen him, a boy in the crowd; but he had seen and heard me 51years ago. A commendatory notice of *Aphorisms, Maxims, Etc*, in the *Weekly Chronicle* a few months ago, brought me into pleasant epistolary relations with the author, and a friendship which I had hoped would continue the rest of my days, not doubting that my junior by 13 years would long survive me. I expect another opportunity of speaking of the late minister's career. I had received a sympathetic letter after the

75 In Co Durham.

commencement of my own illness;[76] and then, within a fortnight, came one of those mournful-looking missives one hesitates to open. 'Who now? What friend gone?' No thought of the name I was to find within. Alas! the Rev James Milligan dead at the age of 62. I have no particulars, save that death came suddenly. He had invited me, if ever again I went North, to accept his hospitality. I had some faint hope of that; but not so; before I could look upon his countenance and grasp his hand, he is torn from me. Alas! the mysteries of Life and of Death ....

Scotland and Scottish Chartism

... I must acknowledge that, from want of experience and lack of interest in novel-reading, I cannot reckon myself a good judge of what is a good novel. For some time there has been before the public the name of a writer who has won a reputation, and seems to be on the high road to fame – more or less lasting – the author of *A Window in Thrums*, *Auld Licht Idylls*, etc, works I have not seen. But I have received and read a new and cheap edition of *The Little Minister*, by J.M. Barrie ... The popularity of the author is attested by the announcement on the title-page that the present is the 'twenty-first thousand' .... *The Little Minister* having been sent to me, I have conscientiously read it from cover to cover, and, having done so, I am tempted to address Mr Barrie in the words of his great countryman: 'Vera guid! But, when are you going to dae something?' If I had the power and 'faculty divine' of writing like Mr Barrie, it would not be to waste my time in producing such concoctions as *The Little Minister* ....

The story of *The Little Minister* is an absurdity – that of an Auld Licht Minister[77] fascinated by a girl who plays the double part of a fine lady and a gipsy, chiefly the latter. Supposing the incidents of the story as probable as I believe them to be all but utterly impossible, I can understand that the Little Minister was led captive, as much greater men have been, but what his gipsy Cleopatra could see fascinating in him I think the author fails to show. The chief value of the book is in the exhibition it offers of the sordid life of an insignificant Scottish town, with its prying and malignant or idiotic gossips, male and female; their hard and truculent religion, the hatred, malice, and all uncharitableness exhibited toward every human being not the elect of the elect – the most stupidly bigoted of the Auld Lichts. As the minister

76 A bad bout of quinsy, it would seem.
77 The Auld Lichts (Old Lights) of the United Original Secession Church of 1822 resulted from an ultra-Calvinist split within the highly schismatic secessions from the Church of Scotland.

is described as a little man, he may be pardoned for having taken to the ministry to earn his living; otherwise the life of a delver and ditcher, a smith or mason, must be infinitely preferable. Much that Scotland possesses has my admiration; but rather than live in such a place as Thrums I would much prefer banishment to the Fiji Islands and would rather take my chance with cannibals than with those dreadful beings, the Auld Lichts of Thrums, or any other spot on the surface of 'braid Scotland'. And, indeed, a good deal of the savage still clings to the orthodox Scotsman. When the semi-naked African, or altogether barbaric South Sea Islander, finds that his prayers are not heeded by his favourite little god, he gives his Mumbo Jumbo a sound flogging; and the way Mr Barrie's staunch believers make free with the Deity will strike the less sophisticated Southern reader as going a long way beyond merely bordering on profanity. As long as all goes smoothly with the Auld Lichts, and they can enjoy the beatitude of believing themselves singled out for eternal bliss, all the rest of mankind going to perdition, they are at least decently respectful to the Powers above; but when anything goes wrong with their own affairs, they evince no more reverence than does the savage when he fogs his Mumbo Jumbo.

To my surprise there is at the beginning of the book a lugging in of the Chartists, by which the time of the story may be guessed; the place looks like some small town in Aberdeenshire, or perhaps in Banff, or Kincardine, or North Forfarshire, for I do not detect certain specialities of the Aberdonian dialect.[78] Mr Barrie knows nothing of the Chartists but their name. He represents them as abandoning their 'physical force' demonstration at the command of the Little Minister. The Caledonian Chartists were made of sterner stuff. Probably one half of them, inheritors of the traditions of 1817-1820, had cut aloof from ministers and any and every kind of kirk; the other half regarded the founder of Christianity as a Radical reformer and the Gospel as – for this world – the great original People's Charter, and they looked upon ministers in general, with but rare exceptions, as mere wolves in sheep's clothing who were false to the mission they had undertaken of preaching the glad tidings of the man of Nazareth. From this latter section sprang the Christian Chartists, who for a time strove to establish Christian Chartist Churches; most of them were 'moral force' men. But the two sections were alike in this: that if either of them had taken up arms they would never have laid them down at the bidding of any minister, Auld Licht or New Licht, or any other kind of Light. Mr Barrie's age I do not know; but I dare say he had no more personal knowledge of the men of 1839 than he could have had of the men of 1819. He has manufactured his

78 Barrie had been born in Kirriemuir, Forfarshire.

Chartists, like the Little Minister and the erratic gipsy … out of his own inner consciousness ….

24 December 1892

Chartist Headgear

[An] Address to Northumberland miners advocating 'the Legal Eight Hours for all persons working in the mines' … in addition … proposed to form 'a Labour party in Parliament, distinct and separate from Tory or Liberal'. Very good! – though it must be said we have not yet seen any indication of such independence on the part of the Labour members who already have seats in Parliament. The paragraph above quoted from, contains this further, lengthy and curious sentence: 'The only successful way to accomplish this is to reject Parliamentary candidates with long hats and big purses, accumulated out of the sweat, and marrow, and sinews of our carcasses, and rally round and record our votes for none other than the honest, cultured, and intelligent toiler with fustians[79] and corduroy'. Whether 'our carcasses' is a cultured form of expression is a matter of taste. Of fustian I will say nothing; and if the toiler is honest and intelligent it matters but little if corduroy is his ordinary wear. In my opinion he will probably be none the less honest, cultured, and intelligent, if he has a suit of broadcloth in which to be married, and to wear on Sundays and other high days and holidays. The only successful way, we are told, to form a Labour party in Parliament, 'is to reject Parliamentary candidates with long hats and big purses'. I am afraid the 'big purses' will be sufficiently difficult to beat, without prescribing the 'long hats' in addition. The adjective is new to me. Here, down south, such hats are designated 'tall', 'topper', or 'chimney pot'. Why the low, the soft, and the slouch should be preferred on the heads of Parliamentary candidates, is not evident, at least to my untutored mind. The felt hat is now a big industry – I think mostly Oldham way – and, for the sake of the makers it is to be hoped will not soon be superseded. But there are other hatters to whom the still surviving 'chimney pot' is of some account.

If, however, Parliamentary candidates are to be rejected because they wear the 'topper', it will not tend to the welfare of the London hat-makers, who, also, are men and brothers. Is it not a little ridiculous to make the 'slouch' the type of Democracy, and the 'long' the natural association of a 'big purse'? The old Chartist leaders were not reputed to be the happy

---

79 Working clothes made out of a coarse, twilled cotton fabric, including corduroy.

possessors of big purses, but Feargus O'Connor, William Lovett, and John Frost – I name these three as typical men – all wore 'long hats'. The only member of the Convention of 1839 who wore a 'slouch' was Dr John Taylor; but he was a little exceptional, not to say eccentric; and a sort of semi-gipsy, semi-brigand costume, well became his fine but swarthy features, glossy black hair, large dark eyes, and rolling gait. I never heard of the men of 1839 being accounted not sufficiently democratic; yet it appears that, if now in the flesh, and abiding by their old headgear, they would be tabooed as Parliamentary candidates for wearing 'long hats'!

26 September 1891

The Free Trade Fetish

The Chartists were right. I never doubted it. Historians of the stamp of Harriet Martineau, who took her 'facts' from the organs of the Anti-Corn Law League, and the dribblers, I will not say drivellers, of historical compendiums following in her wake, have represented the Chartists as frenzied idiots or the dupes of selfish demagogues, indeed both, to account for their opposition to the Anti-Corn Law League! Could anything be more benevolent than the desire of the league to assure every man 'a big loaf'? Could anything be more insane than the Chartist preference for the 'little loaf'? The only way these sapient manufacturers and pedlars of history could account for such aberration, affecting so numerous a party as the Chartists, was to surmise that the Chartist leaders were Tories in disguise, or the recipients of 'Tory gold', and that they were clever enough and unprincipled enough to mislead their too credulous followers. That surmise, if only true, would account for the Chartist opposition to the League. Unluckily for the slanderers of the Chartists, their surmise lacked the necessary ingredient of truth. I know what were the lives of the leaders, nearly all long ago in their graves. What they got at the hands of the Tories was the alacrity with which, as grand and petty jurymen, they found 'true bills', and verdicts of 'guilty', against those accused of 'sedition'. Rarely did a landlord, never did a 'jolterhead', evince the slightest feeling of humanity toward the men who, struggling for justice, perhaps 'not wisely, but too well',[80] found themselves involved in the meshes of the law. Those men suffered, not only within but out of prison. They were not faultless, but they were incorruptible; they suffered and they died, and passed away; no Tory or other 'gold' came to lessen their cares or alleviate their sorrows.

80 Shakespeare, *Othello*, 5, ii.

The 'gold' circulating in those days flowed into the pockets of the writers and lecturers in the pay of the League; and the end of the Anti-Corn Law agitation saw the most of said writers and lecturers comfortably provided for, or rewarded with testimonials.

Rightly or wrongly, I believe rightly, the Chartists opposed the Anti-Corn Law League on principle: for reasons, *firstly*, because one purpose of the Anti-Corn Law League agitation was to obstruct and nullify the agitation for the People's Charter; *secondly*, not because they preferred a small to a big loaf, but because they made use of their thinking faculty and looked beyond the promised benefit of the coming moment to the future, when, as they believed, the doctrines of the Manchester School, fully put into practice, would inflict widespread injury, and lead the way to national decay.

It was very well understood that the repeal of the Corn Laws would be the first step only in the march of Free Trade. The Chartists believed that the first, unconditional repeal, unaccompanied by other necessary measures, would be the ruin of English agriculture and the further displacement of agricultural labourers, banishing them from the land and forcing them into the towns. They believed that the second would flood the country with foreign manufactured goods to the decline or destruction of English crafts, and the ultimate and irrecoverable injury to the country.

The Chartists failed. They were largely disunited; they showed less judgment than zeal; above all, they were poor. The League succeeded, in part because, fully equipped with the sinews of war, commanding more pounds than the Chartists could command pence; but largely the League owed its triumph, its unexpectedly early triumph, to the Irish famine – setting our worthy legislators to do in a panic that which no mere argument could have induced. From that hour the march of Free Trade was rapid and practically unopposed. There was more jubilation! Free Trade was to regenerate Britain, and not only Britain, but most of the civilised world; for it was prophesied that within twenty years all the leading nations of the earth would follow this country's example! Wars would cease, fleets would come to be dismantled and armies disbanded, and all the dreams of the Peace Society[81] would be realised. The first International Exhibition of 1851 was declared to be the inauguration of the New Era.

The first rude shock to these bright anticipations was the war with Russia. Five or six years subsequently came the Secession rupture, the commencement of the great Civil War in the States, and the cotton famine. With this calamity came the adoption in America of a stringent

81 Founded in 1816 as the Society for the Promotion of Permanent and Universal Peace and advocating disarmament and arbitration.

anti-Free Trade tariff, which, never relaxed, has recently been made all but prohibitory. The end of the American Civil War, the renewal of the unchecked exportation of cotton from the Southern ports, brought relief and better times to the manufacturing districts of England; the troubles on the Continent, and the wars that engaged the resources of Austria, Italy, Germany, and France, gave Britain, for a time, almost a monopoly of the world's trade, and enabled the leading statesman of the day, never very judicious in his utterances, to boast of the country's prosperity as advancing 'by leaps and bounds'.[82] Subsequent years brought a reaction, and there is no human probability that there will ever be ground for repeating that vaunt. It is not the example of England that France, Germany, and other leading nations have followed, but that set by the United States. The Cobden prophecy of universal Free Trade has been absolutely falsified, and the very reverse has come to pass. Even our own colonies, with the exception of New South Wales (there is no other exception of any account), have set up barriers against us, imposing duties upon our manufactures as if England were a foreign country. Nor is this all. In Canada a strong party, aiming at supremacy, design, if successful, to enter upon terms of reciprocity with the United States, continuing or even raising the duties on English goods, in order to give the States an advantage over the Mother Country. These Canadian 'Liberals' are a nice set of men, quite worthy of their name. For meanness, for treachery, for alliance with the enemies of Great Britain, the name of 'Liberal' has become synonymous on both sides of the Atlantic.

Let it be acknowledged we have cheap bread, and many items of food in the form of canned meats, fish, fruits, etc. Let it also be acknowledged that there has been a great increase in the mercantile marine of the country, largely owing to the importation of grain and other descriptions of food. So far, so good; but this pleasant obverse of the medal has its reverse.

The farmers were assured by the orators of the League that foreign competition could not injure them; that, indeed, foreign rivalry would but act as a healthy stimulant, and that they would share in the country's general improvement. What has been the result? The land largely abandoned and left to go out of cultivation, and, where that is not the case, the old cultivators superseded by new. It is said that at this time Scotch farmers are beginning to supersede English in Essex and Hertfordshire, probably because they can live more economically than English farmers have been used to do, and, so living, may pay the landlords' rents. As to the labourers, the country has been so far denuded of that class of the population that last harvest time there was an outcry that the necessary labour could not be had in some of

82 Gladstone presumably.

the Southern Counties. Year by year the agricultural labourers throng more and more into the towns, and probably furnish the numerous 'blacklegs' against whom the unionists wage implacable war.

One effect of this thinning of the agricultural population is the falling off in the bodily strength and stamina of our soldiers. Time after time the standard has been reduced, until now the recruiting sergeants are glad to enlist undersized lads of 5ft 4in height, 33in chest measurement, and 8st 3lb weight, with no uncertain prospect of further deterioration. Some of our newspapers, alarmed, are calling out for increased pay to enable the military authorities to command better material in the labour market. If we cannot do without a standing army, such better pay would be as politic as just; but no amount of pay can attract and enlist better men in sufficient numbers whilst the causes of deterioration continue, and continue to more powerfully operate. The bringing back of the labourers to the land, or the securing of those not yet expatriated, they and their families and successors in the future, is a need even more imperative than higher and just pay.

The feeble experiments in the way of allotments, coming into vogue, will have but small appreciable effect. The rehabilitation of the cultivators of the soil will not result from the puny and tentative methods at present pursued. The work is national, and, as such, should be taken in hand by the national authority. To omit that work is to ignore and neglect the very safeguarding of the nation.

As to our commerce, our increase of shipping, the preponderance of our mercantile marine in the Suez Canal, and on every sea; that is not all national gain. Is it not a fact that since the repeal of the Navigation Laws[83] the British sailor has been in course of elimination? Is it not a fact that of the crews sailing from the Thames, the Tyne, and the Wear, from Bristol and Hull, from Glasgow and Dundee, a large proportion are foreigners? The questionable doings [84] of our sailors, firemen, dockers, and others at the present time I fear are calculated to aggravate the evil. Commerce, more than any other human pursuit, has illustrated, and may continue to illustrate, the instability of Fortune. 'Trade's proud Empire hastens to decay',[85] and one of the effects of unrestricted Free Trade has lessened the number and perhaps the quality of our native seamen. A poor defence on shore would be an army of foreign mercenaries, but far worse would be our

83 Originating in 1650-51, the Navigation Acts restricted the importation of non-European goods to vessels belonging to Britons or English colonists and manned by crews at least 75 per cent British; and similarly for all imports to and exports from the colonies. They were repealed in 1849.
84 Organising trade unions and going on strike.
85 Oliver Goldsmith, *The Deserted Village*.

case if, with ships and guns, we could no longer count upon the manning of our navy by the lineal descendants of those who roamed the distant seas of the world with Drake, Anson, and Cook, whom Blake led to victory, and who conquered with Nelson at the Nile and Trafalgar.

I propose to return to this theme.

28 February 1891

The Working of Free Trade

In last Saturday's *Weekly Chronicle*, I commented on the outcome – thus far – of the doctrines of the Manchester school as regards English agriculture. Still more marked have been the consequences in Ireland. Fenianism and Parnellism, with the playful doings of the O'Dynamites and Invincibles,[86] have for a generation occupied the foreground of Irish history; but for fifty years the foundation of the trouble has been mostly agrarian – not merely between tenants and rack-renting landlords, but occasioned by the fall of Irish prices, consequent on the vast importation into England of various food supplies, causing competition with Irish produce, disastrous to the Irish farmers. Those among them willing enough to pay fair rents found themselves without the means. This state of things offered a grand opening to the political agitators. To organise agrarian discontent and turn it to political account, the Land League was founded which, on its nominal suppression, was succeeded by the National League – the same old conspiracy under a new name. Irish discontent and Irish conspiracy may largely be traced to the victory of the Anti-Corn Law League and the introduction of unrestricted Free Trade.

The Chartists were not infallible; like other men, they were liable to error, and they were mistaken in their belief that foreign competition under Free Trade would at once, or very soon, lower wages to the Continental level. In my belief, they were mistaken as to the form in which the consequences of unrestricted Free Trade would tell upon the country; but not as to later and disastrous results. It must be acknowledged that, taking the national industry all round, there has been, so far, instead of a decrease, an increase of wages. The docker with his sixpence an hour is in a far better position than his predecessor of forty years ago. And as with the docker, so with the employed generally. So far as wages are concerned, the calculations of the Chartists have been shown to have been miscalculations.

86 The Invincibles had assassinated Lord Frederick Cavendish, the Liberal Chief Secretary for Ireland, in Dublin in 1882. 'The O'Dynamites' is, of course, a satirical coinage of Harney's.

'Ah, then', will say the champions of Free Trade, 'you must acknowledge that if bread is lower and wages are higher, if food supplies have increased, and the purchasing power of the workers has also increased, Free Trade is justified, and has conferred incalculable benefits on the nation! No more need be said!'

Stop a minute. The previsions of the Chartists in reference to agriculture have been fully confirmed, and their anticipations as to the effect upon manufactures are in course of fulfilment, more slowly, but continually in progress. Instead, however, of lower wages for all, we see the total loss of employment for a large number of the population, compelling the latter to emigrate or to sink into the lowest depths of pauperism.

If the country is not yet 'flooded' with foreign manufactures as well as foreign food, the inflow is persistent and increasing. Christmas cards may be but a small matter, but may be taken as one of the signs of the times. The manufacturers are generally Germans, or Jews, or both; there is but one exception that I know of, the firm of Marcus Ward and Company, whose work is done in Belfast, where, no doubt, the wages of lithographers, printers, and others are lower than in London. The foreign firms, though they have their business centres in London, have the most of their work done in Germany. Readers may have noticed on many of the Christmas and New Year Cards of 1890-91, the words, 'Designed in England, printed in Germany'. The Merchandise Marks Act of 1887 enacts that foreign manufactured goods imported into this country shall bear the name of the country of their origin, as may be seen on (the boxes of) Lucifer matches: 'Made in Belgium', 'Made in Sweden', etc. As regards Christmas cards, 'designed in England', means simply the original sketch. Such sketches are sent to Germany, where they are copied on to the stone by German lithographers, and worked off by German printers. The author of the original sketch may be a German or other foreigner, living in England; but supposing him an Englishman, into the production of the Christmas card there enters the labour, or the skill, of one Englishman – all the rest is the work of underpaid foreign labour. Thus produced, tens and hundreds of thousands of Christmas, New Year's, Easter, and birthday cards are thrown upon the English market. The consequence is that the card-making trade has been abandoned by British lithographic and fancy printers, with the exception of Marcus Ward and Co, and that firm must be unable to pay full or London wages. In photography, the picture books of English and Scottish cities, towns, coast views, and inland scenery, bought by thousands and tens of thousands of tourists and summer holiday-makers, are all nearly of German production.

In Macclesfield[87] I bought a frame for a photograph. I found out, subsequently, that the frame was Swiss made. I could have bought other frames, a trifle dearer, made in Paris, but not an English frame! At another place, in the same town, with 'carver and gilder' inscribed on the shop front, I found the frames on sale were not made by said 'carver and gilder', but came from Manchester. Were they made in Manchester or in London? Not so. They were made in Germany! At the principal tailor's in the town, I sought a certain garment for indoor wear, having been told I would find a good assortment of 'ready-made'. Too large; the offer was made to supply one to fit. About to leave the town, I wanted the garment at once, but was told I must wait what seemed to me an unreasonable time. Why? Said garments came from Germany! At another place in the same town I was told I could be accommodated 'the day after tomorrow' with what I wanted from London. 'English or foreign?' I was told I could have either, the English for a small additional charge. I ordered the English. But I am no judge of English cloth and work versus the foreign; and I did not feel quite sure I had got what I paid for.

Nine-tenths of shopkeepers are free traders. They are distributors, not producers. Their business is to sell. Doubtless there are some not altogether insensible to the promptings of patriotism, who would sell English-made goods by preference, if in demand. But they must sell the cheapest, and so they prefer the 'nimble ninepence' paid for the foreign article, to the 'slow shilling' demanded for the English.

Perhaps it will be said: What matters the disappearance of a few printers, picture-frame makers, etc? But is the process of obliteration restricted to such small sections of the population? Have not whole crafts disappeared, or been reduced to the most meagre proportions, as, for example, glass-workers on the Tyne, and the lead miners of Cumberland? Watchmakers could tell a like tale of the effects of Swiss importation and the competition of the Waterbury watch.[88] Have we not doors and window-frames, and other articles in carpentry and joinery necessary in the construction of houses, imported ready-made, leaving to the English mechanic merely the work of fitting? The carpenters and joiners are now engaged in an agitation for increased pay and reduced hours, and threatening a strike if their demands are not conceded. They will do well to reflect before they engage in a doubtful struggle. From the unemployed will come the so-called 'blacklegs', whilst the increased importation of foreign-wrought work may

87 Harney was much attached to the Cheshire town of Macclesfield and was based there for several months after his permanent return to Britain in 1888.
88 A cheap pocket watch mass-produced in Waterbury, Connecticut.

be looked for, with, too possibly, the addition of foreign mechanics to fill the places of the strikers.

From cradles for the newly-born to coffins for the departed, we see home production is being superseded by foreign. Free Trade has made of England a happy hunting-ground for the enterprising foreigner.

'But the consumer?' Always we hear from Free Traders of the interests of the consumer; not often of those of the producer. It is similar to the cry of the Home Rulers – 'the Irish! the Irish!' i.e., the Irish in revolt, disguised as 'constitutional agitation'. They ignore the Irish who desire peace before all things, who wish quietly to follow their respective callings, and ask only to be protected from boycotters, moonlighters, and assassins. So with the Free Trade cry of 'the consumers'. Every working man is a consumer, but to consume (unless as a pauper, a tramp, or a loafer) he must first be a producer, or be engaged in some kind of work associated indirectly, if not directly, with production. It is an old taunt that we are 'a nation of shopkeepers', but that is true only in a degree. The shopkeepers are but a minority, and must depend for customers on the great working majority. Of what good is it to the unemployed labourer that he may buy a German Christmas card for perhaps half the price he would be charged for one of English make – when, if he can earn any pence, he wants those pence for food? What matters a cheap German frame for his photograph to the unemployed watchmaker, who has no money to spend either on frame or photograph? And is the English frame-maker, superseded by the German, likely to be consoled by the reflection that he may obtain a Waterbury watch for 10s 6d?

If we were a nation of consumers and distributors – the distributors also, of course, being consumers; if we could live without being producers, if as a nation we were, what no nation ever yet has been, like Roman patricians, living on the spoliation of subjugated states and the plunder of foreign nations, with slaves for our domestic uses, then, indeed, our interests as consumers would be all-paramount, and the more of foreign produce and foreign manufactures flowed into the country, the cheaper everything, the better for us – *for a time*; until red-handed Nemesis came to blot out a nation so brutally selfish and utterly despicable.

If foreign produce and manufactures are superseding British, what becomes of our unemployed? The best of them, the most energetic, those who can command the means, emigrate – a goodly number to Australia and the British American provinces,[89] but a far larger number betake them to the United States to further magnify the greatness of that Empire of the West, which has been so largely built up by British Capital and British Skill

89 What were to become Canada.

and Labour. It is no longer the Irish who far exceed in number all other emigrants from the British Isles. In 1868, Scotch emigrants numbered 14,954, English 58,268, Irish 64,965. In 1888, Scotch emigrants numbered 35,873, Irish 73,233, English 170,822. The country is being drained of its life-blood; its best of bone and muscle, blood and brain. A still larger number of the unemployed have no means to emigrate, and largely are wanting in the spirit that would induce them to take that step. From these come the 'blacklegs', so odious to the unionists. Others sink into abject poverty or dire crime. The masses are divided into two great classes – those with higher wages than their predecessors, the other section with no wages at all, save such uncertain windfalls as chance may send.

Free Trade has brought cheap bread; but the agricultural labourers swarm into the towns, and 'the country', as distinct from towns and cities, is denuded of its natural population. Free Trade has not brought cheaper meat or lower house rent. It is bringing in the products of foreign labour, the foreign labourers themselves, and foreign masters. The Chartists were right in repudiating and denouncing the gospel of selfishness: 'Lord love you! We are all for ourselves in this world'.

7 March 1891

RUSSIA

The Latest Russian Atrocity

Thou shalt do no murder

As the correspondence columns of the *Weekly Chronicle* of the past two weeks have not contained anything in relation to the latest Russian atrocity, I ask for brief space for some comment. Surely such a chapter of despotic crime and human suffering should have some less fleeting notice than that of an ordinary murder or the latest railway accident. For Englishmen to look on with torpid indifference is to render themselves liable to the charge of silent acquiescence in, if not approval of, one of the worst examples of autocratic atrocity recorded even on the bloodstained pages of Russia's appalling history.

This time the victims are not Poles or Central Asiatics, neither so-called 'insurgents', nor armed combatants making a last effort to defend their hearths and homes against a ruthless invader. The victims were purely Russians; there is reason for believing men of culture and honourable lives, with the addition of some delicate women and children. They had not been put on trial for any alleged offence against the State or against society. They were simply 'suspects'. They were suspected of not adoring 'the Divine Figure of the North'; they were suspected of cherishing the desire to replace by a régime of constitutional law the barbaric despotism which is the curse of the Russian people, and a standing menace to the peace, the freedom, and the welfare of Europe. On the bare suspicion of longing for some kind of reform, or change, the victims were arrested, torn from their homes, and 'by administrative order' exiled to Siberia.

Siberia is a vast territory, larger than Europe, and in some parts life may be tolerable; but not where the exiles under notice were doomed to pass their unhappy lives. To the number of about thirty they had arrived – after what suffering who but themselves could tell? – at the town of Yakutsk, in the far north-eastern section of Siberia. Many exiles are located there, but the thirty were under the doom of proceeding on and on, over the Verkhoyansk Mountains and the snowy plains beyond, to Kolymsk,[90] near the shore of the Polar Sea. If all goes well, the journey in open sledges occupies sixty days. Of late years, some amelioration of the horrors of the journey had been permitted by the local authority, but a new Vice-Governor, Ostashin – accursed be his name! – had rescinded the more merciful regulations, his object apparently being to torture and kill the exiles by starvation. Alarmed at the terrible prospect before them, the exiles got up a joint petition to the Vice-Governor, entreating a return to the old regulations. To present their petition, they went in a body to the office of the Provincial Administration. Ostashin affected to be alarmed at this demonstration, and ordered the exiles to repair next day to the house of a brother exile, stationed in Yakutsk, and there to receive his answer. They obeyed, Soon an officer of police appeared on the scene, and ordered the thirty to follow him to the office of the Administration. They cried out that that was what they had been forbidden to do, and thereupon he took himself off in a rage, but quickly returned with a detachment of seventy soldiers and police. Without seeking entrance by peaceable means, they broke upon the door, and began striking the unhappy exiles with the butt-ends of rifles. A horrible mêlée ensued. In vain the exiles protested they were willing to go wherever they were ordered. They were fired upon repeatedly, until fully one-half were shot down, dead or wounded; and, says the account in *The Times*, Sofia Gurevich was 'ripped open' by bayonets. Some of the exiles, driven to madness, offered the resistance of despair; the result, for that day, was that, of the thirty, six were killed and nine wounded. Of the assailants, one policeman had been killed, and three officials, Ostashin included, had been wounded. Ostashin

90 Or, more correctly, Srednekolymsk.

had himself previously fired twice upon the exiles.

The brutality of Ostashin (I wish Barclay and Perkins's draymen could 'interview' him for a quarter of an hour!)[91] did not stop with the massacre. He demanded a court martial, on the ground that the petition of the thirty constituted 'an act of insurrection'. And the Governor of Eastern Siberia, General Ignatiev, brother of the too famous (another word would be more suitable) diplomatist,[92] ordered the court martial to be held. That mockery of a trial of course resulted as had been predetermined: three of the exiles were sentenced to death and others to long terms of penal servitude. The three condemned to death were hanged. One of them, Kogan-Bernshtein, who had been wounded by four bullets, was carried to execution on his bed, the bed being drawn from under him when consigned to the gallows! He left a letter, which his friends secured, breathing a spirit of noble resignation, exhorting his compatriots not to despair of 'the great cause'. The letter is printed in *The Times*.

To its honour *The Times* gave all the details received of this Russian atrocity. The account will be found in the daily issue of 26 December (what a commentary on 'Peace on earth and good will to all men'!), and in the weekly edition of 27 December, in which it occupies a full page. Moreover, *The Times* had an admirable 'editorial' denouncing the atrocity in the strongest terms, observing, 'we do not hesitate to call it a tale of blood and horror that has seldom been outdone in the records of those "dark places of earth" which are "full of the habitations of cruelty"'. *The Times* adds, significantly:

> Of course, the account which we print will never reach the bulk of the Russian people. It will be blackened out in every copy of this journal which is allowed to circulate in Russia.

Let us return to our own fast-anchored isle, and, for a moment, suppose the impossible to be possible. There is no proof that the thirty were Republicans; but we know that in this country there are avowed Republicans and avowed Republican papers. Imagine the Cabinet or the Home Secretary (we have no ministry of police) acting in concert with Commissioner Monro,[93] and

91   When Haynau, the Austrian general notorious for his savage suppression of the Hungarian Revolution of 1849, visited Barclay and Perkins's London brewery the following year, he had to be rescued from the draymen and others who assaulted him.
91   The strongly nationalist Count N.P. Ignatiev had worked against British government policy in the Far East, Central Asia and the Balkans, where he had sought in 1878 to build a 'big' Bulgaria.
93   James Monro was Commissioner of the Metropolitan Police, 1886-90.

suddenly arresting all known and all suspected Republicans, say in London, and, without preferring any charge against them in any police or superior court, exiling the arrested 'by administrative order' to the Fiji Islands, or to Labrador. How many days would pass without seeing England seething in the fires of Revolution? Even if such high-handed tyranny were possible, the lot of the English exiles would bear no comparison to that of thousands of Russians, Poles, and others. The Fiji Islands are 11,000 miles from England, but in their climatic conditions are the antipodes to Siberia; they constitute a land of luxuriant vegetation, the home of the breadfruit tree, the banana, and the plantain. In the matter of climate, Labrador, 2,500 miles from England, approaches the nearest of British possessions to that of Siberia. But the British colony should be happy under a Constitutional Administration, and republican exiles could hardly fail to meet with sympathy in a community rejoicing in the exercise of manhood suffrage and vote by ballot. Otashin is as impossible in any British possession as would be Sawney Beane.[94]

But because there is no danger, no possibility of our sharing, is that any reason for ignoring, the sufferings of our Russian brethren?

The crimes and cruelties, the outrages and atrocities, of which the Russian Government has been guilty from the days of Ivan the Terrible to those of Alexander the Third, still guilty, still impenitent, still irreclaimable, defiant of the moral sense of mankind, would justify, nay, calls for a new Peter the Hermit[95] to preach a new crusade to overthrow so dark and bloody a despotism. But where to find the modern Peter? He who might have been prefers the role of the Russian bear's jackal.[96]

It is unfortunate for Russian, as for Polish victims, that their sovereign lord is the autocrat, and not the Sultan. Had the Yakutsk atrocity been committed by a Moslem Pasha, how bitter would have been the denunciation of 'the unspeakable Turk'. And, somehow, it would have been made to appear (to fools) that, in some way, Lord Salisbury had made himself *particeps criminis!*[97] But, as the victims were not Bulgarians (small sympathy would the Bulgars get now!), or Cretans,[98] the Grand Old Boanerges[99] of 'the great Liberal party' is silent – as death! He has no expression of sympathy

94 Alexander 'Sawney' Bean was the semi-mythical clan head in fifteenth- or sixteenth-century Scotland, supposedly executed for the murder and cannibalisation of over a thousand people.
95 The French priest who played a leading role in the First Crusade (and died in 1115).
96 Gladstone?
97 Someone who, though not present, helps with the commission of a crime.
98 Still under Ottoman rule.
99 Gladstone. Boanerges is the name, derived from the New Testament, for a noisy preacher or shouting orator.

or of horror for the heroic martyr Kogan-Bernshtein; he has no bowels of compassion for the horribly murdered Sofia Gurevich. All his denunciatory eloquence is reserved for 'the unspeakable Turk' (it would be a good thing if others besides Turks were 'unspeakable'), apparently for the purpose of helping 'Holy Russia' to fulfil the designs of Peter (not the Hermit), and repair the failure of Nicholas, by establishing the most hateful of tyrannies upon the shores of the Bosphorus.

Cui bono? To what end do I trouble the *Weekly Chronicle* with these remarks? To call upon its readers, and especially its Newcastle readers, to make solemn protest against this latest Russian atrocity. My call may be answered by two sections, hostile or indifferent; the one saying that England cannot protest, for her Government is 'just as bad'; the other asking, querulously, 'What good can it do?' The first may be dismissed in a line. Whoever says our Government is 'just as bad' bears false witness against his own country; and, in the expressive language of Daniel O'Connell, 'lies, and knows he lies'. As to the cold-blooded doubters, it is not worthwhile arguing with them, save to affirm that it is every man's duty by deed if he can, by word if he cannot do more, to protest against wrongdoing and to brand the wrongdoer. We cannot reach the tyrant Romanov nor the miscreants who minister to his cowardly cruelty, but we can arraign him in the Court of Eternal Justice, and, in spite of his purple robe and golden diadem, in spite of his two million armed slaves, pronounce him an execrated, outlawed criminal, with whom not only Russian Nihilists,[100] but all men – worthy of the name – of all nations, are at war, eager for his overthrow, and still more for the overthrow of the hellish system of tyranny of which he is the momentary chief.

> Down to the dust in hopeless ruin hurled,
> Its name, its nature, wither'd from the world.[101]

11 January 1890

Two Books about Russia

Again it is Russia that commands universal attention. Untiring in the pursuit of the policy of Muscovite aggrandisement – having for its end the Sovereignty of Europe and Asia – the Slavonic Colossus necessitates the continuance and increase of the vast armaments which so tax the resources and weigh upon the energies of the Continental States; to

100   That is, Populists or Narodniks.
101   This quotation has not been identified.

which must be added, our own burthens for the protection of our Indian Empire, our colonies, and even our domestic safety. Now creeping with cat-like stealthiness, now springing with tiger-like ferocity, the Autocracy unceasingly aims at universal dominion. But at this moment, it is not the massing of battalions, or the marching of armies, whether on the frontiers of Afghanistan or to the imminent overrunning of the Balkan States, that so much attracts the attention of Europe, as the melancholy tramp of wretched exiles on their way to Siberia, and the half-stifled groans of tyranny's despairing victims. Of the educated classes, all but the fanatical Slavophiles, are eager to share in the freedom of thought and action enjoyed by all nations claiming to be civilised; whilst the peasants, though steeped in ignorance, are anxious to resume their ancient rights, wanting which their nominal emancipation must remain very much of a mockery. From this double cause of disaffection springs danger to the Autocracy, which, refusing concession, must necessarily increase its watchfulness, and be more 'bloody, bold, and resolute', in putting down all signs of revolt. Considering the difficulty of obtaining intelligence of current events within the Russian dominions, it is very desirable to have some trustworthy, even if incomplete, knowledge of that empire's history and resources, and of the character of the peoples and classes subjected to Autocracy's selfish, brutal, and pitiless rule.

The two books [under review] will do something toward imparting that information ....

[Yet] one feels on closing [*Russia* by W.R. Morfill, Reader in the Russian and Slavonic Languages in the University of Oxford] that whilst it has imparted a general outline of Russian history, it has not made us much acquainted with the Russian people. That it should be a 'drum and trumpet' history was probably unavoidable. But a little less glorification of the Tsars and their minions would have been in better taste. Peter was hardly less a great barbarian than a great Autocrat. We are told that

> as regards the private character of Catherine II we must be content to forget it for the sake of great services which she rendered to her country. It would be to no purpose to reiterate of the thousandth time these ancient scandals.

'Great services'! Great acts of brigandage; great murders, from the assassination of her husband to the assassination of Poland. One may excuse the author of *Russia* for avoiding the recital of Ivan the Terrible's cruelties, at once so horrible and so revolting as haunt the memory of those who have once read the accounts handed down from that reign. But there can be no excuse for the absurdly brief notices of the storming of Ismail and of Praga,[102] and the atrocities of Nicholas, Muravyov, and Berg in Poland. Nicholas is credited with 'kindness of heart' – a discovery which should bring to Mr Morfill some Russian Order of Merit ....

The second of the books under notice is very unlike the first. It offers no pretensions to be considered as historical, or to do more than give the author's impressions of the Russian people as derived from some months of contact. To the first part of the volume is added a critical examination of Russian literature, more especially of the works of the famous novelists of the last fifty years. From [*Impressions of Russia* by Dr Georg Brandes[103]] we learn much more than from Mr Morfill's history of the inner life of the Russian nation, and of the blighting, withering influence of the Autocracy.

... there is nothing dry or wearisome about these *Impressions*. They excite curiosity and enchain attention from the first page to the last.

It would take columns to indicate the unquestionable proofs filling these 350 pages of the deadening and damning influences of despotism on all the relations of life, public and private, political and social, moral and religious. The neglect and supineness of our Government and governing classes in relation to the great need of national education previous to 1870, was deservedly condemned. But at its worst our Government did not strive to prevent education. In Russia the settled policy of the Autocracy is the perpetuation of the ignorance of the masses, their brutish ignorance, in order to keep them in willing as well as hopeless servitude, whilst the obstacles to the obtaining of a liberal education by the higher classes are practically insurmountable. To be a student in a Russian university is to be under well nigh as much police surveillance and irritating police regulations as our burglars and other criminals have to endure. There is no public life; there are no public meetings, no popular societies, no freedom of the press.

> There is no press in Russia. There are printing presses and paper, of course, and black marks on a white surface; there are editors and journalists; but a press is not and cannot be found.

Thus spoke the editor of a Russian paper, meaning, of course, no freedom of the press, wanting which it would have better if the discovery of printing, at least the invention of journalism, had never come to pass. Licentiousness

102 Massacres were committed by the Russians in 1791 against Turkish forces at Ismail, Bessarabia (in the present-day Ukraine), and in the suppression of the Polish rising of 1794 in Praga, a Warsaw borough.
103 Georg Brandes (1842-1927) was an influential Danish literary critic, much admired and translated during his lifetime.

pervades the higher classes, and religious fanaticism the lower – these are the natural products of intellectual compression, for human volition will find vent in some direction. The Russians are accused of a propensity to falsehood, but falsehood is ever the accompaniment to slavery. Drinking to excess is another characteristic feature. Very largely the literary class believe that 'the best of life is but intoxication', as proved by acting up to their belief. Place British authors and journalists under like conditions, and they would be no better.

Campbell[104] says that 'body-killing tyrants cannot kill the public soul'. But tyranny can come very near to effecting that consummation. The Autocracy does kill the soul, the spiritual part, or the free intellect of individuals born with capacities to diffuse light and shed glory upon their country, but too often brought to abasement and degradation. See Pushkin, who might have been the Byron of Russia, degraded to the position of pensioner of Nicholas and 'gentleman of the Imperial bedchamber'.[105] Did Byron have his once adorer and imitator[106] prophetically in view when he wrote –

> Who toils for nations may be poor indeed,
> But free; who sweats for monarchs is no more
> Than the gilt chamberlain, who, clothed and fee'd,
> Stands sleek and slavish bowing at his door.[107]

See Zhukovsky,[108] Gogol, Dostoevsky, Leo Tolstoy, and others ending their days as semi or absolutely insane mystics. See the terrible life of Shevchenko,[109] a serf born, but with a genius to rank with the highest masters of thought and expression for his poem – for his poem *Caucasus* condemned to be whipped and to be sent as a common soldier to Orenburg, also strictly forbidden to write; condemned a second time to the lash, and to herd with the lowest dregs of society; not allowed to see a newspaper or book of any kind until he sickened and became all but insane. See the execrable treatment of Chernyshevsky,[110] an art critic and writer on historical and economical subjects, – for example, a criticism on John Stuart Mill's *Political Economy*; arrested, kept in close confinement from July 1862

104 Thomas Campbell (1777-1844), Scottish poet and friend of Scott and Byron.
105 Pushkin was released from internal exile by Nicholas I and appointed as his censor (though still kept under close police surveillance).
106 Pushkin.
107 *The Prophecy of Dante.*
108 V.A. Zhukovsky (1783-1852), the originator of modern Russian poetry.
109 Taras Shevchenko (1814-61), Ukrainian poet.
110 N.G. Chernyshevsky (1828-89), author of *What Is To Be Done?*

to May 1864, then brought on to a scaffold in St Petersburg apparently to be executed, an indictment against him read – the reading of which occupied an hour – accusing him of political offences, the accusation founded on his private papers seized by the police, concluding with his sentence, without trial, without any proof of the charges, to suffer 14 years' hard labour in the mines and then to exile in Siberia for life. The mockery of mercy followed: the Tsar had graciously commuted the 14 years' hard labour to seven. Thus at 35 years of age

> He vanished, never more to be seen among those who admired him, and who were indebted to him for the best part of their intellectual culture. He passed his seven years among the criminals in the mines underground, then 15 years' more in solitary exile in one of the most distant points of Siberia, without books, without men with whom he could exchange ideas, cut off from all communion with Europe. A year or two since they at last found the prisoner sufficiently subdued by his martyrdom of more than twenty years. They transferred him to a milder place of banishment, and allowed him to occupy himself in a harmless way by translations and similar things....It has gone so far in Russia that when a genius, who was the honour of his nation, and the pride of its youth, after having been abused for a quarter of a century with the coarsest cruelty has nevertheless not become an idiot, they do not then think much more of what has happened.

The three concluding chapters treat of the great novelists Turgenev, Dostoevsky and Leo Tolstoy; most interesting these chapters are, but I must leave them without comment. I fancy that of the three novelists, Turgenev, at least as a man, undaunted, and unchangeable to the last, will be the favourite with Englishmen.

Dr Brandes's *Impressions* should be read as an indispensible supplement to Mr Morfill's history; or, read alone, the book cannot fail to inform and interest every English reader.

19 April 1890

Stepniak Speaks

Last week we had our Grand Old Sequah[111] on the platform, accompanied by his 'brass band', perambulating East Anglia, and haranguing the natives on the virtues of his famous medicaments, drawing, not teeth, but brains, and like the American Sequah, presented with addresses of confidence and admiration. As part of the entertainment provided for the 'obfuscation' of the East Anglians, we had a mock exhibition of sympathy for the victims of Russian despotism, and a verdict as regards the misdeeds of that despotism 'this seems bad enough'. When he has to deal with the British Government's sins of commission or omission, he is lion-like in the thunder of his wrath. When he has to deal with atrocities at which the world stands aghast, he calmly observes 'this seems bad enough'! In fact, 'he roars you as gently as any sucking dove'.[112]

It is a relief to turn from the political charlatan to the earnest man – a man who has himself suffered and witnessed the worst sufferings of others. From him there will come no mere lip service, no professed sympathy with human sorrow so presented as to excite 'laughter and applause'. The unthinking crowd at Lowestoft did not laugh at the Russian sufferers; but they laughed at their favourite orator's method of 'giving a dig' to Lord Salisbury's Government under the cover of condemning the Yakutsk tragedy. Another kind of exponent of Russian wrongs is the man whose name heads this column.[113]

In the current number of a current magazine, *East and West* (June), Stepniak writes again on the 'Atrocities of the Russian Exile System'.

However shocking may be the sentences of the Russian political tribunals, the administrative punishments are still more shocking. They are inflicted without any formality of a trial, without *confronting the prisoner with his accusers, often without informing of the charges brought against him, or even giving him the name of the person who denounces him.*

Here we have 'the lion's mouth' of the Venetian oligarchy in its worst days. Stepniak goes on: 'It is a punishment inflicted on suspicion...and has for its avowed object to strike beforehand those who some day *may become*

111 Gladstone again. Sequah was a notorious British quack doctor. He pretended to be a Native American and sold supposedly indigenous medicines, his meteoric rise to celebrity – and wealth – dating from 1887.
112 An adaptation from Shakespeare, *A Midsummer Night's Dream*, I, ii.
113 Sergei (or Sergius) Stepniak (1852-95), Populist, who had escaped from Russia in 1880, eventually settling in London. He was to be killed by a train on the level crossing at Bedford Park, where he lived.

political offenders'.

This villainous system has been going on for many years. In all other nations claiming to be civilised, the tendency of criminal legislation has been to increase the safeguards of the accused, and to lighten and lessen punishments. Russia is the exception, the Russian Government enjoying the bad eminence of deliberately aggravating the penalties inflicted upon those whom it fears. A '*suspect*' is suddenly arrested; after detention in prison perhaps a year, perhaps two, his sentence is made known to him. It may be five years' exile to some point in Siberia, anywhere between Tomsk and the shores of the Frozen Sea. If not dead before the expiration of the prescribed period, the exile at length sees the term of his banishment and suffering approaching its end. Shortly before that end, sometimes even at the last moment, the unhappy exile receives intimation that his punishment is to be prolonged for two or more years. Often under this unexpected blow the sufferer sinks in despair, dies, or worse, loses his reason. On what pretexts are these cumulative penalties inflicted? On this, the re-examination of the old documents, or secret accusation, on which the first administrative order or exile was founded. Let us suppose that before the term of his imprisonment in York Castle had expired, Feargus O'Connor had been notified that the law officers of the Crown, having gone over the great agitator's speeches anterior to the one on which he had been convicted, the Administration had decided to detain him another year in prison! That would have been but a very mild version of what hundreds are in course of experiencing in Russia. Or, let us suppose that, before the end of his imprisonment, as already told in the *Weekly Chronicle*,[114] the Administration had taken into account the well-known fact of George Jacob Holyoake's previous connection with Southwell, Chilton,[115] and other heterodox suspects, and therefore had added another six months' detention to the sentence about to expire, such abominable tyranny would have borne a faint resemblance to some of the illustrative cases recounted by Stepniak in *East and West*. Let us not forget that, although tried before judges not always careful to conceal their prejudices, and condemned by juries taken from classes notoriously hostile to the defendants, both Feargus O'Connor and George Jacob Holyoake had fully availed themselves of their right to cross-examine their accusers, bring up their own witnesses, and been fully and patiently heard in their defence. How different to the treatment of the Russian exiles condemned in secret,

---

114 In the serialisation of Holyoake's *Sixty Years of an Agitator's Life*.
115 Charles Southwell and William Chilton were two other free-thought militants who had published the *Oracle of Reason* with Holyoake in 1841-3. In 1842 Southwell was imprisoned for an article and Holyoake for a lecture.

sentenced by arbitrary authority, and exposed to such suffering as the pen of Stepniak records! ....

A high officer of the Russian Government, interviewed by the correspondent of *The Times*, had the assurance to remark,

> The right of arresting and condemning on suspicion is an inseparable prerogative of autocratic rule. If the supreme power in Russia were to give up this right, it would at once cease to be autocratic.

Well may Stepniak add: 'The bitterest enemies of the existing régime in Russia have not condemned it more decisively'.

A word to our Grand Old Sequah. A dozen years ago,[116] you held up the 'good deeds' of the Russian Government for England's admiration and imitation! Now, with cautious reservation, you admit that the Russian Government's 'deeds' 'seem bad enough'. The insincerity of your 'sympathy' is palpable. Pray, leave the Russian exiles and the Russian political prisoners alone. All they ask is the charity of your silence. Their cause is too noble, their sufferings too intense, their wrongs too real, to be employed as party weapons for unworthy ends. The Ark of Russian Freedom is too sacred for your touch. Hands off!

7 June 1890

The Dead Tsar

'All suffering doth destroy, or is destroyed, and in each case ends'.[117] Watching, as it were, at the bedside of incurable disease, long borne with and hopeless of any relief save that accorded by dissolution, one must pity the sufferer, whether peasant or prince, whether the humble toiler or the potentate obeyed by millions, and it is not in human nature to have refused sympathy to the Russian autocrat through the long protracted agony of his fatal illness.[118] Yet there was something worse than incongruous in the courtly language in which the bulletins and all the accounts of the Tsar's lingering illness were couched. It was always 'his Majesty', or 'the august patient', etc. Yet the cruel disease of which he was the victim no more respected his autocratic rank than would have been the case in that of the humblest moujik in his dominions, or one of our own paupers stretched upon a workhouse pallet. All that unbounded means could command –

116 In *The Bulgarian Horrors and the Question of the East* (1876).
117 Byron, *Childe Harold's Pilgrimage*, 4, xxii.
118 He died of nephritis (inflammation of the kidneys).

doctors the ablest, medical professors summoned from distant parts, nurses the most skilful, every medical appliance, every comfort likely to mitigate pain – made a certain difference between the dying condition of the lord of many palaces and that of the dweller in a wretched hovel, or the inmate of the sick ward of a pauper's refuge. But not much! It is probable even that the Tsar's sufferings were prolonged by the services of his medical attendants, and that to the poor man, the pauper, the only possible relief would have come earlier. It came at last even to the Tsar. But save in its outward trappings Death reduced the autocrat to the level of the poorest of his subjects. One moment he was the lord of everything a human being might command; the next he was lifeless clay. One moment he was the master of life and death over millions; the next all-conquering Death had mastered his life and he was more powerless than even the fettered Nihilist in prison or in mine. He had been in life the lord of a vast empire stretching from the Baltic to the Caspian Sea, from the confines of Germany and Sweden to the frontiers of Persia and Afghanistan; the next moment, though he knew it not, the world saw realised the mournful anticipation of our own wayward, wrong-headed Richard:

> And nothing can we call our own but Death;
> And that small model of the barren earth,
> Which serves as paste and cover to our bones.[119]

True, whilst the unclaimed body of an English pauper may be handed over to the doctors for dissection, that of the Tsar has been embalmed – yet 'all his spices but prolong decay'[120] – and, if it escapes the perils of its Black Sea voyage, will find its resting place in some circumscribed vault in the metropolitan church of St Peter and St Paul, as the great Napoleon lies in his gorgeous but dreadful-looking well, weighted down by tons of marble and bronze; and yet gloomy vault or splendid tomb amounts only in reality to 'the little grave' for which Richard had to change his forfeited kingdom.

Death is so inscrutable a mystery that in the presence of its awful solemnity we must all uncover; and whether the breathless body be that of a friend we lament or of an enemy we forgive, it is but right to ignore the errors of the one and condone the sins of the other – doing justice to the good qualities of both. All that can be fairly said laudatory of the deceased Tsar may pass without question. Much is made of his private virtues, his marital fidelity, his affection for his children, etc. Are these,

119 Shakespeare, *Richard II*, 3, ii.
120 Byron, *The Vision of Judgment*.

then, uncommon virtues in the ranks of royalty? I am far from wishing to depreciate the virtue of conjugal fidelity; but if I must choose between such a ruler as the late Tsar, and Henri Quatre and his fair Gabriella and I know not how many more mistresses, but also with his kindly nature, his liberal ideas, his desire, according to his lights, that the people over whom he ruled should be free and happy, I give my verdict in favour of the hero of Ivry. Out of the domestic circle, I doubt if I can find aught to praise in the life and character of the dead autocrat. He appears to have been a man of violent and dictatorial temper, and if he was tender to his wife and delighted in the infantile happiness of his children such graceful characteristics appear to have been restricted to the domestic circle. His ministers and courtiers could not have had a pleasant time with him. That he earnestly desired to banish corruption and malfeasance from the administrative sections of his Government is unquestionable. But, strong-willed as he was, the task was beyond his strength; though he probably accomplished some genuine reforms calculated to make the Russian military system more effective – hardly a gain for any outside nation. He was the incarnation of Despotism in its most grinding and repulsive form. I could not have blamed him that in view of his father's fearful death he steeled his heart against those who had consigned Alexander II to a gory grave.[121] Nor could I have wondered that his own narrow escape from a like tragical end in the railway explosion at Borki further hardened his heart against the Nihilists. But as the years rolled on, Time wrought no beneficent, no softening change. It was enough to be 'suspect' – suspected of very mild principles of liberalism, such as desiring the liberty of the press, the freedom of association and public meeting, and some kind of representative institutions – however restricted and conservative – to ensure the arrest of the 'suspect', followed by deportation to Siberia. Throughout the 13 years of his reign, Alexander III was pitiless to all who excited his suspicion or incurred his displeasure. Open trial of accused persons with any hope of acquittal or escape there has been none. How many of such have been hanged in private, to say nothing of those semi-publicly executed, it is impossible to say. Enough is known to make any decent man wonder at the servile encomiums lavished upon the dead Tsar by the writers who conduct our public journals. The persecution of the Stundists,[122] the Roman Catholics, and the Jews is a matter of worldwide notoriety; and the late autocrat at least sanctioned, if he did not suggest, that

121 In 1881 a bomb was thrown at Alexander's carriage in St Petersburg. He was uninjured, got out and was mortally wounded by a second bomb.
122 A sect whose theology derived from German Baptists, they were located chiefly in the southern Ukraine, only breaking from the Orthodox Church as late as 1870.

persecution. If, in the internal affairs of Russia, he tried to abate corruption and promote administrative reform, he at the same time strove to intensify the evils of centralisation and bureaucratic rule. He took from the peasants almost the last shred of local management, so that they became more enslaved to the Tsar and the State – convertible terms – than they had been when the serfs of the great landholders. Stealthy, but remorseless filchings of the liberties of the Finlanders – though consecrated by solemn compact – was part of his Russifying policy. From long-suffering Poland the Tsar never lifted his heavy hand; no idea of justice, no sentiment of pity ever moved or touched Alexander III in his dealings with that cruelly-wronged land. The leaden despotism, the irritating police supervision, the brutal displays of crushing military force in Warsaw and elsewhere, instead of being lessened, were rigorously increased during his reign. Yet no doubt the Russian journals, perhaps some of our own, will tell us of the deep sorrow pervading Warsaw!

Disgusted with results of the last Russo-Turkish war, and bitterly disappointed at the failure to seize Constantinople when that great prize of Russian aggression seemed to be within grasp, the late Tsar found compensation for his inactivity in Europe by continuing the march of Russian conquest in Asia, until now only Afghanistan separates the aggressive forces of Russia from the defensive forces of Great Britain. That collision will come some day, and may come any day, no one doubts, with a result it would be useless to attempt to forecast. England may learn to bitterly regret the ostrich-like policy of her statesmen who would not see the inevitable consequences of refusing to arrest the march of Russian aggression; and Germany and Austria may as bitterly repent that they ever cast in their lot with the spoliator and destroyer of Poland.

Alexander III, whilst yet Tsarevich, held high command in the Russian army in the Russo-Turkish war, without earning any special distinction, though some of the troops under his command shared the death-doom of the multitudes of victims mowed down by Osman's cannon ere Plevna fell. It is said that the horrors of that war, the sickening scenes of carnage, and the frightful sufferings of non-combatants whose country was ravaged by the contending armies, made a lasting impression upon him, so that thereafter he shrank from the demoniac task of again letting loose the dogs of war. If true, that was greatly to his credit, and redounds to his honour.

Well, we are told the late Tsar kept the peace; he was what Daniel O'Connell would have termed Head Pacificator of Europe. Whatever his motive or impulse, whether simple humanity – which hardly accords with his treatment of native disturbers of his reign – or that he had misgivings of the result of letting loose the vast and conflicting forces of destruction, the fact that the peace of Europe has not been broken would warrant any reasonable commendation of the Tsar's European policy. But I am amazed at the grossly servile adulation indulged in by some of our English journals. Had the late Tsar been a god, or a Gautama[123] incarnating the Divinity – who, having fulfilled his mission, had been withdrawn from the earth – no more hyberbolical laudation could have been engaged in than that of our foremost journals praising the dead Tsar. Reading our newspapers, the Russians must despise us as a crew of cowardly wretches acknowledging that we owe our continued existence to the magnanimous forbearance of Holy Russia's Tsar.

What is the plain truth? It is a fact that throughout Alexander III's reign Russia was a standing menace to the peace of Europe, is so today, and will be tomorrow. Seeing much of the weakness of the military machine when engaged in war, the Tsar set about its reorganisation to make it invincible and all conquering when next the tocsin of war resounds. He loved peace, we are told; but he took care to keep his army on a peace-footing of 800,000 men, more than half being garrisoned in Europe. On a war-footing the army, it is estimated, would muster more than two and a half millions of fighting men – to say nothing of the navy, etc. Did Alexander III ever indicate any thought of reducing that vast destructive force, even pari passu with the other military powers? Would not Austria, always on the verge of bankruptcy, be only too glad to reduce her military expenditure if assured from deadly surprise on the part of Russia? To what but the menace of Russia do we owe the inception of the Triple Alliance?[124] That alliance has of late been rendered the more indispensable by the ostentatious entente of France with Russia[125] and the aggressive and furious declamation of Gallic politicians and journalists. The mighty armaments of Russia hang like a thunder cloud over Europe; and no one doubts that, whether soon or late, that cloud will burst, and bring upon the entire Continent – this island not escaping – the tempest of horrible desolating war.

That the new Emperor may also play the part of Pacificator is to be desired. But, even if so, the evil day is but postponed. Nominally, the Tsar is absolute; and in many things, and especially in relation to individuals from the highest to the lowest, really so. But there is something stronger than the Tsar in Russia – the system of organised Russia aggression seeking the dominion of the world, which has been growing and consolidating since the

123 Buddha.
124 The military alliance of 1882 between Germany, Austria-Hungary and Italy.
125 A military alliance of 1894.

days of Peter.[126] Any Tsar attempting to set aside that system would probably be the victim of a palace revolution and experience the end of the Emperor Paul.[127] The late Tsar, the Emperor Alexander III, has been gathered to his fathers. It cannot be said that he enjoyed absolute power. His Gatchina Palace was at once a fortress and a prison; closely watched by guards night and day, the roads leading thereto constantly patrolled – Gatchina, in fact, being defended by an entrenched camp. When travelling, the entire length of railway was guarded by soldiers placed at short distances, the soldiers being strictly enjoined, after three challenges, to shoot anyone approaching the line. These were but a few of the precautions taken to protect the Tsar. Soldiers, police, spies – with too often the hangman's services in addition – passed their lives in guarding the life of that one unhappy man who could never have known a moment's peace, hardly assured of a moment's safety; starting at the unexpected rustling of a curtain, on the alert at any unusual sound. Such a life must have been a life of horror. What a moral for the Royalties and the representatives of Royalty gathered at Livadia![128] What an example of the vanity of human grandeur!

> Within the hollow crown
> That rounds the mortal temples of a king,
> Keeps Death his court; and there the antic sits,
> Scoffing his state, and grinning at his pomp –
> Allowing him a breath, a little scene
> To monarchise, be fear'd, and kill with looks;
> Infusing him with self and vain conceit –
> As if this flesh, which walls about our life,
> Were brass impregnable – and humour'd thus
> Comes at the last, and with a little pin
> Bores though his castle wall, and – farewell king![129]

Emperor, Autocrat, Kaiser, Tsar – Vanitas vanitatum![130]

10 November 1894

126 Peter the Great, ruled 1682-1725.
127 Catherine the Great's son and attempting reforms, he was assassinated in 1801.
128 A summer palace in Crimea.
129 Shakespeare, *Richard II*, 3, ii.
130 Vanity of vanities.

TURKEY

The New Crusade

We have all heard of midsummer madness; but whereas that of canines is generally restricted to the hotter months of the year, the madness of humans is liable to break out, like the shafts of Death to fly, at 'all seasons'. Just now a crusading madness is afflicting, not the 'people of England', but a portion of that people; I believe not a large portion ....

'Strike! but hear!' said the illustrious Athenian.[131] Let the word 'reflect' be substituted for 'hear', with the counsel reflect before you strike – the consequence will be a repudiation of rodomontade, and a rational consideration of the facts dictating the line of duty. Of rodomontade respecting Armenians and Cretans we have had quantum suff[132] from small-beer poets and third or fourth-rate politicians posing as philanthropists. But worse still has been the war-whoop of Christian preachers who, beating 'the drum ecclesiastic', have to their sermons added their platform incitements to their audiences to join the new anti-Turkish crusade 'for the deliverance of the Cretan Christians'.

If Crete could be delivered from both Christians and Mussulmans, that would be the best solution of the Cretan question.[133] Paganism, or the worship of nature, had its superstitions, some of which seem very ridiculous to us – we are so wise! – and the forerunners of the Roman augurs knew how to 'work the oracle' for their own profit. But the belief in Pan and the offerings to Zeus entailed no massacres. It is modern religion, the religion of the Greek Church versus that of Islam, that is at the root of all the trouble in Crete. Our people, bamboozled by party spouters and sacerdotal belligerents, believe that the Sultan sends Turkish troops to butcher the Cretans; when the fact is that, outside the Turkish garrisons, the Mussulmans are just as much Cretans as are the Christians. The Mussulmans constitute nearly one-third of the native inhabitants, – in some of the towns a considerable majority, in other parts a small minority. I do not know who were the aggressors at the beginning of the present troubles, but it is certain that foreign intriguers

131 During the war against the Persians the Athenian strategist and statesman Themistocles counselled the Peloponnesians not to retreat from the Bay of Salamis. When his exasperated opponent, the Spartan admiral Eurybiades, raised his staff, he was told 'Strike, but hear me'. The result was the great naval victory the next day (BC 480).
132 An abbreviation – and a favourite term of Harney's – for 'quantum sufficit' (a sufficient quantity).
133 Although an independent Greek state had been set up in 1830, its territory was only about one-third of the modern country – with Crete among the regions remaining under Turkish rule.

have been concocting conspiracies and fomenting outbreaks on the part of the Christians for a long time past. Those conspiracies and outbreaks have constituted a warning and a danger for the Mussulmans, and so the two divisions came to blows. The frequently recurring riots in Belfast, and the anti-Protestant mobs in Cork and elsewhere, show that Ireland might offer a parallel case if the administrative rule in the sister island was as weak as that of the Sultan in Crete. The worst feature of Turkish rule is its weakness. It is not strong enough to defy and repel foreign aggression, nor to curb or crush internal disorder.

Not the least of the sufferers from the misrule of the Porte are the Turks themselves. I speak of the great body of the Turkish people, upon whom mainly falls the weight of taxation, and absolutely the burden of the blood-tax or military service. The idea – pictured by our crusaders – of the typical Turk is that of a lazy lout sitting on his hams all day intent on smoking an everlasting chibouque,[134] excepting when engaged in the pleasant pastime of slaughtering a few Christians! Whereas the typical Turk is hardworking and abstemious (no need for 'local option'[135] in his case!), patient and courteous – so long as you do not touch his religion.   Suspecting that, he revolts, and is very apt in the fury of his orthodox zeal to become, for the time being, a savage. Another of our popular delusions is to confound all Muhammedans with Turks. Under settled, strong, even Christian Governments, millions of Mussulmans – enjoying the full liberty of their own religion – make good law-and-order abiding subjects, as in Algeria under French, and (on a large scale) in India under British rule. The Cretan Mussulmans are not Turks. That they are much worse or more fanatical than the Cretan Christians, may be doubted. Within the last month, when and where the Christians have gained the upper hand, they have ruthlessly massacred the Muhammedans, without calling forth any protest on the part of our crusaders. Indeed, in Parliament, some of our 'Liberals', and especially of the Irish contingent, could not conceal their vexation at the rescue of a Turkish garrison and Cretan Muhammedans – men, women, and children – from imminent massacre. For a Mussulman to kill a Christian is an 'atrocity'; but for a Christian to kill a Mussulman? – Ah! well! let us say nothing about it!

There seems to be an idea abroad – very much abroad! – that the annexation of Crete to Greece would be an act of restitution. I care not to enquire whether the earlier (it is idle to speak of 'originals' anywhere) Cretans were Trojans, or Thracians, or of the Greek race. Let us accept the theory

134 A Turkish tobacco pipe.
135 A local veto on the sale of alcohol (that is, prohibition): a key component of Gladstone's 'Newcastle Programme' of 1891.

that they were Greek colonists; that did not make the island the property of Greece. Never did Crete belong to Greece in the sense that the Australian Colonies belong to Britain. The Dominion of Canada is for all domestic purposes independent. Still the Dominion has for sovereign the Queen of Great Britain, and is by all the world acknowledged as an integral part of the British Empire. But the Greek colonists, when they set up new states, whether on the numerous islands or the Asiatic shore, acknowledged not the sovereignty of Athens or of Sparta. They carried with them Greek culture, and followed Greek experiments in government and social arrangements – sometimes going beyond their originals, as our New Zealand colonists are doing; but the states they formed were politically distinct and separate from the states of the mainland. Sometimes the colonists were allies, sometimes enemies. Some sided with Athens, some with Sparta; and there were Greek colonists who, from policy or compulsion, aided the Persian aggression and the attempts of 'the Great King' to bring Greece under the Asiatic yoke. In those days there was no Kingdom of Greece, or Republic – one and indivisible – to which Crete belonged; and the idea of restitution is preposterous. Still, if the Cretans unanimously wished for annexation to Greece, that should go far to outweigh the claims of Turkey merely founded on conquest; but there can be no pretence of such unanimity. Do the Cretan Mussulmans, nearly one-third of the population, desire annexation to Greece?

Suppose that annexation to come to pass, as indeed it may ultimately, there is not much risk in prophesying that the Cretan Christians will soon be disillusioned. For the best part of fifty years the Ionian Islands were under a British Protectorate – Corfu being the seat of British administration. The islanders said they were Greeks, and nothing would satisfy them but incorporation with Greece. Agitators within, and intriguers and conspirators from without, kept the islands in a constant state of hot water, until this country grew sick of the whole business, and 'let go the painter'. Under the Protectorate roads had been made or kept in repair, bridges built, industries encouraged, libraries founded, education promoted; but now travellers tell us the 'Ionians', especially those of Corfu, regret the loss of the British Administrators. Crete annexed to Greece, a hungry horde of Greek officials would be let loose upon the island, and the Cretans might find, like Aesop's frogs, that they had changed the rule of King Log for that of King Stork with prospect of being 'gobbled up'.

I have not much confidence in the proposed autonomy of Crete with a people so hopelessly and savagely divided by religion as are the Cretans. In the Grecian island of Samos autonomy has existed for some sixty years, and we never hear of trouble there; but I believe there is no such division in

Samos as prevails in Crete. However, the 'Great Powers' have decided that autonomy is to be tried. I confess that I would rather Great Britain had not had part or parcel in the so-called 'European Concert', though, had this country stood aloof, it would have insured the reproach of 'selfish isolation' and the design of 'wholesale grabbing' in the event of the break-up of the Turkish Empire. Anyway, we are in the 'Concert', and to withdraw now would be to provoke the conflict which Europe has reason to dread.

That the British Government earnestly desires the maintenance of the European peace cannot be doubted; but that events provocative to war may suddenly reveal themselves is only too probable. If the newspapers are to be believed, the Government, whilst hoping for the best, is preparing for the worst, as, according to them, naval and military preparations indicate. The thinking man will not restrict his mental vision to Constantinople, Crete, and Athens. He will look at least as far north as St Petersburg for the hand that pulls the strings of the puppets of Diplomacy and that holds the issues of Peace or War. The following, professedly from the pen of 'A Greek', appears in *Lloyd's*,[136] 14 March:

The 'eyes of Europe' have seldom gazed on so puzzling a spectacle as is now presented by the audacity of little Greece in challenging Turkey and defying the Powers. Whether King George[137] took the Tsar into his confidence respecting his designs on Crete or not before taking action, the demonstrative hostility of Russia to Greece and her national aspirations, at this juncture appear most unnatural. Therefore, I will divulge a State secret, known to leading Greek statesmen and diplomatists – which is that Russia is merely pretending. She was never more favourably disposed towards Greece than at present. The Greek expedition[138] to Crete has not only been approved of, but was suggested by Count Mouravieff [Muravyov].[139] Russia's aim is to produce a convulsion in the Balkan States similar to that of 1875-76,[140] to be followed up immediately by a warlike action on her part. It was Servia [Serbia] who opened the ball in 1876, and the same office now devolves upon Greece. While

136 *Lloyd's Weekly Newspaper*, a Sunday paper launched in 1842.
137 King George I of Greece, previously a Danish prince and proclaimed 'King of the Hellenes', ruled 1863-1913.
138 A Greek force invaded Crete in 1897, but although it failed to defeat the Turks, intervention by the European powers in 1898 led the expulsion of Ottoman troops and the creation of an autonomous state. Crete was eventually assimilated into Greece in 1913.
139 Count M.N. Muravyov, Russian Minister of Foreign Affairs, 1897-1900.
140 Revolts against Ottoman rule in Herzegovina, Bosnia and Bulgaria were followed by Serbia declaring war on Turkey. Russia intervened on behalf of her fellow Slavs in 1877.

secretly encouraging the Greeks to seize Crete, Russia is doing her best to disappoint their hopes in that quarter, in the certain expectation that that disappointment will drive them to the desperate course of making war upon Turkey.

The above may be merely a shrewd guess, but that it substantially outlines the game being played by Russia I have no doubt. It should delight our pro-Russian Liberals and Evangelicals. The New Crusade, as preached by the politicians of the opposition is simply a barefaced attempt at a revival of the 'atrocities' agitation which had for object the discrediting of the Beaconsfield[141] Administration and replacing the Gladstonians in power. But the deluded are not likely to be as numerous and as powerful for mischief as twenty years ago. Even the ordinary man in the street must see through the fraud of the parliamentary Opposition's pretended sympathy for Crete and Greece. That 'sympathy' is a mere party manoeuvre to harass the Government; whilst that of the Irish Separatists is simply the rancorous manifestation of their implacable hatred of this country. The gentry of the 'Forward Movement' seek the further acquisition of notoriety, so that when there comes a return of 'Liberals' to power they may not be left out in the cold, but be called to a fair share of the loaves and fishes.

A week ago (6-7 March) the Nonconformists were being urged to send signed postcards to the Marquis of Salisbury[142] with the words – 'No War with Greece'. No War with Lilliput! Far from making war upon Greece, our Government is employing its endeavours to prevent Greece from lighting up the flames of a general European conflict. Priestly effrontery is no new thing; still a sense of decency might have modified the warlike zeal of the sacerdotal belligerents, if they had looked back upon the records of their own religion – records of centuries written in blood, the blood of Christians shed by their fellow Christians.

We want no war; we have war enough at home at present. Well would it be, whether in International Questions or questions at issue between Labour and Capital, Trades Unions and Employers, if all concerned would hear and reflect before they strike. As the Americans say: 'First be sure you are right, and then go ahead!'

20 March 1897

At length all disguise has been thrown off, and the New Crusaders stand

141 Disraeli had been created Earl of Beaconsfield in 1876.
142 Both Prime Minister and Foreign Secretary, 1895-1900.

self-unmasked, like Mokanna[143] revealing himself in his true character. No revelation to some of us. From the inception of the pro-Armenian agitation[144] thinking men understood that the agitators were bent on playing a party game; in fact, repeating the 'atrocity' agitation of twenty years ago for purely party ends. In vain did the speakers who so loudly manifested their 'sympathy' for the Armenians protest that their manifestations were dictated by humanity and had no reference to the chance of ousting the present Administration; that talk might go down with the groundlings, but would not deceive those who had watched the Opposition leaders and who remembered the reckless crusade preached at Blackheath[145] and elsewhere. Then, Lord Beaconsfield was trying to keep the peace of Europe, and then Mr Gladstone was employing all the powers of his mischievous rhetoric to light up the flames of war. The aim of the agitators was to make the then Government odious by representing the Beaconsfield Administration as the ally of 'the unspeakable Turk', and, so far, a sharer in the responsibility for the 'Bulgarian atrocities'. Now, we have Sir William Harcourt[146] boasting that he shared in that fraudulent agitation, or, as he grandiloquently puts it, that he 'carried a musket (!) in the glorious fight which we fought against the Government of Lord Beaconsfield from 1878 to 1880'. If this heroic self-portraiture leads the Cretans or Greeks to think that the rejected of Derby[147] is going to shoulder a rifle in the ranks they will find themselves mightily deceived. There was a double result of that agitation: There came the war which Mr Gladstone had so passionately invoked, one of the most cruel and murderous wars of modern times. For the scores slain in the 'Bulgarian atrocities', thousands were slain in the Russo-Turkish war. That war did not expel 'the unspeakable Turk' from Europe, but it brought 'unspeakable' miseries upon tens of thousands, including non-combatants, women, and children. The 'Bulgarian Atrocities' evoked the Blackheath orator's most frenzied denunciations; but on the awful story of the multitudinous slaughters and widespread desolation of the Russo-Turkish war, as told by the war correspondent of his principal party-organ, the *Daily News*, he was

143 In 'The Veiled Prophet of Khorassan', a poem in Thomas Moore's *Lalla Rookh* (1817), a story is told about Mokanna, loosely modelled on an eighth-century Persian prophet. His adherents claimed he wore a veil to obscure his beauty, his opponents that he needed to hide his ugliness.
144 Massacres of the Armenian population in the Ottoman Empire occurred during 1894-6, leading to a campaign in Britain in support of the Armenians.
145 Gladstone was MP for Greenwich, 1868-80; and within his constituency Blackheath was an open space where he spoke in his anti-Turk campaign in 1876.
146 Liberal politician, who was Home Secretary, 1880-85, and Chancellor of the Exchequer, 1886 and 1892-5. He was leader of the party, 1896-8.
147 Harcourt had lost his seat at Derby in the general election of 1895.

silent. There were those who sympathised with the Bulgarians quite as much as ever did Mr Gladstone, who yet had the sense to see that Turkish misrule and Bashi-Bazouk[148] ferocity insufficiently accounted for the deplorable events in Bulgaria. Of the whole truth the Blackheath rhetorician could not have been ignorant, but his tongue was silent thereon. Why? Because his purpose was to misguide the multitude and lead the electorate 'by the nose, as asses are'. The game was successfully played. At the ensuing General Election the Beaconsfield Administration was defeated, and Mr Gladstone and his followers were again installed in Government offices. We saw in more recent years what became of that 'glorious fight' – the 'trade' with Mr Parnell,[149] and the attempt made twice over, to disintegrate the United Kingdom, to abandon the Irish Loyalists[150] to the tender mercies of their implacable enemies, and actually in the second Home Rule Bill to place the governing power of Parliament in the hands of the Irish members – England to have no voice, no authority, in the Government of Ireland, but an Irish revolutionary faction to have control, the casting vote on English laws and institutions![151] All the other meddling and muddlings of the Gladstonians – such as the Harcourt Local Option scheme[152] – 'pale their ineffectual fires'[153] in the presence of the great treason of the Home Rule Bills. Now it is sought to play the like game again, with Harcourt speeches, Gladstone pamphlets, and the awakening of the 'Nonconformist conscience' preaching the New Crusade to expel the Turks from Europe.

If troublous times for this country are not near at hand, it will not be the fault of that stormy petrel, 'the Grand old man'. He has just issued another sixpenny pamphlet in the form of A Letter to the Duke of Westminster, elaborately calculated to work the greatest possible amount of mischief. His comments on the Russian and German Emperors would be comically refreshing if they were not likely to have the effect of provoking irritation, and so adding to the obstacles to the preservation of peace. Rather late in

148 Turkish irregular soldier.
149 After the commitment of the Liberal Party to Irish Home Rule, while Charles Stewart Parnell and the Irish party had instructed Irish electors in Britain to vote Conservative in the general election of 1885, they were now compelled to support the Liberals (and vice versa), despite the rejection of the First Home Rule Bill and the return of a Conservative administration in 1886.
150 Supporters of the Union with Great Britain.
151 This assertion is incorrect. Under the First Home Rule Bill Ireland was not to be represented at Westminster, but the Second Irish Home Bill had provided for eighty Irish MPs (a reduction from the existing 103) who would only be able to vote on matters of Irish or imperial concern.
152 The Local Liquor Control Bill – the Local Veto – was Harcourt's measure but defeated in the Commons in 1895.
153 An adaptation from Shakespeare, Hamlet, 1, v.

the day, Mr Gladstone has made the discovery that Russia is a pure and perfect despotism. Within a few days past we have had an illustration of how they manage things in that country, even under the present regime, supposed to be 'mild' and 'beneficent'. A girl student, Alisa Vitrov,[154] was arrested last December for having political pamphlets in her possession. Since this she has been confined in one of the fortress-prisons of the capital. Finally, she committed suicide by setting fire to her bed and burning herself to death. It is believed she was driven to the terrible deed by insults and violence on the part of an officer of the prison. Over a thousand of the St Petersburg students were arrested at the doors of the Kazan Cathedral, where they attempted to attend prayers for the soul of Alisa Vitrov. Did ever Mr Gladstone know twenty years ago – sixty years ago – that Russia was a pure and perfect despotism? Of course he did. Yet he had the audacity to proclaim the virtues of 'Holy Russia' and to exalt her as a model for England to imitate; and when on Blackheath one generous voice, from one who had not lost his head, interrupted the orator with the sympathetic cry of 'Poland!' the wily rhetorician ignored and made no response to that accusing cry.

If Russia is a pure and perfect despotism, no man outside of Russia ever did as much as Mr Gladstone has done – from the preaching of his Peter-the-Hermit-like crusade twenty years ago to his swaggering fiasco in connection with 'the Pendjeh incident'[155]– to make Russia the paramount Power of Europe. How often must the forgetful British public be reminded that it matters little who may be Emperor of Russia – whether a strong remorseless tyrant like Nicholas the First, or an 'inexperienced', but probably well-meaning, even kindly young man, like Nicholas the Second – the Russian system, the Russian policy, the Russian aim is always the same: the possession of Constantinople, Russia the dominating power of Europe and Asia with as near an approach to universal empire as the Fates may permit. Sometimes it suits Russia to foster conspiracy and stimulate revolt, as the Greek War of Independence, culminating in the destruction of the Turko-Egyptian fleet in the Bay of Navarino. At other times it best advances Russia's aims to snub her dupes and to pose as the protector of States menaced by revolution or by external enemies. It was in the character of protector that the earliest Russian essays were made in the partition and spoliation of Poland.

154 Her actual name was Maria Fedoseevna Vetrova. She lived from 1870 until 12 February 1897.
155 When Russia had attacked and defeated an Afghan force at Pendjeh in 1885, Britain was for some weeks on the brink of war with the Russians until Gladstone and his Foreign Secretary Granville agreed to them annexing this fertile border region.

The impotency, thus far, of the 'European Concert' is undoubtedly due to the secret workings of Russian policy. A great fuss is now made about turning the Greeks out of Crete; but why were they ever let in? Surely the six Great Powers are strong enough to have prevented the landing of a single Greek trooper, or the anchoring of a single Greek war vessel in Cretan waters, had they so desired. Britain had no interest in prolonging the miseries of Crete. Had the other Powers? Can any sane man doubt which of the Powers was unmistakably interested in that prolongation? And now, the 'coercion' of Crete, and the threatened 'coercion' of Greece, are calculated with Machiavellian subtlety to excite the Greeks to commence war against Turkey on the mainland. Macedonia is likely to be the scene of first hostilities, and no doubt the Greeks will have Mr Gladstone's good wishes. But his former clients, the Bulgarians, have their claim, and the Servians have theirs; and the probability is that the King Log rule of the Turks will be exchanged for a four-corner'd duel of Turks or Albanians, Greeks, Servians, and Bulgarians, and these three Christian powers will have a fine opportunity of showing their brotherly love and their vast moral superiority over the hated Moslem! Lamenting Chœronea's fatal day, one could wish, nevertheless, that Philip and his phalanxes could reappear on the scene to crush the promoters of discord and scatter the forces of anarchy.[156]

The occupation of Crete will furnish a precedent, sooner or later, for other occupations. How would we like the Great Powers, exclusive of Great Britain, to occupy Ireland, on the pretext that the Government of this country could not suppress an Irish insurrection? Of course, there is no more present apprehension of that than of any such insurrection in the Isle of Wight or Eel Pie Island at Twickenham. But States have their vicissitudes, as the most powerful, and empires the mightiest, have known –

> A thousand years scarce serve to form a State,
> An hour may lay it in the dust.[157]

Could we imagine such an Irish insurrection and such intervention of Great Powers, it would be time for every self-respecting Englishman to betake him to the Fiji Islands, or to the interior of Africa, and try to forget he was born in England. What is much more likely to be seen is the occupation of Constantinople. There is an ominous prediction afloat of 'more massacres' in Stamboul.[158] Probably some of the prophets are engaged in engineering movements calculated to lead up to 'more massacres'. If the Ottoman

156 Philip II of Macedonia defeated an alliance of Thebans and Athenians at the Battle of Chœronea in BC 338.
157 Byron, *Childe Harold's Pilgrimage*, 2, lxxxiv.
158 Istanbul – or Constantinople, as it was still named.

Porte cannot maintain order in the capital, the Great Powers, with Crete for a precedent, may determine it is their duty to occupy Constantinople – of course, in the name, and to uphold the authority, of the Sultan (!), who from that hour will have about as much authority as the Queen of Madagascar has enjoyed since the French occupation of that island, or as Stanislaus Augustus, the last King of Poland, enjoyed under the protection of Catherine! Necessarily, the occupation of Constantinople by all the six Powers would have to come to an end. Does any one suppose that Russia would be the first to march out, or march out at all? If so, evergreen must be the sanguine creature credulous enough to entertain such belie ….

I saw in one of the newspapers the other day that Ricciotti, son of General Garibaldi, was enlisting volunteers to serve with the Greeks against the Moslems, and that he counts upon 200,000 Italians to assist the Greeks in expelling the Turks from Europe. That 200,000 seems to be a big number to clothe, victual, arm, and convey across the sea. But suppose the 200,000, or the half, or the fourth, or even the eighth of that number enlisted, and, joining the Greeks, and the combined forces driving the Turks across the Bosphorus and the Hellespont, what next, and next? I suppose Ricciotti Garibaldi does not count upon re-annexing the ancient Byzantium to Rome. Probably he would be content to see Constantinople the seat of a new Greek Empire. The Greeks themselves have had such a dream. But the new Greek Emperor would have first to ask leave at St Petersburg. Of course, up to the last moment of taking possession Russia will protest that she has no burglarious intentions; but about one thing she has never made, or pretended to make, any concealment – namely, her fixed resolve to allow no burlesque Greek Empire to be set up in Constantinople.

With the Turks expelled from Europe, with Russia, not Greece, enthroned at Constantinople, will the crusader Ricciotti Garibaldi tell us in what way that would be an advantage to Italy? Of course, crusaders repudiate all considerations of national 'interests' and 'advantages'. Very well! Tell us, then, please, what advantage will accrue to the general cause of Freedom, so much mouthed about at present, even if largesses of plunder are thrown to Greece, Bulgaria, Servia, and the rest of the hungry lot, by the paramount Muscovite power at Constantinople? 'Freedom and whisky gang thegither', according to Robert Burns; but Russia and Freedom, no! As to our 'Radicals' who ask, 'Who's afraid? if Russia wants Constantinople, let her have it!' it is needless to argue with them. A visitor to a lunatic asylum courteously listens to the speeches of the inmates, their wonderful inventions, their amazing schemes for the world's reformation and the regeneration of the human race – the visitor listens, smiles, and – passes on; he does not discuss. So neither will any sane man discuss with our modern Radicals approval of the seizure of Constantinople by Russia. Those who are not ashamed to express that approval are of the same order, some of them the same individuals as the 'Perish India' gang of twenty years ago. Whatever the issue of the Cretan imbroglio and of Greek pretensions, no true Englishman, at once sane and patriotic, will give aid to any movement calculated to advance the aims of Russian aggression.

27 March 1897

THE USA

Some American Items

When the Revolution of '76 was consummated by Britain's acknowledgment of 'Independence'; when the British Lion had been compelled to turn tail before that 'tarnal'[159] screamer the American Eagle – a humiliation signally avenged within the last thirty years by the triumphant lodgment of the English sparrow, successfully defying State laws, murderous pop-guns, and incitements to the indiscriminate massacre of the perky, pugilistic, and fearless little winged Sayers; when, etc, our old friends Thomas Paine and Clio Rickman,[160] like Mr Silas Wegg,[161] 'dropped into poetry', and sang of the glories of the New Atlantis, the world was promised that so brilliant would be the example of Republican institutions that all nations would hasten to go and do likewise. And very soon the realisation of that promise seemed to be assured by the French Revolution, when our 'English Jacobins' (good and true men, they were) could sing with enthusiasm:

> O'er the vine cover'd hills and fair valleys of France,
> See the day-star of Liberty rise.[162]

But soon, alas! that dream vanished amidst storms and tempest, the downpour of which was torrents of blood. Hence the first check to those bright anticipations with which the American Revolution had been hailed. Soon the European friends of Freedom awoke to the startling incongruity of the 'glittering generalities' of the 'Declaration of Independence' side by side with the monstrous institution of Slavery. From that curse the country was purged by the fires of the greatest civil war ever recorded in the annals

159 Damned.
160 Thomas 'Clio' Rickman (1760-1834), British bookseller, writer of poetry and friend of Paine.
161 Ballad-seller in Dickens's *Our Mutual Friend*.
162 By William Roscoe (1753-1831), historian, poet and abolitionist.

of mankind, compared with which our Wars of the Roses were but as a protracted bloodstained tournament. But though purged of the curse of Slavery, in no other respect has the country commonly called America been reformed, or purified; on the contrary, the very war of the maintenance of the federal pact against the league of slaveholders gave birth to such a system of corruption, political and social, as can be found nowhere else on the face of the earth, unless, possibly, in Russia, and Turkey. In those countries corruption is the unavoidable attendant upon despotic power. The reigning despots may be personally pure; but with all their authority of life and death they are powerless to prevent the demoralising corruption of the official agents of the despotisms, from Ministers of State and Generals of Armies, down to wretchedly-paid policemen and poverty-stricken clerks of Customs. In the States no excuse, such as may be presented for the Russian and Turkish despotisms, can be offered. There the 'sovereign people' rule, and it is not upon kings, or dukes, or privileged classes, or a State Church, that the burden of blame can be laid. Philadelphia and Chicago Exhibitions, notwithstanding the promises of '76' and '83' have not been realised within the States, and in the outside world generally, and Europe in particular, the fulfilments of those promises seems more remote and more unlikely than ever. In South America, where the political revolution effected by Franklin, Jefferson, and Washington has been imitated, the history of the several Republics has been one of continual inter-State wars, varied by domestic insurrections and the despotism of military adventurers, whose one object has been the plunder of the so-called 'sovereign people'. Brazil has presented the latest example. The country was peaceful and prosperous under the limited rule of a nominal Emperor. To have the ideal Republic Dom Pedro[163] (apart from his Royalty, a cultured and very worthy man) was cashiered, and the country has been the theatre of anarchy ever since. Violence, plunder, mutiny, treason, hideous and useless slaughter, have been the results of the Revolution. The lull at present is but for a moment; bad commenced with the expulsion of Dom Pedro, 'and worse remains behind'.[164]

The drunken helot trotted out by the Spartan slaveholder as an 'object lesson' for the edification of his little son, was not more so than is the big Republic for the instruction and warning of mankind. In no other country, not in England, France or Germany, is there such disparity of condition as in

163 Dom Pedro II, second and last emperor of Brazil and grandson of Dom João VI of Portugal, reigned from 1831 to 1889, when he was ousted by a coup d'état instituting a republic.
164 Shakespeare, *Hamlet*, 3, iv.

the States. Hatfield and Hawarden, Alnwick and Alton Towers, Chatsworth and Woburn, are not palaces that any amount of American dollars can create in a day, or a generation; they are the monuments of centuries which the New World cannot command, and never will be able to command. Yet where England has one wealthy aristocrat, like the Earl of Derby or the Dukes of Bedford and Westminster, the States have a dozen or two, wielding a still greater purchasing power – a power not only to buy individuals, but to buy, at least to dominate and manipulate, Governments, and subserve their own purse-proud luxury, unexampled since the days of Imperial Rome. With abounding and increasing wealth on the one hand, there is abounding and increasing poverty on the other. Yet, on the approaching 'glorious Fourth', that bit of ancient history, the Declaration, will be again dusted and brought forth, and Buncombe[165] orators will repeat the sonorous affirmation: 'We hold these truths to be self-evident: that all men are created equal; that they are endowed by their Creator with certain inalienable rights; that amongst these are life, liberty, and the pursuit of happiness. There needs no lengthened Blackstonian commentary;[166] sufficient is the phrase – the Coxeyites.[167]

Of all the 'mighty movements' the nineteenth century has witnessed, the march of the Coxeyites to Washington has proved the most complete failure and absurd fiasco. The tramping of some thousands, or tens of thousands, from California and the faraway West to Washington was practically impossible; and hence the seizures and attempted seizures of trains, with occasional conflicts, resulting, mainly, in the dispersion of the Western forces. Of course, the march from Ohio to Washington was not absolutely impracticable, as proved by the fact that Coxey and three or four hundred of his followers did succeed in reaching the Federal Capital. Three or four hundred, instead of the one hundred thousand he had boasted he would lead! .... Coxey is still encamped, waiting, like Micawber, for 'something to turn up'. I suppose the other 'hundred thousand', which, owing to desertions, arrests by wholesale, dispersions by the application of cold water through fire-engine hose, and other causes, is likely by the time any fraction can reach Washington, if any and ever, to be still more diminutive

165 Humbug – or bombastic speechmaking intended for newspapers rather than to persuade the audience.

166 Sir William Blackstone (1723-80), jurist, was the author of the classic *Commentaries on the Laws of England* (1766-70).

167 'General' Jacob Coxey, a wealthy quarry owner, led hunger marchers from Ohio and Pennsylvania to the grounds of the Capitol in Washington, DC. Other 'Coxeyites' assembled in the Pacific Northwest (Montana, Oregon and Washington State). Coxey's advocacy of paper currency and public works, at the time reviled generally, not just by Harney, now seems admirably prescient.

in point of numbers than 'the army' from Ohio. One result may be the easing of the Western States of some of the unemployed together with not a few professional tramps and loafers, and an increase in the number of these classes in the Middle and Eastern States. The Government will probably issue free passes to the best of 'the army' disposed to return to the places from whence they came; others, as vagrants or criminals, will find their way to durance vile. Meanwhile, 'General' Coxey has got himself well advertised, his name, his portrait, and his spectacles in the newspapers. He has achieved what is dearer to the average American even than dollars – notoriety. We may expect next to hear of him as a Labour candidate; and, if he can succeed in making his dupes believe that the blame of failure rests, not upon him, but upon some others, he may presently pose as a Labour member of Congress. It is melancholy to reflect that thousands of working men, who, presumably, had a common-school education, and many of whom must have been registered voters – could have been duped by such a transparent imposter ....

The brutalities connected with strikes far exceed – so far, happily for us – the incidents of such troubles in this country. In Walker County, Alabama, the miners blew up the machinery and fittings at several mines with dynamite. In must be inferred that they have some other line of business in view. It is reported from Cleveland, Ohio, that the city was all but the scene of an insurrection on the 1st. At Scottdale, Pennsylvania, a number of women attempted to drive off the coke-workers who refused to join the strike. The police resisted the Amazonians, and thereupon the men joined in the mêlée. The Sheriff's deputies used their revolvers freely, fifteen of the strikers and a woman being shot. In the State of Ohio, at Mount Sterling, some Coxeyites having seized a goods train, Colonel Coit placed Gatling guns in such a position as to sweep the train. Then, watch in hand, he gave them three minutes to leave the cars. The Coxeyites wisely scrambled down, and averted a hideous massacre. As in our last coal strike so many hundreds of factories and workshops were brought to a standstill, or, at the least, to short time, involving the lessened or no employment of thousands who had no connection with the strike, so it is in the States: trains are stopped, factories closed, and industry largely paralysed. Whereas the Americans boast, and with reason, of possessing the largest coalfields in the world, and count upon the time when, English coal being exhausted, we shall be dependent upon the States for existence – for existence without coal, or some equivalent, in a country like this, would be impossible – it is significant that Cardiff has received an American order within the past few days for 15,000 tons! One marked feature of these strikes is the bitter hostility against non-strikers carried out by methods of the utmost violence, even to the taking of life. We have seen the like spirit manifested in this country, the strikers being utterly regardless of the rights, wants, and sufferings of others.

The atrocities of lynching continue. Recently from Madison, Louisiana, came intelligence that the manager of a plantation had been murdered by negroes on the estate. It was calmly added – 'During the past week no fewer than eight negroes have been lynched'. Whether 'negroes' connected with 'the estate', or others having nothing to do with the alleged murder, is not stated. Ohio is the oldest settled state subsequent to the Revolution; and originally by settlers from New England: of course their descendants were long since outnumbered by immigrants from other States and from Europe. In educational appliances, in churches, in all the paraphernalia on which morals and religion are supposed to depend, Ohio vies with New England. Well, recently, on a Sunday morning at a place called Sylvania, 1,500 citizens marched to the gaol and demanded that Seymour Newland, a negro, should be handed over to them. He was awaiting trial on an abominable charge of assaulting a lady of 81 years of age. The militia were overpowered, Newland was dragged from his cell, and at once lynched, 'every armed man in the mob apparently regarding it as a duty to discharge his weapon into the negro's body'. If the law of Ohio is death for such an offence as that above indicated, let the perpetrator die – after impartial trial and a verdict of guilty; but not execution before trial, in fact without trial. The reason for the Sunday morning service of the 1,500 virtuous citizens of Sylvania is naively given: 'As she was a white woman, the indignation of the citizens was intense'. Had she been a black woman, outraged or assaulted by a white man, would 1,500 of the white citizens have assembled on a Sunday morning to put him to death without any pretence of a trial? Lately there came to Newcastle 'a coloured lady', who had taken upon herself the mission to make known these lynching atrocities to our people with the view of bringing British opinion to bear upon the Americans in the interests of justice. I do not see that the moral force of such opinion can have any effect upon Judge Lynch's followers, unless to embitter them still more intensely against the 'coloured people' and their advocate – even though a woman. I sincerely hope that her friends in Newcastle and elsewhere in this country will see that she does not return to the place from whence she came, or anywhere within reach of the lynchers. Why do these atrocities go on? Why does President Cleveland make no sign? Why does New England make no pronunciamento? The answer is 'State Rights'! And when an Irish Parliament sits in College Green, no matter what atrocities may be committed in Ireland, whether the massacre of Irish loyalists, the assassination of helpless individuals, or the horrible mutilation of dumb animals,[168] we shall be told that England must not interfere, because Ireland has Home Rule; and the 'Nonconformist conscience' will endorse that cruel, cowardly, and cursed conclusion.

..... Is it true that in model Massachusetts children are taught in the public schools to kill and dissect cats and other animals placed under chloroform? So it is alleged in a petition addressed to the State Legislature by George T. Angell, president of the Massachusetts Society for the Prevention of Cruelty to Animals; and it is stated in the *Rochford Morning Star* (Massachusetts) that the dissecting fad is turning to vivisection. Vivisection in the presence of children in the public schools! Massachusetts, hanging of Quakers two hundred (and more) years ago had the excuse of religious fanaticism. What shall excuse this new barbarism? Lastly, is it true, as stated in *Our Dumb Animals*, a Boston periodical of many years' standing, in fact in its 26th volume, that there is now before the Legislature of Ohio a proposed law by which all criminals sentenced to death are to be turned over to the surgeons for experiments in vivisection?

We owe a great deal to the free and independent States of America: the gradual corruption of our language, the caucus, the example of unscrupulous politicians running 'the political machine' – an example our own shoy-hoy[169] politicians are eager to follow – the new journalism, with its interviewers, and its base pandering to the popular love of scandal and a morbid sensationalism; the cruel Pennsylvania prison system;[170] the debasement of children in public schools as set forth above; the horrors of electrocution as presented by the State of New York;[171] and (omitting many more items) the vivisection of human beings as proposed to be enacted by the Ohio Legislature! Enough! In that capital rattling, good old Scotch song, praised by Burns as 'the best Scotch song Scotland ever saw', 'Tullochgorum', the author invokes 'a' the ills that come frae France' on every enemy to the 'favourite' reel so named. The 'ills frae France' that the Rev John Skinner referred to did us no harm, not even those of a later day when the Revolution was rampant. It will be otherwise when the further 'Americanising of our institutions' will have made Britain an object for the world's mockery and scorn.

19 May 1894

168 The traditional maiming of horses and cattle by agrarian rebels in Ireland.
169 Sham. Cobbett had famously described Brougham and the moderate reformers as shoy-hoys (scarecrows) in 1830.
170 The separate system based on the principle of keeping prisoners in solitary confinement dates from 1829 when the Eastern State Penitentiary was opened at Philadelphia.
171 The first execution by electrocution was in the New York state prison at Auburn in 1890.

Looking Backward

.... That hackneyed simile, 'a bolt from the blue', but faintly indicates the surprise, even astonishment, not to speak of indignation, caused by [President Cleveland's[172]] Message. To speak plainly, without passion or prejudice, the Message was not merely unfriendly, it was a studied act of insult and carefully prepared menace. President Cleveland had no concern with the dispute between Britain and Venezuela, no more than he has any concern with the Alsace-Lorraine trouble between France and Germany. Nor has the dispute between Britain and Venezuela anything to do with the Monroe Doctrine, or the Monroe Doctrine with it.[173] Britain is not seeking to seize Venezuela and to transform it into a new monarchical colony; she merely desires that the boundary line between British Guiana and Venezuela should be as clearly defined as is the boundary line between the Dominion of Canada, or British North America, and the United States.

On the face of the words of 'the Monroe Doctrine' there is no warranty for the action of President Cleveland, independent of the fact that 'said' doctrine has never been accepted by Europe as part and parcel of 'the Law of Nations'. It is true that our Minister, Canning,[174] approved of the Monroe Doctrine and, it is stated in some quarters, even suggested it to the American President! Foolish enough; still it could never have entered into the mind of Canning that he was preparing a trap and a pitfall for his own country. It gives me nausea to see that man spoken of as a 'brilliant statesman'. Not such was the estimate formed by the old-time Radicals. In Hone's *House That Jack Built* we see him described as 'the spouter of froth by the hour',

Who haunts their Bad House a base living to earn,
By playing Jack Pudding and Ruffian in turn.
And William Cobbett never wearied of exposing Canning's mischievous

172 Grover Cleveland, US Democratic President, 1884-8 and 1892-6.
173 President James Monroe declared in 1823: 'The American continents ... are henceforth not to be considered as subjects for future colonisation by any European powers'; but also: 'With the existing colonies or dependencies of the European we ... shall not interfere'. Venezuela and Britain had long disagreed over the former's boundary with British Guiana. When in 1895 Venezuela made an especially extravagant claim, Britain rejected arbitration (fearing arbiters would split the difference) and dispatched troops to the disputed area. The USA invoked the Monroe Doctrine ...
174 George Canning, Tory politician who was Foreign Secretary, 1822-7, and Prime Minister, 1827. It is accepted that he did indeed prompt the formulation of the Monroe Doctrine through the intermediary of the US emissary in London. His motivation was to prevent intervention by other European powers (especially Spain or France) in the affairs of the newly independent Latin American republics, while maintaining British commercial influence and restricting US authority.

incompetence as Foreign Minister. I have no set of Cobbett's *Register*; I wish I had! Canning died on 8 August 1827. Any visitor to the British Museum Library who will take the trouble to look up the *Register* immediately succeeding the above date will find a trenchant review of Canning's political career, terrific in its invective, but as true as terrible. Canning strikingly illustrated the difference between the noisy, showy, party politician and the true statesman. It was to the first category he belonged. His admirers are fond of repeating a special specimen of his histrionic performances, his boast that he called into existence the New World of the Free States of South America to balance the despotic governments of the Old World! Yes: 'A new world' of anarchy and military despotism to which the South American Republics have been a prey – most of them continuously from the beginning of their 'emancipation from the Spanish yoke'. For a time Chile promised to be an exception, and Brazil, as a monarchical state, after its separation from Portugal, enjoyed comparative tranquillity; but events in recent years have added both to the number of anarchical states ruled by military adventurers under the semblance of republican forms, but with no more genuine liberty than is to be found in Russia, or order and safety than is in the worst governed provinces of Turkey. If Canning had been a veritable statesman, brilliant, or not brilliant, he would have refused to give any countenance to a 'doctrine' which by less scrupulous interpreters than President Monroe might be employed as a weapon against his own country, as we see it now sought to be applied by President Cleveland. England has never accepted the Monroe Doctrine as at all applicable to possessions like Canada, held on the American Continent before the world knew anything of the United States as an independent nation; nor as applicable to warrant interference between Britain and any other of the States outside the Union, if seeking rectification of doubtful frontiers, or demanding reparation for any wrong suffered at the hands of aggregations of half-breeds masquerading as South American Republicans.

There is no question in my mind as to the origin of the idea of President Cleveland's message. It is said we should not impute motives! The men who utter that drivel either wilfully ignore or are as blind as bats to the facts of American party politics. President Cleveland desires nomination for a 'third term', a new departure in the history of the American Presidency, and not likely to be achieved unless by making himself the pronounced exponent of the national vanity. Toward the end of his first term, President Cleveland, in his ungenerous treatment of Lord Sackville[175] – which was

175 Baron Sackville, British ambassador in Washington since 1881, was tricked in 1888, six weeks before the presidential election, into apparently advising a United States citizen

too tamely borne with on this side of the Atlantic – affected to exhibit more than Roman virtue in repudiating – not foreign patronage, but – foreign sympathy, solely with the view of getting himself re-elected. Lord Sackville had blundered; but the President ungenerously seized upon the opportunity to pose as above. That dodge was not a success. In the ensuing struggle Mr Cleveland was not elected. Now he deliberately imperils the peace between two great and kindred nations in order as he hopes to be nominated and re-elected for a third term. Perhaps again he may be disappointed.

The proposed commission[176] to inquire into the boundary dispute between Britain and Venezuela, and to report thereon, was not merely an insult, it was the assumption of arbitrary power which I trust Britain will never acknowledge, never yield to. One might have supposed that men of standing and repute in diplomacy, law, and statesmanship would, without exception, have refused to serve on such a commission. However, the commission has been formed. Its report need not be anticipated. If one could feel like indulging in any pleasantry in connection with an affair of such gravity, I should feel impelled to say that it was with considerable amusement I read the expressions of amazement – some real, others, I fancy, simulated – of 'our best possible instructors'[177] at the sudden, and at first apparently general, outbreak of feeling against England manifested by Americans in response to the President's Message. It came as a most unwelcome revelation to all but a few of our people, the great majority for a number of years having been fooled by the sugary assurances of the growing brotherhood of 'the two great branches of the Anglo-Saxon family'. I have known for thirty years what came as a revelation in the closing days of December to the vast majority of the British people. I do not dispute that the members of the Century, the Lotus, and other New York clubs may have been perfectly sincere in their friendly reception of British celebrities, as I am certain of the genuine good feeling of those on this side who at public dinners and receptions, literary and scientific meetings, gave cordial welcome to Americans eminent in diplomacy, politics, science, and literature. Nor do I question the genuine warmth of the private hospitality so many British travellers have experienced in the houses of Americans

on how to vote, a technical breach of international conventions. Salisbury's attempts to exonerate him proved unsuccessful, the US government insisting on terminating his mission, and he was formally retired.
176 In December 1895 Cleveland had asked Congress to set up a commission to determine the boundary, adding that any attempt by Britain to assert jurisdiction beyond that line would be resisted by the USA – by war, if necessary. (The Treaty of Washington of 1897 was to refer the question to arbitration, the eventual award in 1899 finding substantially for the line the British claimed.)
177 The press, presumably.

from Boston Harbour to the Golden Gates of San Francisco. But, though numerous, how many these friends of Britain and 'Britishers', how many, 'all told', compared with the many who responded with eager enthusiasm to the President's Message, regarding it a signal for the explosion (long pent up) of their anti-English feeling?

Our people, unused to look below the surface of international complimentary exhibitions, were startled, astonished, could not understand the savage war-spirit aroused in the States, being conscious of no design to injure, overreach, or annoy the Republic, its territory, government, or people. The outbreak on the one side and the surprise on the other Mr Balfour[178] well set forth in his recent speech at Manchester.

He had been deeply and painfully impressed by the different attitude and different mode in which we on this side of the Atlantic looked at the questions or war from that which appeared to be taken by some sections of the American population. To him the idea of war with the United States carried with it something of the nature of the horror of civil war ....To judge from the newspapers, large sections of the people of the United States seemed to regard a war with this country as a thing to be lightly indulged in, an exhilarating exercise, a gentle stimulus. To him that was a depressing and horrible point of view .... Might no English statesman or English party ever have the responsibility of that crime heavy upon his or their souls!

Gladly I note the outspoken declarations for peace by some of the foremost men of the Republic – outside of politics: authorised exponents of international law, University professors, ministers of the churches, including some of the most eminent, distinguished men of letters, to whom must be added a few (I fear a very few) influential journals, notably the *New York World*. In addition, it may be said that the voice of almost the entire ranks of the educated and cultivated was given for peace. Amongst the remarkable pronouncements for peace was that of Mr Henry George, whose name was at one time so conspicuous as an agrarian revolutionist. Such peace manifestations at least served to show that a numerous body of President Cleveland's constituents refused to bow before the storm of popular fury he had evoked. So far, so good. But the question remains, would public opinion, in the main, declare for, or against, President Cleveland?

I think there can be doubt. Practically the two Houses of Congress,

---

178 Conservative First Lord of the Treasury, 1895-1902.

supposed to represent the nation, 'went solid' in support of the President. Generally the State Legislatures were not in session; but (I believe) all but two of the Governors of States sent their adhesion to the President. The professional politicians of both parties were, with but few individual exceptions, unanimous that the Monroe Doctrine, as enunciated by the President, must be sustained even at the cost of war. The newspapers generally – North, South, East, and West – responded to the President's Message with a war-whoop which would have done no discredit to Cherokees or Choctaws in the days before Red Indian supremacy had been challenged.

I passed some twenty years of my life – say 1863-1883 – in the States, principally in Boston and neighbourhood; and I take this opportunity to record my grateful recollections of the fair play, justice, and kindness I experienced. Most of the personal friends of that time have disappeared, and of those who remain I have no favours to seek, so that my gratitude is not a lively sense of benefits to come. But, whilst personally I have nothing to complain of, on the contrary, much to remember with grateful appreciation, I could not shut my eyes and ears to the disagreeable fact that even in model Massachusetts there was more than enough of hostile feeling towards England, and that in the States generally that feeling was still more marked. Well might I have said at the time: ''Tis true, 'tis pity; and pity 'tis 'tis true'.[179]

I write these words with great reluctance. I know that Lord Playfair,[180] Mr Bryce,[181] and others truly testify when they tell of the kindness and hospitality they have experienced. But what are the stubborn facts? I name only one, but sufficient. The two senators representing Massachusetts in the United States Congress are chosen, as are the senators from all the other States, by the two branches of the State Legislature[182] – elected by what may be termed, in the language of our old-time Radicals, Universal Suffrage. One of these Massachusetts senators (I do not know who at present is the other) is Henry Cabot Lodge,[183] 'a rising man', apparently already posing

179 Shakespeare, *Hamlet*, 2, ii.
180 Lyon Playfair (1819-98), chemist (Professor of Chemistry at Edinburgh, 1858-68) and Liberal politician. His third wife came from the USA.
181 James Bryce, Liberal politician and minister, but also a jurist, historian and author of *The American Commonwealth*, his pioneering study of 1888. He served as British ambassador to the USA, 1907-13.
182 This was the procedure until the introduction of direct election by popular vote in 1913.
183 US Republican politician (1850-1924), descended on both sides from Boston Brahmin families. Although he never ran for President, he was notorious for his chauvinism, leading the opposition to the USA's ratification of the Treaty of Versailles and joining the League of Nations.

as a future Republican candidate for the Presidency, and he is perhaps the most unscrupulous, the most violent, the most virulent of all the avowed enemies of England. Remembering the cultivated, the true gentlemen of the Historical Society, the Genealogical Society, the trustees and officers of the Boston Athenaeum and of many more public institutions in Boston; remembering the genuine friendliness, the kindly hospitality of so many Boston families; remembering the warm interest taken generally by the most cultivated Bostonians in the fortunes of Old England, the land of their forefathers, I would have been delighted could I have believed that Massachusetts, at least, was to be counted on as the unswerving friend of international peace and justice.

But the fact is that the sections of Boston and Massachusetts society above referred to must not be regarded as representing those who have the votes, and in whose hands – indirectly, if not directly – are the issues: peace or war. Unfortunately, though not unnaturally, many of the ablest and best men take no part in politics, the conduct of which they have surrendered to professional demagogues; many not even voting at elections, because regarding themselves as politically 'swamped'. And what is true of Massachusetts is not less true of the other states. It is asked, will the growers of wheat and cotton do themselves immense injury if so they may injure or humiliate England? The answer is 'Yes', if the tide of passion rises high enough. To the million, or well on to that number, of Western cultivators whose farms are mortgaged, and who have to pay exorbitant interest to Eastern usurers, war with England, if it continued three months, would mean ruin. But material interests have rarely, if ever, constituted an obstacle to an insane desire for war. Mr Keir Hardie[184] has stated that wherever he went in the States he found working men entertaining the preposterous idea that a war with England would be a good thing for them! If war ever comes, it will not be the wheat-growers and cotton-growers who will be consulted; it will be town mobs, led by unscrupulous politicians and lying journalists, who will make the war – with a rush; no matter who may suffer and who may have to pay.

The present storm may pass over. Possibly the US Commissioners' report may not be favourable to President Cleveland's views and his suggested course of action. Some kind of settlement with Venezuela may be effected, and peace may be prolonged. But the bitter bad feeling against this country,

184 The former Scottish miner who had been elected MP for South West Ham in 1892, the year before the foundation of the Independent Labour Party in which he was to become dominant. He visited the USA in September 1895 to address the Labour Congress at Chicago but stayed fifteen weeks, travelling widely.

not created, but evoked by the President's Message will remain, and I suspect is much more likely to increase than diminish ....

25 January 1896

.... Mr H.M. Stanley, MP, the African explorer, has given in the January *Nineteenth Century* a clearer exposition of the causes [of American hatred for England] than any one else, so far as I know. I don't think his exposition adequate or complete; but what he says is worth consideration.

He was in the States as recently as last September, 'and it was a disagreeable surprise' to him 'to find that ... there smouldered in certain sections an intense fire of hate' towards England! .... Saddened, astonished, Mr Stanley made enquiries as to the causes of American hatred. The answers indicated the dislike as of long standing, 'and that nothing but war would satisfy the Americans'. Among the counts of the indictment were these:– 1. That the Canadian Pacific Railway might be utilised to transport Imperial troops across the Canadian Dominion to act against a foreign Power, and that Power might be Russia! 2. The supercilious spirit displayed by Englishmen at boat or yacht races, football or cricket matches, etc. 3. English faith in English naval supremacy. 4. English opinion on monetary matters, criticism of American authors and journalism, conduct towards American individuals, and even the capture of American heiresses, 'all contributed to prove our national unfriendliness, despite our profuse expressions of friendship in after-dinner speeches'. Mr Stanley heard nothing about Ireland and her grievances, but it seemed to be the true American spirit that was aroused in 'deep, deep earnest'! Mr Stanley regarded the President's Message as a warning to prepare for war, and could 'not understand why people over here can declare so lightly there will be no war' ....

Never since the war of the Big-Endians and the Little-Endians, described in *Gulliver's Travels*, has there been such a ridiculous assortment of grievances as the above on which to found a casus belli! Perhaps there are other causes. Remembrance of the *Alabama* affair,[185] and the sympathy shown by a number of English, at the head of whom was Mr Gladstone (the son of a slaveholder), for the Secesh[186] cause and Jeff Davis. That

185 The cruiser *Alabama* had been built on the Mersey and supplied to the Confederacy despite the protests of the Northern minister in London that it was intended for the destruction of commercial shipping. The post-war claims for the *Alabama* and two other ships were to be both protracted and immensely expensive. Finally, in 1872, a tribunal of arbitration awarded the US government (even after immense 'indirect claims' had been dropped) $15 million which, although considered outrageously high by the British public, was accepted by Gladstone's administration.
186 Secessionist – or Confederate.

sympathy does not seem to have caused any reciprocal feeling for us 'down South in Dixie'. The *Alabama* affair was long ago settled. It was a foregone conclusion that, thanks to Downing Street red-tapery, England would be cast by the board of arbitration, though the amount of damages awarded was a good deal of surprise. However, the award announced, payment was made in full and instanter. No haggling, no murmuring. As to the above-mentioned sympathy of certain sections, there was a great and memorable offset, in the effective attitude of the English working classes. Owing to the cotton famine, there were, in the cotton manufacturing districts, starving thousands and tens of thousands, whilst throughout the country the workers generally were but poorly employed. The agents of the South were busy: 'Recognise the Confederates; break the blockade; and you may have all the cotton needed to set every spinning-jenny going!' Thus spoke the tempter. But everywhere the 'clemming'[187] multitude repudiated the counsel and stood for the North and against slavery. I say that conduct of the English working people was to their eternal honour, and should have assured them the grateful appreciation and lasting friendship of the Americans who fought to maintain the Union.

I rather think we must go further back, even to the Revolution of 1776-83. It is curious that any rancour arising against England at that time should still exist. When Napoleon was crushed at Waterloo, it was but natural that the French felt soreness that continued perhaps forty years. That soreness was not increased by any undue exultation on the part of the victors. On the contrary, the first flush of excitement, the illuminations, etc, over, the reaction favourable to France at once set in. When some years later Napoleon died,[188] the expressions of sympathy were general among the British masses, especially discharged soldiers and naval seamen. Ten years later the 'Three Glorious Days'[189] evoked English enthusiasm to a startling degree –

> All hail to thee, land of the Gaul!
> All hail to thee fearless and free!
> For bravely thy children have broken the thrall,
> That the despots had placed upon thee.[190]

and so on. Had the issue of the American struggle been the opposite to what it was, American bitterness would have been natural. But it was not so.

187 Starving.
188 In 1821.
189 The French Revolution of 1830.
190 This quotation has not been traced.

Defeat and humiliation fell to the lot of Britain. If ever there was a share of bitterness on this side, it was of brief duration. Why should the victors' bitter hostility, in and after their success, have exceeded the bitterness of other peoples in their defeat? There are two answers. In the first place, as in the case of the Canning endorsement of the Monroe Doctrine, we have ourselves to blame. The recognition of the independence of the colonies evoked a jeremiad on the part of our then 'Liberals' on the decline and approaching fall of England. From the Whigs led by Fox, to the Republicans who swore by Paine, there was a general agreement that the loss of the colonies was a fatal blow. It was natural for the Americans to believe in the lugubrious anticipations of an England destined to become as powerless as Venice. For a time, especially some fifteen years subsequently, those vaticinations seemed to be likely to be fulfilled, judging by the Duke of York's military performances,[191] the fierce rebellion in Ireland,[192] and, more than aught else, the great naval mutinies.[193] But England had not yet fulfilled her mission. The splendid victories of Nelson on the sea were followed by the decisive victories of Wellington on land; Canada had remained steadfastly loyal; the advance of British power in India had been rapid and brilliant; and the early years of the century witnessed the beginnings of colonial growth we now witness in Australia, New Zealand, South Africa, and elsewhere. In fact, far from dying, Britain had taken a new lease of life; and at the fall of Napoleon was in the forefront of European nations; and since that date her power has certainly not lessened. When doctors demonstrate that a man cannot live, it is very provoking that he will not die. If the prognostications of our 'Liberals' of 1780-1800 had been fulfilled, probably what might have been left of England would have been accorded the sympathetic protectorate at present ostentatiously offered to, if not proposed to be forced upon, the South American States. But history has a perverse way of not suiting itself to the needs of political prophets, and so our American Cousins found they had been deceived by the prophecies of our English 'Liberals'. Very provoking; but so it was!

A more potent cause remains to be named – the get up of American school histories, depicting the past connection of Britain with the States, and, more especially, British acts in the Revolutionary War, in the blackest colours. Thus American children are nurtured in hostility to the country which originally founded the colonies from whence sprang the present

191 Prince Frederick, Duke of York and Albany (1763-1827), second son of George III, commanded the British troops in the disastrous Flanders campaign of 1793-5 and then, as Commander-in-Chief, presided over the equally calamitous invasion of Holland in 1799.
192 Of the United Irishmen, 1798.
193 At Spithead and the Nore, 1797.

United States. Therein is the great cause, as it seems to me, of the hostile feeling so much to be deplored. It is more than ten years since I looked into an American schoolbook, and I might have indulged in the hope that American compilers of manuals for schools had become ashamed of such travesties of the past; but I see in the *Literary World* (London) that Dr Conan Doyle, who has returned from the States, admits 'the bitter feeling against England as a country'. The cause, he thinks,

> must be sought first in the schools where American history is taught. This resolves itself almost entirely into a series of wrangles with Great Britain which occupy space out of all proportion to what they get in an English history.

The seed sown in schoolbooks is carefully and persistently cultivated in three-fourths (and more) of the American newspapers. Of the anti-British sentiment permeating those journals, neither whole columns, nor even pages, of the *Weekly Chronicle* could give any adequate representation ....

1 February 1896

CONTEMPORARY BRITISH POLITICS AND SOCIETY

'Am I Not a Man, and a Brother?'

It must have been when I was eight or nine, possibly nine or ten years old, that I plunged, up to my armpits, into politics, in consequence of finding myself in the midst of election contests in the ancient borough of Southwark. I was at first puzzled between the claims of 'Polhill and our glorious constitution', and 'Farncombe, the Man of the People'. But 'Wilson and Reform', 'Wilson and the Abolition of Slavery', captured me beyond recall. There was some fun in electioneering when elections continued over 14, or it might be 21, days; and though my boyish insignificance saved me from any temptation to share in the guzzling and other gross forms of influencing 'the worthy and independent electors', that could not deprive me of, perhaps, rather lent a zest to, any enjoyment of the more harmless concomitants of the time, such as the processions, the bands, the banners, the ribbons, the party-coloured cards, and the thrilling excitement consequent on the hourly announcements of the votes recorded, and how the tide of fortune flowed or ebbed as regarded the popular favourite, who generally, at the conclusion, found himself at the bottom of the poll!

It was not so with the Southwark favourite in the pre-Reform days. As a defender of Queen Caroline and a victim of Fum the Fourth's hatred,[194] General Sir Robert Wilson[195] was popular alike with the non-voting masses, and with a majority of the then very circumscribed electorate. I see him now in my mind's eye, like a Roman conqueror in his triumphal car, standing up in his carriage on the day of 'chairing', and bowing responsively to the cheers of his admirers. He had been very handsome in his youth, but the toils of war and the cares incidental to civil strife had told upon him, and, if memory serves, he appeared to my boyish eyes as a man of middle age, tall, spare, and pale, the beau-ideal of the soldier and the gentleman. Among the many flags and banners carried by his supporters there was one I have never forgotten, bearing an anti-slavery device – on a white ground the figure of a black man in chains, and with clasped hands asking, in the inscription above his head, 'Am I Not a Man, and a Brother?' There needed not the speeches of a Wilberforce or a Clarkson, or the writings of a Granville Sharp, to make me an Abolitionist forthwith, and the humble well-wisher to a cause which within ten years[196] came to a triumphal issue.

Of the general poverty and hopelessness of the working people around me I knew quantum suff., but of the special wrongs of the 'White Slaves' immured in Manchester and other factories I then knew nothing. Yet a few years, and the *Poor Man's Guardian* and similar publications enlightened me as to those wrongs; and then I discovered that a good many manufacturing 'philanthropists', whose sympathies had been enlisted on the side of the negroes, had been quite oblivious to the sufferings of women and children in their own factories, and had opposed, and continued, unyielding opposition to the efforts of Michael Thomas Sadler, Lord Ashley, Richard Oastler, and other champions of the factory workers in their efforts to redeem the white slaves of England from what was, in some respects, worse than Jamaica or Barbadoes slavery. The factory system had been productive not only of the individual sufferings of thousands, but also of such semi-savage wretchedness pervading Lancashire generally, as to make Sir William Napier, when conducting Marshal Soult[197] through the factory districts, blush for his country. That the old spirit of lustful gain, no matter at what cost of blood and tears, is still rampant among certain of our leviathan

194 Fum the Fourth was a radical nickname for George IV. See 'The Conflict' below.
195 Radical MP for Southwark, 1818-31. Dismissed from the army (as lieutenant-colonel) for remonstrating with the troops at Queen Caroline's funeral in 1821, but later reinstated, becoming a full general in 1841.
196 Slavery was abolished in British colonies in 1833.
197 One of Napoleon's marshals, but weathered the restoration of the monarchy by being reappointed marshal in both 1820 and 1830 and serving as Louis Philippe's minister of war and prime minister.

manufacturers and capitalists was shown, in its appalling features, by John Burns,[198] in his address at Battersea, mentioned in the *Weekly Chronicle* of 1 November.

As the reader is aware, the opposition to the 'Legal Eight Hours Day' in the Liverpool Congress[199] was led by the Northumberland and Durham miners' delegates, and the delegates, notably Messrs Birtwistle and Maudslay, representing the textile trades of Lancashire, who argued that an eight hours day would mean the ruin of the manufactures on which some 600,000 male and female operatives are dependant for their bread; in like manner affecting probably a million and a quarter of other workers directly or indirectly dependent upon, or associated with, the 600,000 mill-hands. In his address Mr Burns shows, first, that in spite of the ever-growing competition of foreign nations – French, German, American, and others – the exports of cotton yarn and cotton goods have largely increased since 1870-74, when the manufacturers made fortunes with a rapidity rarely, if ever, before equalled, and he gives examples of 11 mills which in the first quarter of this year were paying dividends of ten, and, in one instance, of 15 per cent. He gives a list of another 19 mills paying a dividend of from 7½ to 12½ per cent. He also gives a list of 14 new mills at present in course of erection which, when completed, will comprise a power of 1,019,000 spindles. And yet it is pretended that money is being lost at the present time! If exports have diminished in certain directions, they have expanded to the extent of 15 per cent to Australasia, 25 per cent to China, and 125 per cent to Japan. But Mr Burns admits there is a formidable and growing competition on the part of India. With eight hours a day it would be impossible for Lancashire to compete with India, say the textile delegates. Why? Because the Indian operatives already work nearly double the hours the English work, and live, *somehow*, on wages which, if offered in Manchester, would summon Luddites and Chartists from their graves 'to make a new Thermopylae',[200] rather than there should be abject submission to such a servitude of woe. The reader whose only knowledge of Indian textiles is derived from the sight of the beautiful fabrics he has seen in exhibitions, with specimens

198 Burns's overall career could serve as an object-lesson in Harney's warnings as to the perils of the embrace of the Liberal Party. John Burns (1858-1943), a Battersea engineer, became a Marxist and member of the SDF, was imprisoned in 1887 for leading an assault on a police cordon on 'Bloody Sunday', and was an important figure in the New Unionism of 1889-91. He was elected MP for Battersea in 1892, but soon lapsed into Lib-Labism, becoming the first working-class Cabinet minister, 1906-14, as President of the Local Government Board – and hence responsible for the administration of the Poor Law.
199 The Trades Union Congress of 1890 had been held in Liverpool.
200 Byron, 'The Isles of Greece'. At the Battle of Thermopylae, although a defeat for the Greeks, 7,000 men held off a vast Persian army for seven days in 480 BC.

or pictures of the rudimentary machines wrought by the Hindu workers, may sigh to think that England, with all her power, has not yet redeemed that dependent people from the wasting toil inherited from countless ages! What will be his surprise to learn that it is not the ancient injury which thus bows down the unhappy people, and which presents a growing competition likely to embarrass and injure English trade, but is a modern and English infliction, a species, and a very dreadful species, permitted by England as a nation and perpetuated by English capitalists! Here is Mr John Burns's startling statement:

The 97 Indian cotton mills, with 19,000 looms and 81,000 operatives, are owned by the proprietors of the Lancashire mills, and these men, who urge the Lancashire operatives not to reduce their hours because of Indian competition, are the cause, through their greed, of making that competition possible by working the Indian operatives brutally excessive hours and paying low wages. In the race of long hours and low wages between Lancashire and Indian operatives, death and degradation are their rewards. The employers secure the prize by exploiting both.

Mr Burns goes on to speak of the progress of Indian competition, as shown by the increase of exports from 2,450,000 lbs of cotton in 1874 to 150,000,000 lbs in 1889. That this increase is a serious matter is shown by the estimate that whereas between 1874 and 1889 England's increased exports amounted to 100 per cent, India's increase amounted to 700 per cent! India has the advantage of the raw cotton being at hand, but pays more than the cost of England for coal, and is under other disadvantages. India can beat us only because, as Mr Burns says, 'the Indian operatives are ruthlessly overworked and underpaid'. 'The advantage an Indian mill of 30,000 spindles has over a Lancashire mill of a similar number is £3,000 per annum, brought about entirely by long hours and low wages'.

The next two pages of Mr Burns's address will not bear compression. The pamphlet should be ordered in 'bulk' by every Trades Union, but especially by the textile workers of Lancashire and elsewhere, and be sown broadcast through the land. The statements as to the hours of work in the Indian mills and the miserable wages paid are appalling. Let me repeat specimens only:- Men, women, and children in Lancashire are protected by law from working more than 56½ hours per week; in India they work from 72 to 100 hours, and often labour 12, 14, and 16 hours at a stretch! Including Sundays, Saturday half-holidays, Bank holidays, etc, the Lancashire operatives have 88 days of cessation from labour out of 365. The Indian operatives work seven days per week, and have 15 holidays in the entire year!

Observe the utility of having 'heathen' workers to whom the Christian Sabbath is naught. I am reminded of the story of two Hebrew brothers in the Houndsditch district.[201] One turned Christian. He kept the shop open on Saturday whilst his brother religiously abstained from work. On Sunday the shop was kept going by the Jewish brother, in whose eyes the Christian Sabbath was of no more account than any other day. It is pleasant to see brethren dwell together in unity; and these two brethren knew how to make the best of both worlds!

But what are we to think of the hypocrisy of our broadcloth-robed, canon-lined, wealthy pillars of the church or chapel, who subscribe handsomely to send out missionaries for the conversion of the followers of Brahma or Buddha, when their Christian brethren, if not themselves, take advantage of the 'heathenism' of the natives of India to work them with such excessive brutality as would justify a jacquerie, and would certainly cause one in Lancashire?

'The average wage of the Lancashire operative is £61 10s for 277 days in the year, or a daily average of 4s 4d. In India for 350 days the average wage is £8 10s or 6d per day'. Mr Burns quotes in support of his statements from the Report of the Bombay Factory Commission, and his quotations exhibit facts far worse than can be gathered from the above selections. Missionaries, forsooth! Before they embark for India let them enter the halls and villas of the English masters, of the wretched slaves on 'India's Coral Strand'.[202] Let them tackle the Christian capitalists who 'grind the faces of the poor',[203] and who make a double profit by pitting the labour of the poor 'heathen' against that of their own country's people.

Who are they? Is it behind the law of libel they slink, safeguarded by the infamous dictum: 'The greater the truth, the greater the libel'? Would that their names could be pilloried – 'the climax of all scorn',

> Exalted o'er their less abhorr'd compeers,
> And festering in the infamy of years.[204]

There is a movement in India among certain of the educated Hindus for a species of Indian Home Rule. There are many objections to be taken to any such scheme in the present stage of our Indian Empire's history. But welcome Home Rule for India, with all its perils, if our Government, moved by the Unpaid Parliament,[205] will not come to the rescue of India's

201 In East London, between Bishopsgate and Aldgate.
202 From Reginald Heber's hymn, 'From Greenland's icy mountains'.
203 Isaiah, 3, xv.
204 Byron, 'A Sketch'.
205 The Chartist demand for payment of MPs was not enacted until 1911.

cotton slaves. Could Russia impose worse serfdom upon the victims whose sufferings are set forth in the Bombay report? 'Am I not a man, and a brother?' may be demanded by the Hindu cotton-mill hand with as much justice as ever it was demanded by a negro 'chattel'.

Who will be the new Wilberforce to lift up the banner of Freedom, and arouse the conscience of England to a sense of the 'blood-guiltiness' of the slavery in which Englishmen, to their shame, dare to hold the subjects of the Empress of India? John Burns is invited to Australia. I doubt the wisdom of that call. If he accepts, let him not fail to visit India on his way and investigate the actual state of things in the cotton mills of India. If he finds that state to be as bad as he believes at present, to say nothing of possibly being worse, let him on his return to England kindle that flame of national indignation which shall not be quenched until the claims of Justice and Mercy have been satisfied, and our fellow subjects be redeemed from worse than Egyptian bondage.

15 November 1890

Theocracy

The Sligo election, like the North Kilkenny election,[206] has afforded further evidence of the onward march of sacerdotal ascendancy in Ireland. My concern is not with the doctrines or the ritual of the Roman Catholic Church in Ireland or out of Ireland. I have a good deal of respect for our old Catholic families, of whom there are many in our North-Eastern English counties. Though I could not share, I can esteem the devotion with which those families have clung to the ancient faith held by Stephen Langton,[207] and unquestioned on the glorious field of Runnymede. I take quite another view of modern 'perverts'[208] to Rome – if honest, the victims of their own sophisms. It was not the Roman Catholic defenders of the realm in the days of the Spanish Armada who enunciated the slavish doctrine: 'Roman Catholics first, Englishmen afterwards'. But though I decline to discuss creeds and ritualistic performances, I cannot view the course of the Irish priesthood with indifference. If the communicants of the Roman Catholic

206 After the scandal in November 1890 of the O'Shea divorce, in which Parnell was cited as co-respondent, the opposition of both the British Liberal Party and the Catholic Church in Ireland to his leadership led to the Irish party's splitting into Parnellites and Anti-Parnellites. The first two by-elections were at Kilkenny (December 1890) and North Sligo (April 1891), in both of which Parnellite candidates lost badly.
207 Archbishop of Canterbury, 1207-28, a leader in the struggle against King John, culminating in the signing of Magna Carta at Runnymede in 1215.
208 That is, converts.

Church in Ireland are satisfied that their bishops should give the law as to what is orthodox and what heterodox in Irish politics, and are satisfied to see their priests participating in election brawls and sharing in the filth and violence of Parnellites and anti-Parnellites engaged in deadly conflict, so be it. If the Roman Catholic Irish like to submit their necks to the yoke of such a Theocracy, so be it. But it should be our concern to see that the Irish who are not of the Church of Rome shall not be abandoned, bound hand and foot, to the tender mercies of a priest-elected, priest-governed Home Rule Parliament. To see illiterate electors brought up in companies and battalions headed by priests, and voting as dictated to by the priests, is a sight sad enough; but that is a small matter compared with compelling the free, intelligent, Protestant minority of the country to submit to the racial and sacerdotal rule of a tyrant majority. The English Nonconformists who wilfully, with their eyes open, adhere to any scheme of government for Ireland that would place one-third of the people of that country under the absolute rule of a Parliament elected after the manner in which the Kilkenny and Sligo vacancies have been filled, are nothing less than traitors to the traditions of their churches, the principles of their fathers, the Protestantism which their ancestors vindicated, and that devotion to 'Civil and Religious Liberty' which was their boast until recent times, but the very wording of which boast has now become 'as sounding brass or a tinkling cymbal'.[209]

11 April 1891

The Labour Congress

The delegates to the 1891 Labour Congress[210] must have been more than satisfied with the reception they experienced in the Tyneside capital. Never before have Trades Unionists been accorded so hearty a welcome, been so officially honoured, and hospitably entertained. How great the contrast between 1839 and 1891! How signal the difference between the days of Mayor Fife and those of Mayor Ellis. *Then* 'specials', infantry, cavalry, and cannon to charge and disperse the Chartists; *now*, the Mayor in his robes and 'collar of gold',[211] with that awful emblem of authority, the mace, borne before him, welcoming the invaders from all parts of the island; feasting them at breakfast, and entertaining them at a garden party; and directing the mounted police to escort the procession to the great meeting on the

209 1 Corinthians 13, i.
210 The Trades Union Congress of 1891 met in Newcastle upon Tyne.
211 Thomas Moore , 'Let Erin remember the days of old'.

Town Moor. Let me admit that the Chartists in their 1839 mood were a trial to the authorities; on the other hand, those authorities showed the most lamentable ignorance of how to deal with an excited people smarting under centuries of wrong and seeking the acknowledgment of those rights, which their successors now so largely enjoy. Now there is no cause for 'seditious agitation', and no excuse for the constituted authorities to take coercive measures for 'the maintenance of order'. Still the Mayor and Corporation of Newcastle, in this year of grace, deserve grateful recognition and warm laudation for the generous, kindly, and hospitable reception, which the delegates to the great Labour Congress of 1891 can never forget.

Two great facts have marked the Congress of 1891. 1, the evidence of the rapid and formidable growth of the Trades Unions; 2, the advance of the eight hours idea as, for the time being, the prime article of the Trade Union programme. No. 1 needs no comment, save this, that the formidable organisation of labour has already given rise to not less formidable organisations of capital – a fact the most ardent trades leaders are not blind to, and which will probably have a steadying effect in staying them from counselling or approving any ill-advised conflict; and inducing, rather, recourse to less belligerent means of settling any of the vexed questions still existing, and likely to exist, between Labour and Capital. It is to be hoped that the trades leaders and counsellors may see their way, in future, to prevent any such senseless quarrels as those which are said to have been responsible for the heavy loss shown by the balance sheet of Palmer's Shipbuilding Company.

As to the eight hours' question a wide divergence of opinion still exists. The advocates of the Legal Eight Hours Day did indeed obtain a signal success, but only after much vacillation on the part of the Congress, and it may be assumed that the defeated were by no means converted. Still the Eight Hours idea has unquestionably advanced, and it may be believed that as regards the miners an Eight Hours' Bill is one of the questions with which the next House of Commons will have to grapple.[212] It may be expected that, in addition to the labour candidates in the next General Election, a considerable number of the old parties' candidates will promise to support a miners' Eight Hours' Bill, at least in constituencies where miners preponderate or are numerous. As regards a general Eight Hours' Bill, said candidates will have no difficulty in promising to keep 'an open mind' for its consideration. The 'open mind' dodgery is not likely to eventuate in any Act of Parliament on the lines of Mr Keir Hardie's resolution before the next meeting of Congress, so that there will be ample opportunity for the

212 The only Eight Hours' Bill to be enacted was for coalminers in 1908.

revision of that awkward, not to say despotic, scheme, which would impose the Eight Hours rule upon all trades and callings, save those organised trades who might determine to vote themselves out of its operation. This form of the Eight Hours scheme can hardly fail to be challenged at the next Congress, and meanwhile is not likely to seriously commend itself to politicians of the 'open mind'.

Next to the Eight Hours Working Day, the most prominent test question is to be Payment of Members of Parliament, Members of County Councils, School Boards, 'and all local bodies returning representatives', meaning, I suppose, Town Councillors, Boards of Guardians, and Parish Councils when called into being. It will be well to bear in mind that all these payments will involve a considerable Budget, to be provided for out of the general taxation as regards Members of Parliament, and out of the rates as regards other representative officials. The general taxes, apart from the Income Tax, are not so directly felt as the rates – already a heavy burthen upon struggling householders. When County Councillors, Town Councillors, and members of other representative bodies are all paid for their services, the burthen of local taxation will be well-nigh intolerable. 'Good and Cheap Government' was the old popular demand; but the *cheap* will certainly have to be eliminated. Democratic Government has its advantages; but these are not likely to include economy, retrenchment, and a lowering of taxation. 'Payment of Members' was one of the points of the Charter; and there is no gainsaying the fact that it follows as a necessary sequel and complement to the Abolition of the Property Qualification.[213] It is not to be expected, nor is it to be desired, that other trades should follow the example of the Northern miners in subscribing the salaries of Parliamentary representatives. Not to be desired because not desirable that Members of Parliament in general should sit as the direct representatives of special trades or particular sections of the population, instead of the people at large. Payment of Members has been inevitable from the day of the Abolition of the Property Qualification. It is, however, much to be desired that the 'mob' of (nearly) 700 MPs should be reduced by one half. At £500 a year each, the bill will be quite heavy enough for the payment of the 300 to which the People's Charter proposed to reduce the number of Members. Whilst such a lessening of the present number could not fail to contribute to the greater efficiency of the legislative body.

The cost of paying Members of Parliament and members of other representative bodies is not the most important consideration. Unfortunately, there is very little of unalloyed good in this world; and whilst

213 The first of the Six Points of the Charter to become law (in 1858).

payment of members is just, necessary, and inevitable, it will be well to bear in mind that one effect will certainly be to increase the number of professional and unscrupulous politicians. Doubtless men of the stamp of Mr Burt,[214] honourable and patriotic – according to their lights – will be found among the paid members; it is morally certain there will be as many, and, probably, very many more, of a very different stamp, adventurers to whom the yearly stipend will be a strong inducement to play the part of courtiers to the people; men who will be ready to make any bid for votes likely to bring them into contacts with the shekels and sequins. That the people will have the intelligence and public spirit to see through and repudiate such knaves and charlatans is more to be desired than to be expected.

It is remarkable how easily, rapidly, and naturally the democrat develops into the despot. Mr Burt has been the recipient of much and deserved praise for his ability, decision, and firmness as President of the Congress. But it should be said that if the member for Morpeth and his associates in the representation of the North experienced no more merciful consideration than was shown to the delegates in general under 'the ruling of the Chair' in the Newcastle Town Hall, terrible would be the outcry against the tyranny of 'Mr Speaker'. Mr Burt's sufficient defence is the necessity of his position. Precisely the justification of Cromwell for dissolving the Long Parliament and making himself practically the Dictator of the Commonwealth. Mr Burt's despotism was not caused by any desire on his part to play the despot; he was obliged to do so through being called upon to preside over a cumbersome and unwieldy assembly, packed into a most unsuitable place of meeting, and assembled to debate questions of the gravest importance, all to be disposed of within a week, when a month would not have been too much for their thorough and necessary consideration.

A year ago I noted the unsatisfactory proceedings and scenes of disorder at the Liverpool Congress. The cause was palpable enough – too many delegates and too little time. Aggravation instead of moderation has marked the first of these untoward circumstances. Last year the delegates numbered about 450; this year they numbered 552; an excess of one hundred members over last year. The accommodation for the sittings at Liverpool was complained as inadequate and irritating; the same complaint has been made this year against the Newcastle Town Hall, which, hideous in its outward aspect, is by common consent condemned as totally unsuitable in its interior for any such purpose as the meetings of the recent Congress. Again, the mistake of

214 Thomas Burt (1837-1922), miner, elected for Morpeth in 1874 and (with Alexander MacDonald) one of the first two working-class MPs. A lifelong Liberal, he represented Morpeth until 1918.

crowding the 'agenda' with all sorts and sizes of resolutions on all conceivable subjects having reference to the claims of Labour has been repeated with the like result as at Liverpool. There would have been no objection to the number of resolutions, nor to the almost numberless amendments, had there been sufficient time for their serious consideration. But there was not. There was a good deal of speechmaking under difficulties, but the use of the word 'debates' would be an absurdity. Why is the Congress restricted to a week? Probably to avoid increasing the expense. Reduce the number of members and the reduced expense of sending delegates will leave means to prolong their sittings. A fortnight's session should be the minimum; three weeks would be better ....

19 September 1891

The Conflict

Exactly 62 years ago, on 27 June, William Cobbett, being then in Bristol, engaged on the first number of his *Two-Penny Trash*, was writing with the clanging of church bells in his ears, dolefully tolling for the death of his Sacred Majesty George – by Tom Moore[215] and other irreverent writers facetiously named 'Fum the Fourth'. Exactly a month subsequently occurred the 'Three Glorious Days' of Paris. Then followed the 'Reform' agitation – fierce and violent – all but passing from agitation into revolution, and, culminating in the royal assent to 'the Bill, the whole Bill, and nothing but the Bill', on 7 June 1832. Since that time, with some pauses, the march of 'Reform' has been onward, until, as we frequently hear, most of the points of the Charter have obtained legislative recognition, and with a free press and national education – not to be speak of many other acquired advantages – 'the masses' today occupy a widely different position to that held 62 years ago. Whether 'Progress', so extraordinary, has made the millions better qualified to take part in governing the country, in providing for its safety, the security of its trade, and the advancing of their own welfare whilst respecting and conserving the just rights of other 'classes', the electoral turmoil now in full swing will show between this [week?] and the middle of July.

I am but an onlooker. I have no share in this game; personally it matters nothing to me which side wins. Nevertheless, it is sometimes incumbent upon a man who has some thought, and to that thought can give expression, to do so. Two parties present themselves before the electors; the

215 Thomas Moore (1779-1852), Irish poet and friend of Byron.

supporters of the present Administration,[216] and the Opposition who desire the restoration of Mr Gladstone to power. The one appeals to the last six years' record of what has been done and attempted, and offers that record as evidence of the desire and intentions of the party to continue the work of national reform and well-considered progress; the other party points to a programme of innumerable changes, more or less drastic, calculated, it is averred, to promote the general welfare and shower blessings upon the working classes – more especially the agricultural labourers. Between these biddings for the popular vote John Bull (if 'the masses' may be so typified) must be in the quandary of a jackass between two bundles of hay, or a bundle of hay and a crop of thistles, reminding one of a certain noble poet's quatrain:

> The world is a bundle of hay,
> Mankind are the asses who pull;
> Each tugs it a different way,
> And the greatest of all is John Bull.[217]

The supporters of the present Administration point to what they have done; their opponents to what they will do. If the first acknowledge shortcomings, they may truthfully plead that they have been hampered, and to some extent reduced to powerlessness, by the systemic obstruction placed in their way by their opponents. Until within the last month it has been the game of the Opposition to as much as possible prevent beneficial legislation, so as to have some colour for the charge of neglect or incompetence to level at the Administration. But when that Opposition had concluded that it was a matter of policy to hasten the Dissolution, then every bill was to be hurried forward, every money-vote adopted with indecent precipitancy. The Lords, generally by the 'Liberals' assailed for too closely scanning the measures sent for their consideration, have been violently assailed for passing recent bills without any examination whatever. The cry against the House of Lords, got up by Gladstonian candidates, has not the slightest justification in any recent action of that branch of the Legislature. Without going over the items of six years' legislation, let it suffice to say that, in my judgment, the conduct of public affairs, domestic and foreign, is an honourable record that should command public approval and confidence.

216 Salisbury's Conservative government of 1886 which was replaced by Gladstone's Liberal administration in August 1892.
217 Byron, 'Epigram', quoted in full by Harney.

In Ireland almost unbroken order has taken the place of general lawlessness, and in that country there would now be absolute peace, as there is a steady advance in general prosperity, were it not for the mischief-making labours of professional agitators, encouraged by the patronage and incitements of our own politicians. In England's relations with other countries the Administration has given us 'peace with honour', signally and strikingly contrasting with the last Gladstone Administration's record – a record of shame, of gross extravagance, of petty but sanguinary wars, or irreparable losses in gallant soldiers, of whom General Gordon was the most famous, but far from being the only conspicuous victim.

I am old enough to remember the funeral of Queen Caroline, 71 years ago, and I can look back over sixty years of intelligent interest in political questions and public affairs, and I affirm that the present has been the best Administration within that time.

This affirmation may excite a howl. Be it so. I am not denying that there have been epochs when organic changes more important than the County Councils Bill have been enacted – though that measure will have far-reaching consequences. But it does not follow that a Ministry presiding over or inaugurating revolutionary changes must, therefore, have been a better Administration than that of that of the last six years. The most notable of organic changes was the Parliamentary Reform Bill of 1831-32; the most notable, for it was the forerunner of the more sweeping changes of subsequent years. Well, the Reform Bill Administration of 1831-35 was a hard and cruel Administration. The first work of the new and Reformed Parliament was a strong and stringent Coercion Bill for Ireland. Home Secretary – my Lord Melbourne – had the people bludgeoned in Coldbath Fields.[218] The most memorable performance of the Reform Administration was the enactment of the New Poor Law, erecting bastilles over the land and barbarously punishing the poor for their poverty. Doubtless, gross abuses existed under the old system of parish relief; but the harsh, brutal, and damnable procedure under New Poor Law did more than all other grievances to drive the working people well-nigh to despair. It was that brutal law and the brutalities of those engaged in carrying it into effect, in conjunction with the then atrocities of the factory system, that fired the imagination and lent terror to the winged words of Joseph Rayner Stephens who in an earlier age would have been a second John Ball, who was not a

218 A meeting convened in 1833 by the National Union of the Working Classes at Coldbath Fields, Clerkenwell, was declared illegal by Melbourne and broken up by the new Metropolitan Police. Constable Robert Culley was stabbed to death in the mêlée, a coroner's jury returning the verdict of 'justifiable homicide'.

Chartist, but whose thunderbolts of passionate wrath against tyrants and wrongdoers made him a welcome ally at Chartist meetings – his speeches mainly contributing to that charge of 'violence' with which the Martineaus and McCarthys,[219] and such 'historians', have labelled the righteous agitation for the People's Charter. In more recent times we have seen Mr Gladstone, in spite of his 'Reforms', filling Irish gaols with 'suspects' never brought to trial – to the extent, it is said, of twelve hundred persons! I repeat that Lord Salisbury's Administration has promoted the country's welfare, sustained the nation's reputation, and will remain a record of honour when the politicians of all parties have disappeared, and the turmoil of the present day is hushed in everlasting peace.

Refraining from further notice of the Gladstone past, what, may I ask, is the promise held out by the Opposition as regards the future? I decline to discuss the Newcastle programme[220] – disestablishment, House of Lords abolition, local option, eight hours, parish councils, and that state of beatitude for the agricultural labourers, of which 'three acres and a cow'[221] constituted but the faint premonition. I decline to discuss these 'burning questions', for the sufficient reason that, whatever they may become, at present they are not 'burning', they are not in presence at all, they are but *in nubibus*;[222] for so the Grand Old Man has determined, and it is enough: '*Le roi le veut*'.[223] The one great aim to be accomplished by the Gladstonian restoration is Home Rule! All the other items of the Liberal programme are mere 'springes to catch woodcocks'[224] – mere gabble à la Mrs Bond: 'Dilly! dilly! dilly! come – and be killed!'[225]

Concerning Home Rule, a few more words presently. I may be found fault with if I do not notice a third section of candidates, representatives of the Labour Party.[226]

Hitherto the Labour Party has been but a barely tolerated adjunct to 'the

219 The reference is to Harriet Martineau and Justin McCarthy.
220 At Newcastle in October 1891 the National Liberal Federation had adopted the 'Newcastle Programme', which included Irish Home Rule, disestablishment of the church in Scotland and Wales, local veto, abolition of plural voting, reform of the Lords, shorter Parliaments, employers' liability for industrial accidents, district and parish councils, reform of the land laws and new powers to acquire land for allotments.
221 Joseph Chamberlain's 'Unauthorised Programme' of 1885, pitching for the votes of the newly enfranchised agricultural labourers, featured the promise of 'three acres and a cow', very much a descendant of the aspirations of the Chartist Land Plan.
222 Literally 'in the clouds'; hence 'nebulous', 'uncertain'.
223 The king wills it.
224 Shakespeare, *Hamlet*, 1, iii.
225 From the nursery song, 'Oh, what have you got for dinner, Mrs. Bond?'
226 Neither the Labour Party nor even the Independent Labour Party yet existed. Harney is referring to all working-class MPs – and complains about their affiliation to the Liberal Party.

great Liberal party'. That Mr Burt and the other miners' members will be re-elected, I do not doubt. There are a few other candidates, representing the New Trades Unionism. The election of the chief of these candidates, John Burns, seems almost certain. I think that Mr Burns, and Messrs Tillett, Mann, and others, should be in Parliament, so that their practical knowledge may be utilised in the discussion of measures directly affecting the welfare of the working classes. But while I think John Burns should be in Parliament, I cannot rejoice that he will enter as a member of the Labour Party. We have too many parties already. Party spirit is one of the prime curses of the land. Parliament should be composed of men representing the Commonweal, not delegates of class or party. Moreover, as far as we have revelations of the aims of the Labour Party, the prospect is not exhilarating. I fear very gross tyranny is more than possible under a 'Labour' regime. I must name another objection. If I am not misinformed, Mr Burns, if elected, will owe his election in some measure to the Irish vote, in return, I assume, for a pledge to vote for Home Rule. That is to say, Mr Burns will enter Parliament to add one vote more in support of a scheme which can only result in rekindling disorder in Ireland, causing infinite trouble to Great Britain, and very likely eventuating in the disintegration of the United Kingdom and imperilling the existence of the Empire. It is nothing to the purpose to tell me that it is not for the sake of a seat in Parliament that Mr Burns bids for the Irish vote, but because he honestly believes in Home Rule as a measure of justice and pacification. I will not dispute his honesty, but I will his judgment. A public, as a private, man should be honest before all things; but something in addition to honesty is needed to make an efficient legislator. A man meddling with medicines might in all honesty poison his dearest friend, his beloved child. The skill of the trained practitioner as well as the honesty of the man is needed in practising the medical art. Honesty! Why, I have no doubt of the honesty of the great mass of the Gladstonians. What then? As Pierre says –

> Honest men
> Are the soft easy cushions on which
> Rogues repose and fatten![227]

Home Rule! I have said over and over again, and I repeat it, let it be shown that the Irish are unanimous, or anything like unanimous, in desiring separation from Britain, I will say, Let them go. Let them show that they are as unanimous as were the Greeks against the Turks, the Italians against the

---

227 Thomas Otway, *Venice Preserved.*

Austrians, and our own kith and kin in the 13 provinces against England, and, if I have vote or voice, it shall be given for separation. That separation would not alarm me. With the 'brass band'[228] turned out of Parliament, and every Irishman who would not give his allegiance to this country sent back to his own, England would be none the poorer, none the worse – in peace. In time of war, if war came and it was found that Ireland was to be made a point d'appui against Britain, the remedy, the safeguard against that danger, would be short, sharp, and decisive.

But the Irish are not unanimous. The party name of 'Nationalist' is an absurdity. Always in tribal discord, there are now at least two nations (if the term is at all allowable) in Ireland. It is the larger of these sections for whose exclusive benefit Home Rule is proposed. Ulster will have nothing to do with it. It will resist a College Green Parliament. 'Well', say the Gladstonians, following their chief, 'that resistance will be put down'. How? By the Queen's forces? Mark these lovers of liberty! It will be a bad day for us all, and not the least for the chiefs of the Liberal Party, when the soil of Ulster is reddened with the blood of Ulstermen shed by the Queen's troops at the dictation of the bitter enemies of this country, its throne, its constitution, and its laws. The rent in Ireland will have its corresponding rent here, and Anarchy will be the direct outcome of the attempt to enforce Home Rule.

On a memorable occasion the late Prince Consort observed that Parliamentary institutions were on their trial. Now the working-class electors are on their trial. If they vote to bring about a Gladstonian restoration, and that restoration is effected, they will have voted for the postponement of reforms they profess to have at heart; for, they may rest assured, it will not be in one Parliamentary session, nor by one Parliament, that Home Rule will be enacted. They will have voted for the gratification of Britain's enemies in France, in Russia, in America, wherever Britain has an enemy. In France it will be expected that England will scuttle out of Egypt; in Russia Mr Gladstone's return to office will be hailed as a check to the Triple Alliance[229] and the Tsardom will count upon working with a free hand; in the States the Irish-American conspiracy, demoralised by the split in Ireland, will recover confidence and courage, and recommence its nefarious designs against this country with all its former audacity and fiendish procedure. If the working men vote the Gladstonian ticket, they will have done all in their power to plunge Ireland into fresh disorders, and will have voted to accentuate our own lamentable divisions. The choice is simple: Union and Progress, or Disintegration and Anarchy.

2 July 1892

228 The Irish party.
229 The alliance of Germany, Austria-Hungary and Italy in opposition to Russia.

Illusions

'They came like Truth, and disappeared like dreams'. Byron[230]

When I was young, as Coleridge says, the reform and regeneration of the world – at least of this little world of ours called Britain – seemed by no means a labour of Hercules, but comparatively easy of performance and attainment! The prescription to effect the desired cure was simplicity itself. The people were ignorant, suffering under social wrong, and unrepresented in the council of lawmakers. Give them knowledge and recognise their rights as men and citizens, the march of regeneration would be swift and sure; all that was oppressive would be overthrown, and triumphant Justice would take the place of extirpated Wrong. Had it not been said and firmly believed – 'For a people to love Liberty it is sufficient that they know it; to be free, it is sufficient that they will it'?[231]

When I was young!

And now?

When I look around, and seeing what I see, knowing what I know of passing events, I would fain drink of the Lethean stream fabled by poets, that I might forget the past, and be oblivious, or at least indifferent, to the present. That draught will come, and to all in turn; only when it comes the drinker will not be writing letters to the *Weekly Chronicle*.

'Knowledge is power', said Bacon, and, having perfect faith in that aphorism, we of 'the Thirties' strove to make political knowledge free as air. Sixty years ago the newspaper press was fettered by fiscal exactions and tyrannical restrictions, and subject to ferocious prosecutions on the part of the Government. The self-sacrifice, the heroic devotion of a few men, changed all that. The press has enjoyed unrestricted freedom for well nigh fifty years: freedom from the stamp duty, the paper duty, the advertisement duty, and a string of meddlesome and exasperating regulations. We have all that Junius[232] clamoured for, and never beheld. And the result? We have an abundance of penny and even halfpenny newspapers, many of monster size, and continually enlarging. We have in those papers editorial matter that in one day far exceeds the quantity of printed thought given to the public in a month in all the days of the *Freeholder* and the *Craftsman*, and all the rest of

230 In *Child Harold's Pilgrimage*, 4, vi.
231 From Lafayette's presentation of the 'Declaration of the Rights of Man and of the Citizen' to the National Assembly, 11 July 1789.
232 The pseudonymous author of a series of seventy letters published, 1769-72, attacking the ministries of Grafton and North and the personal government of George III. His elegant invective exercised considerable influence over later political and newspaper writing. Sir Philip Francis (1740-1818) is thought most likely to have been 'Junius'.

the pamphleteering periodicals of the reigns of Anne and the early Georges. As regards quality, there can be no question of the high standard of the editorials of *The Times* and *Pall Mall Gazette*, the *Spectator* and *National Observer*,[233] but, somehow, the best writing fails to impart the patriotic earnestness inspired by a Junius or a Cobbett. In addition to the daily journals we have a multitude of publications weekly or more frequently published, to enumerate which would require a catalogue. Reading must be incessant and universal. Every week some new publication is launched, and nearly all the ventures appear to pay. The railway stalls are weighed down with what to a great extent is the merest printed 'rubbidge'; but all is eagerly devoured by insatiable readers, with this striking result – apparently the more reading the less thinking; and the consequent deterioration of public spirit, and well nigh the absolute death of patriotism. When daily newspapers were seven pence, weeklies from sixpence to a shilling, *Cobbett's Register* fourteen pence, and only unstamped publications like Hetherington's *Poor Man's Guardian*, could be had for a penny, said *Guardian* not being above one-fourth of the size of the penny 'rubbidge' now on the stalls; then the middle classes were not devoid of public spirit, and at least the elite of the working men had an ideal beyond and above that which is now presented to them by the bog lights of cheap and nasty journalism.

Seventy years ago, the toilers in mills, factories, and workshops, in mines and on shipboard, in town and in country, were absolutely at the mercy of the capitalists; and the law provided so many snares and pitfalls to entrap would-be unionists that no effective labour organisations were then possible. All lovers of freedom and justice rejoiced when the first successful breach was made in the old and tyrannical Combination Laws, and all such have rejoiced at the further successful efforts in the same direction, until at length, and for a number of years, working men have come to enjoy perfect liberty to combine for self-protection. But those who rejoiced, and who are still living, must now mourn over the gross abuse of that liberty. The ever-recurring strikes, in addition to the personal suffering they cause, are assuredly undermining the country's manufacturing and commercial supremacy; and perseverance in such a cause must entail national ruin. The method of conducting strikes is to be strongly deprecated. Picketing is as gross tyranny as Irish boycotting, and should never have been permitted.[234] The outrages in the late strike in the county of Durham were most reprehensible. Their recurrence in the greater strike of the Miners'

---

233 Conservative newspaper, formerly *Scots Observer*, published as *National Observer*, 1888-97, and edited by W.E. Henley, 1889-93.
234 Peaceful picketing had been legalised in 1875 by the Conservatives.

Federation[235] has already commenced, and may be expected to be repeated on a greater scale, at least over a much wider territory. It is not necessary to discuss the conduct of the employers; their demands may have been unwarranted, and calling for resistance; but the leaders of the Federation have outlawed their own clients by refusing in advance to submit the question at issue to arbitration; and, worse, by calling out numbers of miners who were not under any notice of reduction, and who, therefore, were without the specified grievance on account of which the great strike was proclaimed. That men so ordered slavishly obeyed, abandoning their work without any justification, shows the degradation to which the new Trades Union tyranny has succeeded in reducing its abject vassals. If the strike lasts two months, and it may continue double that time, thousands and tens of thousands of other workers in iron, in glass, in pottery, in textile goods, in short, manufactures generally, must be deprived of employment and be reduced to pauperism or absolute beggary. I say nothing now of the pressure upon the London poor, who, probably, to the extent of a million souls, always, and in the best of times, suffer from an insufficiency of fuel. The leaders of the strike seem to have entered upon the conflict, or, as more properly termed by themselves, 'war', with as light hearts as that of Monsieur Ollivier[236] previous to the Napoleonic bouleversement of 1870. A four months' struggle, which may be, will certainly cause heavy hearts in many thousands of destitute homes. 'War'! Yes, too much like the wars waged by kings and governments. In such wars the spectacle has been too often witnessed of a belligerent subjecting non-combatants to martial law, burning defenceless villages, and bombarding fortified cities, taking no care to avoid, or even purposely aiming at, hospitals containing hundreds of sick and wounded, and churches in which women and children may have taken refuge; the plea in excuse being that the greater the suffering the sooner the war would end. I suppose the same plea will be urged by the Miners' Federation. Such war, whether waged by kings or agitators, is execrable. The old inscription on Trades Unions banners, 'United to protect; not combined to injure' (if it still exists), should be effaced as no longer applicable, as having now become a grotesque mockery.

I approach, without having the space to do justice to, the most signal

235 This was a national lockout by the coal owners, who were demanding a 25 percent reduction in wages. Beginning on 26 July 1893, it was by far the largest industrial dispute the country had seen. Gladstone finally approached both sides, suggesting a conference chaired by the Earl of Rosebery, the Foreign Secretary. Agreement was reached at the first session – on 17 November.
236 Emile Ollivier was Napoleon III's prime minister at the outbreak of the Franco-Prussian War.

example of 'hopes laid waste' as presented by the popular exercise of the suffrage – the touchstone, as was admitted in advance, testing the capacity of the working classes for self-government and the compatibility of democratic institutions with the safety and life of the nation. Has the success of the experiment – fondly hoped for and believed in by honest advocates of the democratic suffrage – been realised? I trow not. True, popular sovereignty is still young, and there may yet be such a chance as will justify and confirm the bright anticipations of fifty or sixty years ago. But to my vision the prospect is not hopeful; the outlook is gloomy in the extreme. How assured we felt of the glorious results of lifting the working man to the plane of citizenship!

> Fierce in his eye the fire of valour burns,
> And as the slave departs, the man returns.[237]

Vanity of vanities! The new electorate is largely composed of slaves of the Caucus, dupes of professional politicians, and credulous worshippers of inflated vanity and unscrupulous ambition. Admitting that deception was largely and too successfully practised in the last General Election, events since then should have corrected the mistakes and follies of a year ago. A people loving liberty, and determined to be and remain free, would have risen as one man against the imposition of the 'gag'[238] in Parliament and the monstrous betrayal of the country by making the Irish members masters of Britain. There is no such uprising at present – whatever the future may witness. Even the members of Parliament mainly elected by working-class votes are content to be numbered with 'the gang of gaggers', and, voting Irish Home Rule, have voted, at the dictation of the Grand Panjandrum,[239] to deprive Britain of Home Rule, placing this Imperial Island, this Mother of Nations, under the heel of a sordid phalanx of agitators steeped in treason, and bound to carry out the mandate of foreign paymasters – the implacable enemies of this country.

We are now at half-past the eleventh hour; there is yet a brief, though very brief, term for reflection and for final patriotic action. The mute subserviency in voting clause after clause of the Gladstone scheme for promoting disintegration and anarchy – three-fourths of which have been voted without discussion – even the shameful voting of the 'gag' may be forgiven, if, at the last moment, some of those who call themselves

---

237 Thomas Campbell, *The Pleasures of Hope*.
238 The Second Irish Home Bill was immensely complex and time-consuming and there was necessarily recourse to the Parliamentary 'guillotine', restricting debate. The procedure was still relatively unfamiliar, only being made permanent in 1887 when the Conservatives had needed to carry their Irish Crimes Bill.
239 Yet another name for Gladstone.

Englishmen or Scotsmen will so far follow the example set by Mr Grenfell[240] as – without resigning their seats – to vote against the third reading of the iniquitous Gladstone scheme. So doing, they will deserve well of their country. Doing otherwise, still voting as the janissaries of the Dictator, and consummating their mute subserviency by participating in an act of treason to the Country, their classification and designation will admit of no question, and they will amply deserve to be treated accordingly.

12 August 1893

Two Periodicals

Two periodical publications claim mention. They widely differ from one another, but both have the now rare merit of calling a spade a spade. Of 'Labour organs', and political broadsheets professing to advocate 'the cause of Labour', there cannot be said to be any lack. Unfortunately, the bog-light shed by the luminaries referred to, but darkens counsel, and is calculated to lead astray. Of another kind is the *Labour Elector* …. This publication, which has existed, on and off, for some years,[241] was originally, and probably still is, conducted by Mr Champion,[242] Labour candidate for South Aberdeen at the last general election. It appears to be now published monthly, price one penny. With its denunciations of 'blacklegs'; and its references – more or less truculent – to the recent Free Labour Congress,[243] I have no sympathy. Surely the right to labour cannot be restricted to trades unionists? No trades union has any more moral right than Kaiser or Autocrat[244] could have to deny the right of any men to labour. The editor of the *Labour Elector* seems to be strenuously striving to form a Labour party really independent of both the great political parties, and especially disassociated from those platform politicians who, masquerading as Labour members and Labour leaders, have shown themselves to be mere traffickers in the votes of the new electorate for the benefit of 'the great Liberal party'. Their imposture is pitilessly exposed by the *Labour Elector*, whether with any prospect of

240 William Grenfell was returned as Liberal MP for Hereford City in 1892; but, unable to support Irish Home Rule, he resigned in 1893. He then sat for the Wycombe division of Buckinghamshire as a Unionist, 1900-05, until raised to the peerage as Baron Desborough.
241 It ran 1888-90. A new series began in 1893.
242 H.H. Champion (1859-1928), publisher and editor, a former artillery officer who had joined the SDF. Intensely antipathetic to the Liberals, he urged the creation of a genuinely independent party of the working class – his outlook was identical to Harney's. In 1894 he emigrated to Australia, where he spent the remainder of his life.
243 This launched the National Free Labour Association, which assisted employers in strikebreaking – particularly by supplying blackleg labour.
244 That is, the German Emperor or Russian Tsar.

opening the eyes of the duped multitude is doubtful, inasmuch as 'the masses' seem to be bent upon illustrating the old couplet:

> Surely the pleasure is as great
> In being cheated, as to cheat.[245]

The *Liberty Review*, weekly … is a new departure, the *Liberty Review* having been, hitherto, issued quarterly. The editor is Mr Frederick Millar,[246] of whose capacity as the wielder of a trenchant pen I recently made mention …. An article on the Great Coal Strike is severely critical. The *Liberty Review* is a sign of the times, a sign of the beginning of the reaction against trades-union tyranny, and the growing and ignoble despotism of the Faddists. I cannot agree with everything in the *Review*, but I acknowledge the need and utility of such an outspoken champion of freedom.

Indeed of both the above-named publications I may say that their perusal is refreshing. They remind me in their plain-speaking of the times of Chartism and 'the Unstamped' and of the famous *Register* of 'that most English of Englishmen', William Cobbett, who, as the editor of the *Liberty Review* reminds his readers, once said, 'Thank God there is a House of Lords!'

9 December 1893

The New Crusade: A Prelude to …?

Mark Twain's *Innocents Abroad* I never read, though, like everyone else, I have heard of it. If contemplating a new and enlarged edition, Mark should have been in Newcastle during Easter week and among the occupants of the gallery in the Lovaine Place Institute, during the sittings of the Independent Labour Conference. Without waiting to consider whether purely personal ambition, or an uneasy desire for notoriety, may have actuated some of the prominent leaders, assuming that all were sincere even to beyond the verge of fanaticism, it is nevertheless difficult to regard the conference as a serious political manifestation. The whole thing is in my eyes a kind of gratuitous imitation of the Salvationist methods of bringing the New Jerusalem down to the earth and set a-going in this workaday world. I could understand that a number of persons should get together with the view of establishing a new religion, or a return to the supposed primitive state of the present prevailing religion. 'Gods must change', and prophets also; and, to limit our

---

245 Samuel Butler, *Hudibras*, Part II, Canto 3.
246 One of the driving forces behind the Liberty and Property Defence League – of which *Liberty Review* was the journal – and secretary after its founder's death in 1914. See also n63.

backward look to the past sixty years, we have seen the wonderful success of Joe Smith and the second of the Caliphs, Brigham Young; and, following the Yankee prophets, we have had, and still have, our own 'General' Booth with his vast array of 'Blood-and-Fire' worshippers. There is also, I believe, in Manchester and elsewhere, a 'Labour Church' – no other than a revival of an old acquaintance, the 'Chartist Church' of the early 'forties', one distinguished pastor of which, I am glad to say, still survives – the Rev Arthur O'Neill of Birmingham, one of the few friends of the late Thomas Cooper to the end of the poet-shoemaker's erratic but very conscientious career. Mr O'Neill, a man of remarkable talent and earnest belief in the simplicity, justice, and righteousness of Christianity's primitive teachings, long adorned a Birmingham pulpit, from which he has now withdrawn to enjoy well-earned repose. If the Independent Labour Conference had been convened to found a new religion, or a new religious organisation under the Pope-dom of Mr Keir Hardie, I could have understood its raison d'être. There is something about the honourable member for South-West Ham which to my fancy smacks strongly of 'General' Booth, and I imagine he would be admirably in place as the generalissimo of a new religious propaganda; whilst, judging by the speeches and other manifestations at the conference, he seems to have already a corps of efficient supporters, needing only the epaulettes or shoulder-straps to blossom forth into full-blown colonels, majors, captains, and lieutenants. With civilian added to these military missionaries, there might be some prospect of Keir Hardie's influence rivalling that of 'General' Booth; and if the two could only be induced to pull together there might be a chance of the millennium arriving some time before Tib's Eve.[247] But to treat the conference as a serious political manifestation is quite another matter. In times of heated political excitement, Wisdom may cry in the streets in vain. But of all the movements inaugurated in this country since the times of Cromwell, no one was ever so carefully designed by its promoters – as the Independent Labour Party – to promote hostility to its aims and to create such bitter opposition as to ensure its failure.

That many of the trades unionists became dissatisfied with the political course of their leaders, in and out of Parliament, during the past few years, was quite natural. Those leaders had shown themselves Gladstonians first and always, and Labour representatives only semi-occasionally. As regards the Parliamentary corps, there was hardly a pin's difference between them. On the very question on which they might have been expected to show some independence of spirit, the most ultra of them were quite as subservient

247 Never.

as the most abject 'item' that ever meekly responded to the crack of the Gladstonian whip. If I mistake not, the members for Battersea, West Ham, and North-West Norfolk[248] went into the Ministerial lobby when such questions as agricultural distress and the devastation of Essex were brought before the Commons, only to be burked by a tyrant majority, to which the Labour members contributed their quota. The member for South-West Ham has of late been more and more separating himself from his Labour colleagues; and whether he will show corresponding independence in the performance of his Parliamentary duties remains to be seen.

But to the Conference. There was a strong majority in favour of changing [the] name from Independent Labour to National Socialist Party. The proposed change was rejected avowedly because it might have injurious consequences in view of the next General Election. Of what avail the rejection of the proposed name when the creed, the thing itself, is openly adopted, avowed, and strenuously 'demanded'? If the aim and end, the ultimate issue of the agitation, is to be the total subversion of present society and the substitution of Collectivist Socialism, in vain will Mr Keir Hardie and his associate fowlers spread their Independent Labour net in sight of the bird they desire to capture and make prey of. No speeches of competing candidates, however eloquent, no manifestos of hostile parties, can be so damaging to the Independent Labour candidates as the simple reprinting, placarding, and distributing of the Norwich Congress Collectivist resolution, and the resolutions and demands formulated at the Newcastle Conference.

I suppose the calculation is that working-class voters are now the majority in general. Given the conversion of that majority to the Socialist programme, then 'Ça Ira,[249] all will go right'. According to the council's annual report, the party has now 35,000 members. According to the speeches made at the conference, of 40,000,000 in the United Kingdom, thirty-five are the prey of five millions. Consequently, all that is wanted to bring Paradise within the reach of all men is the conversion of the 35,000,000 – minus the 35,000 already converted. But it will be answered there is a much quicker way of arriving at the like end, namely, the return to Parliament of from twenty to fifty Independents, who will hold the balance of power. Supposing the two old parties are nearly equal in number, neither having a sweeping majority, the Independents – following the tactics of the late Charles Parnell – will vote with the Gladstonians, or with Conservatives and Unionists, according as they may be able to make the best bargain, or desire to turn any existing

248 Burns, Hardie and Joseph Arch.
249 French Revolutionary song of 1790, its title translating indeed as 'All will go right' – or 'It'll be fine'.

Administration out of office. Pursuing these tactics, they speculate that some fine day the grand Collectivist resolution embodied in law will be enacted, declaring all the means of production – land, capital, mines, factories, shipping, canals, harbours, machinery, implements, etc – national or public property. This grand bouleversement, dwarfing and eclipsing all other revolutions the world has ever yet seen, is not, I believe, expected by the most sanguine to come to pass in less than ten years from the present time; but, meanwhile, a whole series of pioneer measures are confidently expected. For example, a Legal Eight Hours Day applied to every description of labour; free, primary, secondary, and university education; free maintenance for schoolchildren – I suppose maintenance means at least meals and clothing; pensions for workers from the age of fifty; employment for the unemployed on trades-union conditions as to hours and wages; a direct cumulative tax on all incomes exceeding £300 a year; taxation to extinction of all unearned incomes.

The Independent Labour Party should be attractive in 'the City', seeing that, as Yankee speculators say, there must be 'millions in it'! At least so I judge by the recklessness with which schemes were endorsed by the conference involving the expenditure of incalculable millions. In their lavish dealing with millions upon millions, they remind me of the description in *The Course of Time* of Byron's terrific scattering of the thoughts, creeds, feelings, passions, and beliefs of men – even Time, Eternity – which, according to Pollok,[250]

> He tossed about, as tempest-withered leaves;
> Then, smiling, looked upon the wreck he made.

Is there any man outside the Socialist circle and not inside Bedlam or Colney Hatch[251] who believes in the feasibility of such a programme? Suppose the immoral tactics of siding, now with this, then with that party, could possibly eventuate in any such Parliamentary results, to say nothing about the Upper House or the Monarchy being in the way; supposing even both had disappeared, and that the Commons had become a revolutionary convention, have these dreamers reflected that there is something stronger than Parliament, than Government of any kind – Society? Society may be paralysed for a moment, possibly a few months, even a year or two; but who believes it could be lastingly subdued and be forced to submit to the dictation and despotism so cheerfully heralded by the Independent Labour Party?

250 Robert Pollok (1798 -1827), Scottish poet best known for *The Course of Time*, published in the year of his death.
251 Lunatic asylum in Friern Barnet, North London.

The delegates to the Conference have been complimented on the manner of conducting their strange business and amazing performances. I suspect their comparative unanimity and freedom from a brawling spirit was simply owing to the absence of representatives of the other Socialist sections. Among those who were conspicuous by their absence were the Battersea Rienzi and the Norfolk Spartacus,[252] Mr Alderman Ben Tillett, and other Labour leaders; Mr Hyndman, the father of the Socialist Democrats, the recognised leaders of the Marx section,[253] Mr Clarion Blatchford,[254] the Moses of the New Dispensation, and all the choice spirits of Literary Socialism. There were a few past and intending Parliamentary candidates – not including the Bristol Socialist candidate.[255] The only member present, in addition to Mr Keir Hardie, widely known, was Mr Tom Mann. Whether his speeches will help the Independent candidate for Newcastle remains to be seen. Had the above-named and other absentees been present, there would have been 'wigs upon the green'[256] – for if there is any one fact more unquestionable than another in connection with the English Socialists, it is that, much as they detest landlords and bloated capitalists, they detest each other still more. In fact, they rival the good old Christians, say, of two centuries ago, 'hating each other for the love of God'.

Among the performances above referred to, not the least amazing was the membership test – 'I hereby declare myself a Socialist, pledge myself to sever all connection with any other political party, and to vote in the case of local elections as my branch of the Independent Labour Party may determine, and in the case of Parliamentary elections as a conference specially convened for that purpose may decide'. Why they should have boggled at the name for the party of 'National Socialists' when no one can be admitted without first declaring himself a Socialist, is not easy to determine, unless conscious that other sections of Socialists would dispute the title 'National'. I have always, and from its inception, condemned and denounced the Caucus; but the above pledge indicates a still more despotic and unendurable kind of Caucus. The members of the party cling to the name Independents whilst renouncing their independence. They place their voting privilege at the command of delegates and leaders who may be faithful, but who may have been 'squared' by those interested in capturing or, at least, disarming, the

252 Burns and – most improbably, since he was a dedicated Lib-Lab – Arch.
253 The SDF.
254 Robert Blatchford, editor-proprietor of *Clarion*, around which the Clarion Movement developed.
255 H.H. Gore, a Christian Socialist who was narrowly defeated by a Liberal at the East Bristol by-election of March 1895.
256 A fight or brawl.

Labour vote. And the men who subject themselves to the will of a parcel of delegates – and delegates probably wire-pulled by a secret council – farcically call themselves 'Independents'. Such self-stultification might make Heraclitus laugh and Democritus weep,[257] or, as Feargus[258] would have put it in more modern comparison, might make a Quaker kick his grandmother!

'One man, one vote'! Rather one ballot, one slave. To what end all this burlesque of 'Independent' agitation? The prelude – to what? Possibly to the banishment of some Liberal shams and shoy-hoys to the sweets of domestic retirement. So far, so good. Bon voyage! But as to the aims and ends so explicitly put forth by the conference? At the best there can be but one result – bitter disappointment. Should there be any chance of nominal success, the consequences would be still worse. First a period of anarchy, to be followed by strongly established Caesarism. Every man of commonsense can see that the French Socialists are but preparing the way for another Napoleon, though he may not be a Bonaparte. In this country, there are men who, in quest of an impossible millennium by unendurably despotic methods, seem equally bent upon demonstrating the absolute necessity of finding a new Cromwell. In any event, the misguided votaries of the new gospel of 'Independent Labour-cum-Socialism' are naught likely to gather aught more substantial in return for their pains than

> Dead Sea fruits that tempt the eye,
> And turn to ashes on the lips.[259]

27 April 1895

THE PRESS

The Liberty of the Press

'The Liberty of the Press is like the air we breathe; if we have it not, we politically die'. Some such sentiment will, I believe, be found in Junius; but I have no Junius to hand. The verifying may interest the gentlemen on the look-out for errors in quotations, or mistakes in names, titles, etc. Such pastime amuses them, and hurts nobody. Conversely, if the air we breathe is like the liberty of the press, there is wonder that we are living in alarm at the dreaded approach of cholera, to say nothing of the thousand other natural

---

257 Both pre-Socratic Greeks, Heraclitus became known as the 'weeping philosopher' in contrast to Democritus, the 'laughing philosopher'.
258 O'Connor.
259 Thomas Moore, *Lalla Rookh*, 'The Fire-Worshippers', Part 6.

and unnatural ills that flesh is heir to. One can hardly take up any newspaper without finding learned-looking references to germs, bacilli, microbes, and other uncomfortable propagators of disease, supposed to largely have their origin in the air we breathe, as well as in the water we drink. The press is responsible for much moral disease and mental deterioration, arising from the abuse of that liberty which our fathers worked for, fought for, suffered for, and desired as the most precious of all liberties, the preservative, as they believed, of all other liberties. The authors and producers of books have no censorship to fear; the editors and proprietors of newspapers have no government persecutions to contend with. The law of libel is only in defence of private character and personal reputation. The multitude of publications from six shilling quarterlies to halfpenny ephemera is, like the ocean, boundless, endless, fathomless; and as regards the great majority of these publications, though you search 'deeper than e'er plummet sounded',[260] you will fail to find the smallest modicum of commonsense, or the least vestige of that useful knowledge which Lord Brougham and his associates deemed the first of duties to provide for 'the million'. *Tit Bits, Rare Bits, Funny Bits, Snap Shots, Ally Slopers*, etc, are as multitudinous as the plague of frogs in Egypt – 'and the land stank so numerous was the fry'[261] – with the inevitable consequence of the wider and wider spreading of softening of the brain. In Massachusetts they have an institution for the care and treatment of 'idiotic and feeble-minded youth', and travellers on our railways – where I am but seldom – must see how much called for is such an institution in most of our towns, though, as regards London, especially, it may be feared that no building has ever yet been designed, or even thought of, large enough to accommodate the innumerable victims of our cheap periodical literature. I am sorry to add not confined to the immature, but numbering many middle-aged, with the lamentable addition of a large contingent of the softer sex, though that that sex can be any more soft than the male devourers of the typographical hash above referred to, may well be disputed.

In last Saturday's *Weekly Chronicle* appeared an article announcing the approaching demise of the *National Reformer*, long associated with the name, and under the editorship of the late Charles Bradlaugh. I was never an admirer of Mr Bradlaugh's aims and methods, and but rarely saw the publication identified with his name. But this may be conceded that the *National Reformer* appealed to the thinking faculties of its readers, and in ability and fearlessness was as much above the wretched publications in

260 Shakespeare, *The Tempest*, 3, iii
261 William Cowper, *The Task*, Book 2.

general that encumber W.H. Smith and Son's book and news stands as Mont Blanc is to a molehill. It was not to be expected that the *National Reformer* would long survive the decease of its founder, however able his successor in the editorship. The death of an editor or contributor may make no difference in the case of an impersonal journal like *The Times*, but makes all the difference to a journal associated with some pronounced personality, in or out of Parliament. When William Cobbett died, his eldest son attempted to carry on the *Register*; but the attempt signally failed, and after a few weeks of feeble existence, the *Register*, which had so long gridironed leading Whigs, Tories, and sham Radicals, to their great discomfort, but to the nation's gain and amusement, ceased to exist. Such, it might have been foreseen, would necessarily be the fate of the *National Reformer*. Perhaps its existence would have been prolonged for a season under its present management, but for the adverse surrounding circumstances marking the present time.[262] Apparently, the main result of the so-called national education, now approaching the term of the first quarter of a century,[263] has been to create an appetite for printed 'rubbidge' to the almost complete extinction of that thoughtful reading which sustained Cobbett, and which was still existing when the *National Reformer* was launched.[264] In the article already mentioned, the editor of the *Reformer* refers to the general taste for scrappy papers, and 'so we have a multiplication of the snippy, the snappy, the frothy, the flimsy, the entertaining, out of all proportion to the solid, the scholarly, the thoughtful, the educative …. The point of all this is that becomes harder and harder for a journal like the *National Reformer* to pay'. No more need be said. It is doubtful, even had Mr Bradlaugh been still in the land of the living, if he could for long have prevented the submerging of the *Reformer* by the flood of 'the snippy, the snappy, the frothy, and the flimsy'. Robert Owen had strong misgivings as to the sanity of the world. What would he have thought and said if he had lived until now and witnessed the effects of popular education and the triumphs of a free and cheap press!

It is bad enough that the printing-press is employed to supply rubbish by the ton, and many tons' weight, week by week and day by day; but there are some publications of a still viler order. These may mostly be seen in the shop windows of newsvendors in poverty-stricken districts, and where the mental appetite, such as it is, requires to be served with highly-spiced narratives from the police, criminal, and divorce courts, garnished with a

262 The economy was suffering from a sharp downturn of the trade cycle in 1893.
263 The Education Act, 1870, enabled local authorities to institute compulsory elementary education, but not until 1880 did it become universal.
264 In 1860.

profusion of pictures of the most 'outré' character. That these publications do infinite harm in familiarising their ignorant readers with the details of debauchery, plunder, and murder, there can be no doubt ....

23 September 1893

Milton

Milton's 'Plea for the Liberty of Unlicensed Printing'[265] will never be out of date. The press, freed from political shackles, is still liable to be turned from its proper mission to be made the instrument of rich men, or to be the tool of party organisations, or to be overawed by the boycotting tendencies of those who would like to silence all truth but what they conceive to be the truth, who, clamouring for freedom for themselves, would deny like freedom to all not of their class, party, or association ....

.... Truly it may be said, 'Milton, thou should'st be living at this hour; England has need of thee',[266] to help to restore to Englishmen their manhood, and to smite and wither the Jesuitical intriguers and agents of priestcraft at work to turn back the clock of time, to restore superstitious servitude, and to bring England again under the degradation of 'the Babylonian woe'.[267]

13 June 1891

LITERATURE

Byron

The Pilgrim of Eternity, whose fame
Over his living head like heaven is bent,
An early but enduring monument,
Came veiling all the lightnings of his song
In sorrow.

Shelley, 1821[268]

A new *Life* of Byron is an event commanding the attention and exciting the expectations of the admirers and lovers of the great revolutionary Poet of the eighteenth and nineteenth centuries. True, before Byron's name had

265 The sub-title of *Areopagitica.*
266 Wordsworth, 'London, 1802'.
267 Milton, 'Sonnet: On the Late Massacher in Piemont'.
268 *Adonais.*

been heard, the Revolution – which signifies much more than the terrible upheaval commonly designated 'The French Revolution' – had apparently been crushed by the armies of the coalesced Emperors and Kings; but amidst the jubilation of the victors, and the sullen moaning of the vanquished – whose defeat had been too well deserved – there rang out, clear and sonorous, the trumpet voice of a Poet destined to be known – admired and feared, adored and hated – as the Incarnate Spirit of Revolt. Though his birth dates only from the year before that of the fall of the Bastille, though not the adult contemporary of the Titans of the Convention, he had imbibed not so much their principles as their spirit, and at his summons the nations of Europe, re-inspired by Hope, resumed the struggle, shattering the Holy Alliance of Despots, and laying the foundations broad and deep of that Freedom which, though yet far from being fully established, will assuredly be so. And when Mankind shall come to recognise the debt of gratitude owed to the benefactors, heroes, and martyrs who strove to leave the world better than they found it, in one of the loftiest niches in the Temple of Fame's Immortality will proudly stand the glorious figure of Byron.

The new *Life* [*of Lord Byron*, by the Hon Roden Noel] is, on the whole, a pleasant book, yet not altogether what might have been. It is rather a review of the life, than a consecutive satisfactory biography of the great Poet. Yet small as the book is, and to be easily run through in the course of a few hours, it might have been made some pages fewer with no loss, unless those pages had been turned to better account. What is the use, at this time of day, of discussing the relations between Byron and his wife, and trying to account for their mysterious separation? What is the whole pother to us? Even if we could get at 'the rights' of the story, of what use would it be? The 'dull, cold ear of death'[269] of each of the parties concerned is now deaf alike to censure as to praise. If there is to be reconcilement in the grave, or beyond the grave, it is not to be effected by human means; and only the most contemptible of creatures can find pleasure in seeking gratification of their prurient tendencies by searching for proofs of the eccentricities, follies, and sins of those who have passed beyond the bar of mortal responsibility. The author of this volume wishes 'we knew a great deal more of Shakespeare's private life than we do'. I do not share that wish. 'We should probably find a great deal of human nature in him', says our author. No doubt. And it is not improbable that we are much better off without that knowledge. We have Shakespeare's Works. That is enough. If we knew in addition to Byron's works, only that he was born, and died for Greece and Freedom, that would be better than it is. The like may be said of Shelley and Burns and others.

269 Thomas Gray, 'Elegy Written in a Country Churchyard'.

The author of this *Life* also occupies needless space in noticing the hostile animadversions of the Shelleyites in relation to some alleged errors or negligences on the part of Byron. If anything could weaken one's admiration for the author of *Queen Mab* – if the first, certainly not the least of his works[270] – it would be the fanatical exclusiveness of his worshippers. Not content with exalting the author of *The Cenci*, they must needs try to depreciate the author of *Childe Harold*. Why? Shelley himself would certainly not have sanctioned their offensive exclusiveness. The two Poets were fast friends, admired and loved each other in life, and no sacrilegious hand should try to separate them in death – or rather in their immortality. With all fairly constituted minds they will continue to rank together, like 'the Great Twin Brethren who fought so well for Rome'.[271] ....

That the Hon Roden Noel desired to write this *Life* in a spirit of impartiality and justice to his hero, that he has written without fear of Mrs Grundy before his eyes, there can be no question; yet there are, here and there, admissions of the 'candid friend' order that might well have been spared. I would not have had him attempt the impossible performance of presenting Byron as a sort of demigod, or any approach to a 'faultless monster';[272] I would not have had him gloss over the graver faults of the poet nor shrink from condemning acts not defensible; but some absurdities and eccentricities, and I must add regrettable littlenesses, might well have been allowed to sink into oblivion. In the Third Canto of *Don Juan*, Byron ridicules the propensity of biographers to belittle their heroes. After reference to Johnson's not too agreeably drawn picture of Milton, he adds:

> All these are, *certes*, entertaining facts,
> Like Shakespeare's stealing deer, Lord Bacon's bribes;
> Like Titus' youth, and Caesar's earliest acts;
> Like Burns (whom Doctor Currie well describes);
> Like Cromwell's pranks; but although truth exacts
> These amiable descriptions from the scribes
> As most essential to their hero's story,
> They do not much contribute to his glory.

The reprinting of these small matters is like the reprinting of scraps of no merit simply because written by a famous hand. This has been done, I believe, in the case of Shelley; and in Murray's edition of Byron's poems

270 Although not the first of his poems to be written, Queen Mab was the first of Shelley's significant works. It was especially popular with Chartists and other radicals.
271 See n33.
272 John Sheffield, Duke of Buckingham (1648-1721), *Essay on Poetry*.

may be found 'versicles' (they are called) on Castlereagh (and others) which would have been much better omitted. It is not because I have respect for Castlereagh that I would desire their omission; it is from regard for Byron that I would not see his works disfigured by paltry rhymes unworthy of his genius and doing no honour to his name.

Our author recognises Byron's supremacy as the Poet of the Revolution. But he much underestimates *Marino Faliero*; not to be compared as an acting piece with Otway's *Venice Preserv'd*; but as a dramatic poem setting forth the aims of conspirators for the overthrow of an oligarchical despotism of the worst kind, it is a very arsenal of revolutionary weapons and explosives. Of course it would be as foolish to read the sentiments of Bertuccio and Calendaro as Byron's own, as to pretend to identify him with Conrad and Lara,[273] as many of his critics have done; about as rational a conclusion as it would be to make Milton a personal sharer in Satan's defiant hatred, or Shakespeare in the villainy of Iago. It may be acknowledged that, if the ill-fated Doge's speeches are not tedious, they are too lengthy; but the whole poem abounds in brilliant rhetoric devoted to the anathematising of Tyranny and the exaltation of Freedom. Where, for force and beauty, in the whole range of English poetry, can be found anything to excel these magnificent lines:

> We must forget all feelings save the *one* –
> We must resign all passions save our purpose –
> We must behold no object save our country –
> And only look on death as beautiful,
> So that the sacrifice ascend to heaven,
> And draw down freedom on her evermore!

Although Byron was, pre-eminently, the poet of Revolution, he was still more essentially the Poet of Freedom. He was the Poet of Free Thought, by which I mean not any mere tract-and-lecture propaganda, but that free exercise of man's mental powers which refuses to accept gods or kings, superstitions or customs, on the ipse dixit of mere authority. He was an agnostic. How could he be otherwise, looking abroad upon the world, seeing everywhere the triumph of Ahrimanës and the martyrdom of man?[274]

> Well, did'st thou speak, Athena's wisest son,
> All that we know is, nothing can be known.

273 The heroes of *The Corsair* and *Lara* respectively.
274 Winwood Reade had published his remarkable *The Martyrdom of Man*, a universal history for rationalists, in 1872. Ahriman was a Zoroastrian demon and the embodiment of evil, whom Reade believed would be ultimately vanquished.

*****

> Yet let us ponder boldly – 'tis a base
> Abandonment of reason to resign
> Our right of thought, – our last and only place
> Of refuge; – this, at least, shall still be mine.[275]

A Republican, he was not a fanatic. In Greece he showed himself the most practical of all the Philhellenes, and in council was as wise as in battle he would have been valiant had untimely Death postponed the sweep of his scythe and allowed him the opportunity to emulate the heroes whose glory he has interwoven with his song. His death was to the Greeks an immeasurable calamity. He had the fullest conception of true freedom. He would tolerate no usurpation, whether by one or by the many.

> … I wish men to be free
> As much from mobs as kings – from you as me.[276]

Much more might be said, but lack of space forbids. I have not attempted to give any outline of the story told by the Hon Roden Noel; would that more of our honourables and right honourables were as well employed. The book costs but a shilling, and the return will be infinitely beyond a shillingsworth. Well printed on excellent paper, this book – in handy form – possesses one unique feature, a bibliography of the poems of, and works, reviews, articles, etc, etc, relating to the Poet. This bibliography, by Mr John P. Anderson, of the British Museum, is a wonderful compilation, filling 38 elaborated printed pages in double columns. It alone is worth far more than the price charged for the volume. Mr Anderson's work has been admirably executed, and he will have warm thanks of all admirers and lovers of Byron.

I may be pardoned if I adapt Byron's lines about Tasso and apply them to himself:

> Peace to great Byron's injured shade! 'twas his
> In life and death to be the mark where Wrong
> Aim'd with her poison'd arrows; but to miss.
> Oh, victor unsurpassed in modern song!

*****

'The day will come', wrote Mazzini,
when Democracy will remember all that it owes to Byron. England, too,

---

275 Byron, *Childe Harold's Pilgrimage*, 2, vii, and 4, cxxvi.
276 Byron, *Don Juan*, 9, xxv.

will, I hope, one day remember the mission so entirely English which Byron fulfilled on the Continent; and the European role given by him to English literature, and the appreciation and sympathy for England which he awakened among us …. He led the genius of Britain on a pilgrimage through Europe …. I know no more beautiful symbol of the future destiny and mission of Art than the death of Byron in Greece.

✳✳✳✳✳

> Thy name, our charging hosts along,
> Shall be the battle-word!
> To weep would do thy glory wrong,
> Thou shalt not be deplored.[277]

14 June 1890

Primrose Day: Byron and Disraeli

Although the name of the primrose indicates its early appearance, and is spoken of in English poetry as 'merry spring time's harbinger',[278] it may be questioned whether it is not preceded by the daffodil – the snowdrop is rather a pioneer of both than a spring flower. On Good Friday of this year (23 March) I saw thousands of the wild daffodil on the slopes in Kew Gardens. Indeed, in *The Winter's Tale* precedence seems to be claimed for

> Daffodils
> That come before the swallow dares, and take
> The winds of March with beauty.

Be that as it may, the primrose is as welcome as lovely, and seems to attain perfection about the middle of April (perhaps last, and this year, earlier), very conveniently for a certain memorial celebration which next week will witness – very interesting to one half of the political population of 'this realm, this England',[279] though by no means welcome to the other half. To the Bermondsey boomer –

> A primrose by the river's brim
> A yellow primrose is to him,
> And it is nothing more.[280]

277   Byron, 'Thy Days Are Done'.
278 Shakespeare and John Fletcher, *The Two Noble Kinsmen*, 1, i.
279 Shakespeare, *Richard II*, 2, i.
280 Wordsworth, 'Peter Bell', Part 1.

But to another kind of Englishman, truly so, and not merely nominally from the accident of birth, the Primrose on 19 April is very much more; for it recalls a memorable event, the death of Benjamin Disraeli, Earl of Beaconsfield, 13 years ago (how time flies!), in the year 1881.

As I have said before in this journal, the name of Benjamin Disraeli is of special interest to true Englishmen, not so much on account of his exceptional talents and the strange romance of his political career, as on account of the position he so tenaciously and gallantly held in opposition to the party chief,[281] who in the course of the last 13 years has confirmed and fulfilled not only the sinister apprehensions entertained at the beginning of the Eighties, but much more and much worse. In view of what occurred in 1885-86,[282] and what has transpired since, the death of the Earl of Beaconsfield was a loss and a calamity. He was of Jewish descent, and although he had been baptised into the Christian communion, he always upheld the intellectual character of his race, and was disposed to magnify the peculiar qualities which have made a once generally despised and still persecuted people a power in modern society, not to be gainsaid. Born in London, he achieved the highest eminence a British subject can attain to: and so did the ex-chief still with us. But the man of Jewish race, born in London, was a truer Briton than his rival of 'purely Scotch' family, born in Liverpool. The Dirty Little Englanders, the unscrupulous propagandists of anarchy – and the proper ganders they lead – may revile and sneer; but all who love this isle 'encompassed by the inviolate sea',[283] will remember Primrose Day and honour the memory of Benjamin Disraeli.

To me 19 April is of interest mainly in connection with a mightier name, a name owing its fame to none of the arts of the politician, nor associated with those accursed party conflicts which are the country's bane.

No man unless he deliberately sets about long-designed suicide can foresee the date of his own life's ending; and, not foreseeing his own death, Byron could not anticipate that on another 19 April there would depart from this life the eldest son of that Isaac D'Israeli to whom he makes frequent and pleasant reference in his diary, speaking of him as 'that most interesting and researching writer', and to whom, as 'the amiable and ingenious' author of the Calamities and Quarrels of Authors he dedicated his forty pages of 'Some Observations upon an Article in Blackwood's Magazine' (August 1819); but so the Fates willed it. Yet, probably, but few of those who will offer their

281 Gladstone.
282 The understanding reached between the Conservatives and Parnell; the conversion of Gladstone and the bulk of his party to Irish Home Rule; the introduction and defeat of the First Home Rule Bill.
283 From Alfred, Lord Tennyson's dedication of his poetry 'To the Queen'.

floral tributes in Palace Yard, will remember that it was on 19 April that Byron passed away.

Next Thursday will complete the term of seventy years since, at Missolonghi, the great poet drew his last breath, the poet known to his contemporaries as George Gordon, Lord Byron; but now elevated above the passing show of aristocratic distinctions, his Norman blood counts for naught; he is infinitely greater than the progenitor who came over with the Bastard of Falaise,[284] or the remote ancestor whose loyalty to Charles brought him elevation from the rank of knight baronet to that of baron. In the early days of his poetic career the author of *Childe Harold* was hailed as a poet among lords and a lord among poets! That lordship will be his for evermore. Possibly some time in the future the House of Lords will disappear, or no longer occupy the position it has held for ages as part and parcel of the British Constitution; possibly party spite and the juggling fraud of party politicians will obliterate that ancient constituent of the 'three estates of the realm'; but history and literature are not to be so effaced. Even though it should be made penal to accept, assume, or cling to the title of 'Lord', the name of Byron will continue in luminous glory in the firmament of fame as a star of the first magnitude.

In one sense his life was too brief. He illustrated Bulwer Lytton's line (or, rather, Byron's career, no doubt, suggested the line): 'A morn too glowing sets in storm at noon'. His life was too brief for the great work to which he had devoted his last energies and all his worldly means. Had he lived and could he have united the factious Greeks and moulding them into one patriotic phalanx, the independence of Hellas might have been earlier achieved, and the 'untoward event' three years and six months subsequently – the battle of Navarino, in which England helped Russia to destroy the naval strength of Turkey, never since that day restored – might have been averted. As for his fame as a poet, further prolongation of his life was not essential. Like most poets, he wrote too much. Burns was wiser, or more fortunate; not, we may be sure, from forethought, but by accident. There is just enough of his poetry to read and revel in, admire and remember. Dryden and Pope wrote too much. Cowper wrote sufficient. Gray's poetry, by no means voluminous, would have been none the less effective if restricted to the 'Elegy'. Goldsmith wrote enough: *The Traveller* contains some fine passages; but had he written only *The Deserted Village*, he would have written enough for all time. Of the French poets, Béranger, who essayed nothing beyond some simple songs, has the moral certainty of being read as well as remembered with the greatest of his country's poets. Rouget de

284 William the Conqueror.

Lisle, with his one song, his revolutionary hymn, 'La Marseillaise', is surely of earthly immortality, which, perhaps would have been less sure if he had buried his one great composition in a volume or two of poems.

Take any half-dozen or so of Byron's poems – *The Giaour, The Corsair, Lara, Mazeppa, The Prisoner of Chillon*, 'Darkness', 'The Dream', that seem as if they had been written with a pen of lightning – where is to be found their equal among the puling or mouthing strains of our present-day bards? The man whose prejudice or negligence has caused him to neglect perusal of the poems I have named is to be pitied; but the pity is akin to contempt.

I am not writing a biography of Byron, I am not writing a criticism of his poetry, and so I am not called on to examine the faults of the one or the defects of the other. As to the errors and regrettable incidents of his life, I am content to remember Shakespeare's injunction: 'Forbear to judge, for we are sinners all'.[285] If our sins are not those of Byron, let us not be too sure that they are any more excusable. There are those who 'excuse the sins they are inclined to by damning those they have no mind to'.[286] There are those who hold up the victims of a natural appetite abased to scorn and loathing; yet themselves are drunk with fanaticism, or even more odious for their palpable cant and transparent hypocrisy. As for Byron's poetry, I have read quantum suff. of carping criticism and dreary diatribes on his want of form and finish and all that marks the sing-song perfection of the poets of the latter half, and, more especially, the concluding quarter of the nineteenth century; poets who are called 'sweet singers', I suppose, because their flow of verse resembles the '*eau sucre*' supped with seeming relish by our Gallic neighbours. How often have I read the self-satisfied criticism delighting in exposing the incongruity of 'there let him lay'![287] – all the said critics being able to 'lay' being addled eggs. Turning to the opening stanza of the Fourth Canto of *Childe Harold*, I am invited to note the terrible solecism: 'A palace and a prison on each hand' being incorrect! The poet should have said there was a palace on one side of the canal and at one end of the bridge, and a prison on the other side and at the other end; or, that standing midway on the Bridge of Sighs, the traveller might have said there is a palace on one hand and a prison on the other. Sublime criticism! Sublime humbug! But read the twenty stanzas, or thereabouts, relating to Venice, and then say where can be found in descriptive poetry anything to excel their truth, force, and beauty? All the little imperfections discovered by the critics eager to find faults and flaws are forgotten the moment the eye and the mind and the heart rest upon such poetry as the sonnet on Chillon (preceding *The Prisoner*):

285 *2 Henry VI*, 3, iii.
286 Adapted from Samuel Butler, *Hudibras*, Part 1, Canto 1.
287 Byron, *Childe Harold's Pilgrimage*, 4, clxxxi.

Eternal spirit of the chainless mind!
Brightest in dungeons, Liberty! thou art,
For there thy habitation is the heart,-
The heart which love of thee alone can bring;
And when thy sons to fetters are consign'd,-
To fetters, and the damp vault's dayless gloom,
Their country conquers with their martyrdom,
And Freedom's fame finds wings on every wind.
Chillon! thy prison is a holy place,
And thy sad floor an altar; for 't was trod,
Until his very steps have left a trace
Worn, as if thy cold pavement were a sod,
By Bonivard! May none those marks efface!
For they appeal from tyranny to God.

An American writer has said that the above sonnet 'deserves a place in the centre of the Charter of American liberty'. That is, to my thinking, praise not exactly apposite; probably Byron would have smiled at so hyperbolical a compliment; but it may be allowed to stand in contrast to the carpings and reviling of some of Byron's own countrymen.

His countrymen! Hard measure has been dealt to Swift and Sterne, and other masters of the pen who could be named, but the treatment of Byron has far exceeded previous examples of unscrupulous virulence and malignant hatred. It was Byron's loss – save in one important exception – though it was our gain, that he was born an Englishman. Had he been born a native of France, Germany, Italy, or Spain, his compatriots would have known how to pay him honour as we English have not known. He would have made a splendid Hungarian magnate, and the land of the Magyar would have held him in the most exalted regard. The exception above referred to is the fact of Byron's writings being in the English language. That has made his fame much wider known than could have been the case if his verse had been composed in any other European tongue; but the advantage has not been exclusively on the side of the poet. Mazzini and others have certified that – at least outside of Germany – Byron has made more Continental students of English than has any other British poet; in Germany Shakespeare takes the lead. The popularity, the influence of Byron's name and poetry have suffered no decline among Continental nations. His is still a name to conjure with. It has been said that the verdict of foreign nations anticipates that of posterity. Whether in two thousand years the language of the Court of Victoria will have become like that of the Court of Augustus, a 'dead language' (it is to our shame that Latin is not at this day a living language, binding all the European nations together) I do not know, but of this I feel assured: just as we now turn to Horace for glimpses of the life of the Romans in the days of Caesar's successor, and to Juvenal for the like knowledge of Roman life in the days of Domitian, Trajan, and Hadrian, so two thousand years hence will critical enquirers into the life of Scotland in the last quarter of the eighteenth century turn to the poetry of Burns, and for the life of England in the first quarter of the nineteenth century turn to the poetry of Byron. Eliminate from his longest poem all the story of *Don Juan*, and take only the opening and the closing stanzas of each canto, you will have a body of satirical poetry of the first order descriptive of the manners, morals, corruptions, and aspirations of the age, not to be found in any other poet of the time or since that time. Speaking of satire, where is there to be found since the days of Pope anything approaching to the vigour and completeness, the scarifying ridicule and sledgehammer blows of *The Vision of Judgment*?

Byron was, and is, the poet of Freedom, the poet of combat for Freedom; bear witness the clarion-like invocation to Greece in *The Giaour*. 'Clime of the unforgotten brave', preceded by some of the most pathetically beautiful lines in the language, as in the section commencing 'No breath of air to break the wave', and 'he who bent him o'er the dead'. The same spirit breathes throughout *Childe Harold*, and ennobles *Don Juan* – as in 'The Isles of Greece'. And as regards Italy, there should be noted the Fourth Canto of *Childe Harold*, *The Prophecy of Dante*, the 'Ode to Venice', and the sombre resolve of the conspirators in *Marino Faliero*. What of the defects of form? What of such trivialities? As well disparage the sun in the heavens because of its 'spots', unmindful of the splendour and glory shed upon our earth by his matchless light and vivifying rays.

Byron did not die in combat, as he might have done if spared but a few weeks longer. But slain by the malaria of Missilonghi, he died for Greece, no less than if he had fallen sword in hand at the head of his Souliotes[288] charging upon the Turkish entrenchments. He realised the two concluding stanzas of the lines on completing his 36th year:

> If thou regret's thy youth, why live?
> The land of honourable death
> Is here: – up to the field, and give
> Away thy breath!

288 Greek warlike community; irregulars.

> Seek out – less often sought than found –
> A soldier's grave, for thee the best;
> Then look around, and choose thy ground,
> And take thy rest.

He passed away as Cromwell passed, amidst the crash of a thunderstorm. To the Greeks his death was a calamity beyond words to adequately describe, as proved by the official acts of the Greek Government and the universal mourning of the Greek people. Said the *Examiner*:

He was pursuing a career of glory, labouring hand and heart in the purest cause of modern times, on the most illustrious soil in the world. His celebrity as a patriot was bidding fair to rival his reputation as a poet – a rare conjunction of honours.

To the ghoulish crew who ransack the graves of the illustrious dead to find materials for the gratification of their venomous hatred, who 'distort the truth, accumulate the lie, and pile the pyramid of calumny',[289] I commend the words of Samuel Rogers:

> He is now at rest;
> And praise and blame fall on his ear alike,
> Now dull in death. Yes, Byron, thou art gone,
>   .... if in thy life
> Not happy, in thy death thou surely wert,
> Thy wish accomplished: dying in the land
> Where thy young mind had caught ethereal fire,
> Dying in Greece, and in a cause so glorious!
> They in thy train – ah, little did they think
> That they so soon should hear the minute-gun.
> As morning gleam'd on what remain'd of thee,
> Roll o'er the sea, the mountains, numbering
> Thy years of joy and sorrow.
>
>   Thou art gone;
> And he who would assail thee in thy grave,
> Oh, let him pause!

14 April 1894

---

289 Byron, 'Monody on the Death of the Right Hon R.B. Sheridan'.

Burns – and Harney in Dumfries

At first sight it appears to be incongruous and looks unseemly that the admirers of a great poet should celebrate his death. Birth-day celebrations are of ancient date; but death-day celebrations are a recent innovation which we owe, I think, to the French who memorialised the centenary of the death of Rousseau (1778-1878), and that of Voltaire (1778-1878). It is, however, a commendable innovation. There have been nations or tribes who wept at a birth and rejoiced at a death. Sensible people! The birth cannot foretell the future of any one. Shakespeare and Scott, Burns and Byron, as newborn babies were like every other infant – 'mewling and puking in its nurse's arms'.[290] But of the wasted figure in the repose of death – 'the first dark day of nothingness, the last of danger and distress' [291] – it can be pronounced whether the departed had been a success or a failure, had achieved the fame of the few or must share the oblivion of the many. 25 January is, year by year, duly celebrated as the birth-day of Robert Burns; but it is 21 July that sealed his name with the stamp of immortality. 'It may be, Jean', said Burns to his wife, in almost his expiring hours, 'they may think more of me in a hundred years to come!' A prophecy! – amply fulfilled in the July now (as I write) passing away. The Dumfries demonstration must have more than have fulfilled the dying poet's most sanguine anticipations. It is idle to recall the bitterness of Burns's last years in Dumfries, or to comment on the neglect and ungenerous treatment of which he believed himself the victim. The present inhabitants of the Border town cannot be held accountable for the sins – whether of commission or of omission – of their predecessors of over a hundred years ago. It is enough that on the centenary of the poet's death, the 'Queen of the South'[292] performed her part in a right queenly manner.

'And', if, as Byron says, '"Auld Lang Syne" brings Scotland to my view', the Dumfries manifestation in honour of Burns recalls the time when I first saw that town. It was on the last day of 1839 that, leaving Carlisle, crossing the Border, and not tarrying at Annan, I entered Dumfries with a letter of introduction from Dr John Taylor, of Chartist fame, to Mr Johnson, 'writer',[293] and the most active and ardent of the Dumfries Chartists – not, I fear, to his professional advantage. I received a hearty welcome. A windfall in the shape of the unexpected payment of a bill for professional services had stimulated my new-found friend to indulge his natural inclination to

290 Shakespeare, *As You Like It*, 2, vii.
291 Byron, *The Giaour*.
292 Victoria.
293 In Scotland, a lawyer.

hospitality, and in the evening a score of friends sat down to dinner and to 'see the Old Year out and the New Year in'. Among the guests was Mr Robert Burns, the eldest son of the poet, then, for some six or seven years, retired from the Stamp Office and living on a pension. He had a good voice and sang one or two of his father's songs; and, being pressed, one of his own: for he had some talent for verse, though I believe his verses have never been printed. 'The night drave on wi' sangs an' clatter',[294] and there was no lack of hilarity up to 'the wee sma' hours ayont the twal'.[295] I believe I am correct in saying that any personal resemblance of the son to the father was not striking – judged by the portraits of Burns then and since current. A few years subsequently I became acquainted with an illegitimate daughter of the poet, born in Dumfries, but who when I came to know her was living at Pollockshaws, near Glasgow – a matron, mother of a considerable family; an excellent woman, and who was said to have been in her youth the best human likeness of her father. She was long past her youth when I knew her, but judging by the contemporary descriptions and portraits of the poet, I could have no doubt that in the stately figure, somewhat massive features, dark complexion, and dark and brilliant eyes, I beheld – as far as might be in feminine guise – the features, the look of Highland Mary's lover and Jean Armour's husband. She passed away a good many years ago. Her youngest daughter was married to David Wingate, the collier poet. He, too, has been dead some years. Of my Dumfries friends 56 years ago I know of only one survivor, Mr P.M. Gray, long connected with the Press in Dumfries and elsewhere, but who is now an invalid, happily, though, returned to the place of his birth, there to spend the evening of his days, and to finish, I hope, his *History of Nithsdale*, of which, I believe, one volume has appeared, or is ready for the press. Of the men of 1839-40 whom I knew, Mr William McDowall, local editor, and author of a *History of Dumfries*, some poems, etc, passed away only a short time ago. 'But', as Burns says, 'why of death begin a tale?' I was at the time of which I am speaking nearing the completion of my twenty-third year. Having paid my devotions at the Burns Mausoleum, but one of the striking features of that wonderful kirkyard with its almost innumerable monuments and memorials – a veritable city of the dead – having reverently visited the last living home of the poet, I proceeded to carry out my intended pilgrimage to the 'Land of Burns' from the Nith to the Doon. Small matter then whether I walked or rode, the former often from preference.

294 Burns, 'Tam o'Shanter'.
295 Burns, 'Death and Doctor Hornbook'.

O Life! how pleasant is thy morning,
Young Fancy's rays the hills adorning!
Cold-passing Caution's lesson scorning,
                We frisk away,
Like schoolboys, at th'expected warning,
                To joy and play.

We wander there, we wander here,
We eye the rose upon the brier,
Unmindful that the thorn is near,
                Among the leaves;
And though the puny wound appear,
                Short while it grieves.[296]

True, I had another mission in addition to seeing the 'Land of Burns'; but that comes not within the compass of my present theme.

I doubt if any newspaper published north of the Tweed, from the Edinburgh *Scotsman* to *John o' Groat's Journal*, north, and to the *Ecclefechan Echo*, south, more fittingly commemorated the centenary of the death of Burns than did the *Newcastle Daily Chronicle* in its pictorial supplement on 21 July, and by its Dumfries reports, articles, and contributions, in preceding and succeeding issues – largely reproduced in the *Weekly*. Above all, must be noticed the *Chronicle*'s edition of *The Songs of Burns* which will long remain a precious souvenir of the centenary of the poet's death ….

It contains … close upon a hundred songs with accompaniments. The list appropriately begins with 'There was a Lad was born in Kyle', and as appropriately ends with 'Auld Lang Syne'. Between this Alpha and Omega what a wealth of poetic beauty in the form of songs of love, friendship, patriotism, humanity, and humour! If I had room and verge enough – I would not be greedy, I only ask for the entire of this page[297] – how pleasant it would be to indulge in an old man's loquacity on the varied beauties of these delicious songs, to roam, like the honey-bee, from flower to flower of poetic loveliness, culling a stanza here and quoting an entire song there, including 'The Lass o' Ballochmyle', 'Highland Mary', 'Bonnie Jean', 'Mary Morrison', 'My Nannie O!', 'Lassie wi' the Lint-White Locks', 'O lay thy roof in mine, Luve', 'Corn Rigs'; and passing to the more humorous aspects of love, 'O! for ane and twenty, Tam!', 'Last May a braw Wooer', 'Duncan Gray', and 'Tam Glen'. Of love's sorrowful phases I would specially note

296 Burns, 'To J. S****'.
297 This article, very slightly reduced here, occupied 1⅔ columns of a five-column page.

'Ye Banks and Braes o' Bonnie Doon', a more powerful persuasive against unguarded feminine love and man's inhumanity to woman than ever fell from lips of priest or preacher. With this should be coupled 'O! let me in this ae Night' and the admirable answer in refusal of the maiden within. Then pass we to 'Willie Brew'd a Peck o' Maut', 'Scots Wha Hae', and 'A Man's a Man for a' That!' ....

The Songs of Burns are often spoken of as certain to keep his memory perpetually green and flourishing. The critics are right in their estimate of his songs, but wrong if they entertain any misgiving as to the equal vitality and endurance of his other writings. 'The Twa Dogs', containing as it does a vivid picture of the life of the toil-worn peasantry, with a bitter satire on 'Society' in the last quarter of the eighteenth century – here and there, it must be admitted, needlessly coarse – will never lose its interest. 'The Cottar's Saturday Night', though a poem which might have been written by another than the Master's hand, will always and strongly appeal to the domestic virtues and affections. Probably there are ascetics who would like to see 'Scotch Drink' and 'Willie Brew'd a Peck o' Maut', and similar pieces, expurged and withdrawn from the poet's works; but they never will be. Even under a 'Maine Law'[298] were such a monstrosity possible, Scotsmen would rise to resist such an outrage. 'The Holy Fair' and 'Holy Willie's Prayer' with much more to the same effect will be cherished for their unmasking of cant, hypocrisy and sacerdotal tyranny. As to 'Tam o' Shanter' it is unique, a complete and finished production of its kind, which probably no poet but Burns could have conceived and brought to such perfection. The 'Epistles' I class among Burns's best work. The influence of Pope is evident enough, but the form, the sparkling effect, and, above all, their relation, not to statesmen, great wits, or rival authors, but to our common humanity in the generally lowly but lovable persons to whom they were addressed must be allowed to be all Burns's own. The 'Epistles' are full of wit, wisdom, and humour, and are my favourite reading in the works of Burns. Still, all that is said of the superior attraction and universal popularity of the songs must be admitted. 'See how the mighty shrink into a song', wrote Byron. Yes; and mighty or great and brilliant poems become superseded or passed by in favour of some simple song. In France the poems of Victor Hugo will be for long carefully searched and intensely enjoyed by students of poetry, and, I may add, of revolution. But in the memories, on the tongues – books or no books – of the French people, the songs of Béranger will long maintain their supremacy. Be it understood I am not pretending to believe the song the highest form of poetry. I do not. But it is the most attractive, the most

298 An early example of the 'local veto', introduced in Maine in 1851 but repealed in 1856.

acceptable, the most certain to endure.

One secret of Burns's popularity is that he did not write too much; and all that he wrote was marked by brevity. He never fatigues. The reader never looks to the end of a poem or song to see how much more there is to read. Even songs may be made too lengthy and then they fall flat – whatever their merits which would have been visible enough, if their authors had wisely known when to stop. It is often regretted Burns died at 37. 'Look what he did, and how much more he might have done had he lived thirty years longer'. Yes, and his popularity been all the less. He wrote enough for his fame and for our delectation, for we cannot live altogether on Burns; we must have some time for other masters of the divine art.

Reverting to the Dumfries demonstration, I notice that Lord Rosebery[299] laid particular stress upon Burns's patriotic service in raising the Scottish Lowland tongue from the obscurity into which (according to Lord Rosebery) it had fallen from the time of the Union. I see it stated, too, that Lowland Scotch has of late achieved such a commanding position in consequence of the popularity of the 'Kailyard'[300] literature that the English language may possibly find itself superseded by 'braid Scotch' – when, I suppose, Shakespeare and Milton, Gibbon and Macaulay will be translated into the lingo of the Goose-clubs![301] I will begin to believe that when I see the Edinburgh *Scotsman* and the *Glasgow Herald* printed in the vernacular of the Coogate and the Caudlerigs. Without questioning Burns's patriotic adherence to his native tongue, I affirm that he did much better and greater service. He was the first Scotsman since the days of John Knox to rebel against a sacerdotal tyranny only less hateful than that which had afflicted and ruined Spain. Omitting the torture-chamber and the stake, Scottish Calvinism was yet a most grinding tyranny, worse than 'Edward, chains, and slavery'.[302] In his 'Holy Fair', 'Holy Willie's Prayer', the 'Dedication to Gavin Hamilton', and other satirical pieces, the poet raised the slogan of revolt against bigotry and intolerance, and was the first to awaken the Scottish people to a sense of the shameful degradation to which they had been induced to submit under the pretence of 'serving God and keeping his commandments'! The seed sown by Burns surely but slowly bore fruit.

299 Himself Scottish.
300 Literally, 'cabbage-patch', it refers to the sentimental Scots writing of the late-nineteenth century: the obverse of Burns a hundred years earlier and Hugh MacDiarmid in the twentieth century.
301 Very basic friendly societies in which the members paid small sums over several months in order to have a goose for Christmas.
302 Adaptation of Burns, 'Robert Bruce's March to Bannockburn ...' ('Scots, wha hae wi' Wallace bled ...').

It was from twenty to forty years subsequent to his death that men arose to act up to the lessons he had taught them – to assert the freedom of mind, of thought, and expression. Old-time Radicals, Six-Points Chartists, and Parallelogram Owenites dared to set at defiance 'the lads in black'. They were humble men, but they could read and they could think; they were enthusiasts, and, almost without exception, of blameless lives, and they lived down the bitter hostility which met them at the outset and long continued. They were inspired by Burns, dauntless, and, in the end, successful. 'They broke the fetters of usurped control and hewed them link from link'. Even now the Scottish 'Sawbath' is gloomy enough; but it is brightness itself compared with what it was in the days of Burns and even fifty years ago. The old time dominating, inquisitorial, irritating, oppressive power of the priesthood was been signally lessened – thanks, grateful thanks, largely and originally to Robert Burns.

Another great service calls for mention and applause. In his poetry he did more, far more, to bring Englishmen and Scotsmen together as an united people than had ever been done by Royal Proclamation or Act of Parliament. The like may be said of Scott. In his Waverley Novels, as in Burns's poems and songs, there is nothing to feed fat the ancient grudge between the people North and the people South of the Border. Any trifling gibe at England or Englishmen is but rare, and so palpably of the character of a small joke, merely, that it can move Englishmen only to smiles or laughter. Both the poet and the story-teller did a noble work – whether consciously or unconsciously – when they employed their heaven-gifted genius and the ink of their pens to cement the union of those whose fathers had unhappily shed each others' blood at Bannockburn and Flodden Field.

As was to be expected, there was some pro-Robin[303] extravagance in the manifestation at Dumfries. 'The greatest of poets' may be held to be on a par with the outburst of the patriotic Scot in the Edinburgh Theatre, who, on the successful production of Home's *Douglas*, roared out 'Whaur's your Wullie Shakespeare noo?' More wisely at the splendid reception given to the sons of Burns on the banks of the Doon, under the presidency of Professor Wilson ('Christopher North')[304] it was claimed by one of the speakers, I think the Professor, that the Ayrshire bard was fated 'to rival all but Shakespeare's name below'.[305] There can be no objection to hailing Burns as Scotland's greatest poet, if Scotsmen will it; but in exalting the author of

303 That is, Robert (Burns).
304 John Wilson (1785-1854) used the pseudonym of 'Christopher North'. A voluminous contributor to *Blackwood's Magazine* and Professor of Moral Philosophy at Edinburgh.
305 Actually Thomas Campbell in *The Pleasures of Hope* (1799).

'Tam o' Shanter' and the glorious galaxy of songs, it is not necessary to do so in a way which seems to detract from the greatness of the author[306] of *The Lady of the Lake* and *Marmion*, not to speak of the magnificent series of stories which have done certainly no less than the poetry of Burns to make Scottish literature known over all the regions of the earth.

Scotsmen may be excused if on 21 July they showed themselves under the intoxication of their exuberant idolatry of Burns. If they erred, it was on the right side. Better warmth, even to blood-heat, than coldness; better extravagance than indifference. Enough! I repeat the 'Queen of the South' did her work right queenly. Stratford-on-Avon, Westminster Abbey, Cripplegate Church,[307] the solitary grave in the precincts of the Temple Church,[308] the sward 'where Moore lies sleeping from his land afar',[309] the scene of the Elegy in a Country Churchyard, beautiful Newstead and anti-beautiful Hucknall Torkard,[310] beautiful Abbotsford and Melrose,[311] the banks an braes o' bonnie Doon, Mauchline and Mossgiel, and last, not least Dumfries[312] – such spots as these

> Are pilgrim-shrines,
> Shrines to no clime or creed confined –
> The Delphian vales, the Palestines,
> The meccas of the mind.[313]

1 August 1896

Leigh Hunt – and Chartist Imprisonment

To the valuable and popular list of 'Great Writers', Mr Walter Scott has recently added a *Life of Leigh Hunt*, by Cosmo Monkhouse ....

That Leigh Hunt was one of England's great writers cannot be sustained. Still his place in Mr Walter Scott's series may be admitted, partly on account of his own achievements, and partly because of his association with great and eminent names – Byron, Shelley, and Keats; Hazlitt, Lamb, and Carlyle.

306 Sir Walter Scott.
307 Milton is buried there.
308 Of Oliver Goldsmith.
309 The line is by the Irish poet, Denis Florence MacCarthy (1817–82). Moore is buried in Bromham, Wiltshire.
310 Newstead Abbey was Byron's ancestral home; he is buried in the church at Hucknall (Torkard).
311 Both associated with Scott.
312 All with Burns associations.
313 Fitz-Greene Halleck, 'Burns'.

Strictly estimated by the personal incidents of his career, a page of the new biographical dictionary[314] ought fairly to summarise all there is to tell of the life of Leigh Hunt. His imprisonment and his connection with Byron and Shelley in Italy bare the only incidents of first-class interest in the story of his career. He must have had certain engaging traits of character to have enlisted the sympathy of Shelley, the friendship of Hazlitt and other contemporaries, and, at least, the tolerance of Carlyle. But for those items in his favour, and apart from his literary performances, he would appear to have been a good deal of a 'Miss Nancy'[315] sort of man, with a specially lax idea of the duty of self-reliance. It is only fair to add that his natural failings were confirmed and intensified by the silly worship of a coterie of male and female sentimentalists whose foolish adoration might have turned a wiser head than Nature had planted upon Leigh Hunt's shoulders. As a poet, he was really below the second class; not to be ranked with Thomson,[316] Goldsmith, or Gray. If he was not a 'small-beer poet', like the once notorious W.T. Fitzgerald – embalmed in Byron's *English Bards and Scottish Reviewers*, and in *The Rejected Addresses*[317] – his Hippocrene was certainly not Yorkshire Stingo, but, rather, was like unto the questionable beverage sold forty or fifty years ago under the name of 'Intermediate'. Unquestionably his poetry contains some lines of power and more of beauty, and his oft-reprinted 'Abou Ben Adhem' is perfect of its kind. That, however, is but a small affair. It owed its immediate popularity to the fact that it appealed to a sentimental religion and philanthropy just then coming into fashion, as much easier and more agreeable than the rugged realities and stern demands of the creed of Cromwell and Bunyan. It was hailed with rapture by the weaklings who a few years subsequently welcomed the Crystal Place Exhibition as the surety of universal and perpetual peace! 'Abou Ben Adhem' has the merit of extreme brevity, is 'nice' for quotation and recitation, and has done more than any other composition in verse to make the author admired as a poet by readers of *Selections, Beauties*, etc. Leigh Hunt's real power was not in verse, but in poetical prose – as an essayist, or rather gossip. Regarded as a gossip in print, Goodman Hunt is usually delightful, and his fame, if abiding, will rest mainly upon his genial talk in the *Indicator*, the *London Journal*, and similar publications, and his literary contributions in the *Examiner*, the *Spectator*, etc; to which should be added *The Town*, his *Autobiography*, and *Correspondence*. As to his *Autobiography*, which should,

314 The *Dictionary of National Biography* had begun publication in 1885.
315 Very effeminate.
316 James Thomson (1700-48), author of *The Seasons*.
317 Extremely popular and accomplished collection of 1812 of poetic parodies by the brothers James and Horace Smith.

like Thomas Cooper's, have rendered any 'life' unnecessary, it is 'a thing of shreds and patches', a kind of Joseph's Coat of many colours, but is sadly wanting in coherence, clearness, and reliability. It is lengthy without being full; says much, but imparts little – save picturing the idiosyncrasies of the author. Still it is readable, on the whole amusing, and, in so far, interesting.

In the Leigh Hunt coterie he was known as the 'patriot poet'. Of his poetry no more need be said. His patriotism may be classed as of a like character. To his credit he was resolute enough in disdaining compromise when he had to answer for his writing in the *Examiner*; but his patriotism was not of the lifelong and sturdy type of a Milton or a Marvell. His trial for libel on the Prince Regent was the most interesting event of his life. With his brother John he had been publishing the *Examiner*, a politico-literary weekly journal, for some time (1808-1812), when the paper was brought into notoriety and peril by a scathing criticism on the Prince Regent – 'a dandy of fifty', as he appears in Hone's *Political House That Jack Built*. The prince was described in terms that would do no discredit to the objurgatory powers of some of our present halfpenny evening and penny weekly luminaries: 'A violator of his word, a libertine, over head and ears in disgrace, a despiser of domestic ties, the companion of idlers and demireps, a man who has just closed half a century without one single claim on the gratitude of his country or the respect of posterity!' 'Viewed calmly at this distance of time', says Mr Monkhouse,

> the article appears very possible, very true, but also very foolish. It was a deliberate challenge to a prosecution in the then state of the parties and the law .... and, as Mr Saintsbury[318] has pointed out, it would not have been tolerated by the Government of any country at the time,

nor, it may be added, at any date since that time.

The trial took place 9 December 1812. There occurs a strange hiatus in Mr Monkhouse's narrative – not the briefest account of the trial! Henry (afterwards Lord) Brougham had engaged to defend the Hunts: John as printer and publisher, Leigh as editor and writer of the article or 'libel'. Not a word concerning Brougham's speech, which, surely, should have been worth recalling. It is in vain to turn to the *Autobiography*, which is almost as barren, giving two or three minor incidents, such as the demeanour of Lord Ellenborough, but no mention of Brougham. Unluckily my copy of the *Annual Register* for 1812 is three thousand miles away. The result of the trial was that each of the defendants was sentenced to two years'

318 George Saintsbury (1845-1933), widely-read literary scholar and critic.

imprisonment and a fine (each) of five hundred pounds. A severe sentence. The brothers were sent to different prisons. John to Clerkenwell, and Leigh to Horsemonger Lane. No man ever sent to prison came nearer (or perhaps so near) to achieving in realistic form the lines which had quite another meaning for luckless Lovelace:[319]

> Stone walls do not a prison make,
> Nor iron bars a cage,

than did Leigh Hunt. 'At first', says Mr Monkhouse,

> he was lodged in dismal rooms … But soon this severity was relaxed. He was removed to rooms in the infirmary, his wife and children were allowed to share his captivity, and visitors were allowed to be with him until 10 o'clock. The rooms consisted of a ward which had never been used and a smaller room for a bedroom.

He soon effected a remarkable transformation, 'not very providently', he says, 'for I had not yet learned to think of money'. He continues: 'I papered the walls with a trellis of roses; I had the ceiling coloured with clouds and sky; the barred windows I screened with Venetian blinds; and when my bookcases were set up with their busts and flowers, and a pianoforte, perhaps there was not a handsomer room on that side of the water'.[320] Then a yard he turned into a flower garden, with a grass plot, and even trees ….

Here in the gaol his eldest daughter was born. He had troops of friends to visit him. Besides Byron and Moore, there came the Lambs, Hazlitt, Sir John Swinburne, and many more, including Jeremy Bentham. Imagine the great prophet of Utilitarianism playing at battledore and shuttlecock with Leigh Hunt in his prison garden. He continued to write for the *Examiner*, and composed most of *The Story of Rimini* and other poetry in the course of his two years' seclusion. If there was any 'martyrdom', it was, save in the matter of time, very much like that of the Dowager Duchess of Sutherland – a species of rosewater martyrdom.

Another oversight in this narrative. Not a line as to brother John's imprisonment, as to how he fared in Clerkenwell. The *Autobiography* is equally barren. I find not a word of sympathetic reference to John Hunt's weary, two years' incarceration. John Hunt deserved better treatment than that of absolute silence. Whether he was a writer I do not know, but he was the businessman of the *Examiner*, which must soon have foundered

319 Richard Lovelace (1617-57), royalist poet, twice imprisoned in the 1640s.
320 That is, south of the Thames.

had Leigh Hunt been manager as well as editor. John Hunt was an intrepid printer and publisher. In addition to printing *The Vision of Judgment* in the *Liberal,* he shared with Benbow[321] in publishing *Don Juan* (printed by Reynell, a friend of the Hunts) when Murray would have nothing to do with it. I think he was, too, the publisher of an English translation of Voltaire's *Philosophical Dictionary* in six volumes, with other works of an ultra-Liberal character. Of the two brothers Byron seems to have had much the higher opinion of John.

Recalling Leigh Hunt's imprisonment, it is impossible to avoid brief mention of the striking contrast between his treatment and that of the Chartists thirty years subsequently. Let the reader take down from his shelf, or borrow from the Public Library, Thomas Cooper's Autobiography, and note Cooper's first month's experiences in prison, experiences that would have been his lot during the whole term of his sentence had he not, goaded by his natural nervous impetuosity, wrung ameliorations from his gaolers by means that must be classed as violent. If there was any difference in Ernest Jones's treatment, it was still worse, and, I believe, substantially continued to the bitter end. Scores of less known men had to endure the plank bed, the dark and solitary cell, prison garb, coarse and insufficient food, cold, and all the miseries and vilenesses of prison life. A solitary visitor allowed once in three months, a grating between the visitor and the visited, with a turnkey standing by to note every word uttered. No books (but the Bible and religious tracts), no writing materials; and, last refinement of cruelty, permission to petition Parliament and 'the authorities' for some amelioration of treatment sternly refused. A month of Cooper's or Ernest Jones's imprisonment was far worse than Leigh Hunt's two years. Yet the editor of the *Examiner,* was imprisoned under a rank Tory Ministry, admittedly a bad and corrupt Administration, whilst the Chartists suffered mostly under Liberal Ministries and Reform Administrations!

I must forego any lengthy comment on the second leading incident in Leigh Hunt's life: his sojourn in Italy, associated with Byron and Shelley in connection with the ill-fated *Liberal.* That was a foolish enterprise, the most foolish item of which was Leigh Hunt's absurd emigration to Italy, 'bag and baggage', with his wife and seven children! Moore in vain protested, but his previsions – as had previously been the case in connection with Byron's ill-assorted marriage – were amply justified by the event. Shelley was drowned; the *Liberal* did not pay its expenses; Byron with his mind and aspirations turned to the Greek War of Independence, grew tired of

---

321 William Benbow (1784-c.1852), insurrectionary and pornographer, former shoemaker who became a London bookseller and publisher. Author of the famous (and influential) *Grand National Holiday and Congress of the Productive Classes* (1832).

the unfortunate experiment, which was abandoned at the fourth number (one year); and, finally, Hunt returned to England bitterly disappointed and discontented. In 1824, Byron died amidst the swamps of Missolonghi, and in 1828 Leigh Hunt published his one discreditable book, *Lord Byron and Some of His Contemporaries*. The blow aimed at Byron recoiled upon himself, and brought down upon his own head a very cyclone of indignant censure. The *Quarterly* knew how to be unjust; but in its animadversion on Hunt's conduct it was perfectly just. Of all the pelting of the pitiless storm the author of the denounced book must have most keenly felt the shafts of Moore, commencing:

> Next week will be published (as 'Lives' are the rage)
> The whole 'Reminiscences' wondrous and strange,
> Of a small puppy-dog, that liv'd once in the cage
> Of the late noble Lion at the Exeter Change.

But the strongest condemnation of the book is from Leigh Hunt's own hand in his *Autobiography*, his references being of the most humble, apologetic, and pitiable order.

The Liberals or Whigs in office, never very liberal to any one but themselves, were slow to recognise Leigh Hunt's former services. At length he received two grants from the Royal Bounty of £200 each, one from William IV and one from Queen Victoria: windfalls, but of little account in view of Hunt's everlasting impecuniosity. However, he had something more substantial in an allowance of £120 yearly, commencing in 1844, generously provided by the Shelley family, and in 1847 his name was added to the Pension List as recipient of £200 a year. So with the addition of occasional subscriptions, and, it may be assumed, some profits from his published works, his last years were spent in comparative comfort and security.

Born in the village of Southgate (near Enfield), Middlesex, on 19 October 1784, Leigh Hunt died at Hammersmith on 28 August 1859, and was buried in Kensal Green Cemetery. There he is at rest under the benison of his own words. Beneath his bust is inscribed the line from 'Abou Ben Adhem': 'Write me as one who loved his fellow-men'.

This neat and desirable volume is enriched with a copious bibliography of 15 pages, supplied by the practised hand of Mr John P. Anderson of the British Museum, whose head, full of books, must bear a corresponding likeness to the glorious Library where I could be well content to be sentenced to pass the remainder of my days.

3 June 1893

Heinrich Heine – and James Thomson (BV)

My first acquaintance with Heine's work was as far back as some thirty years ago or a little more, when I was editing the *Jersey Independent*. A company of the Royal Artillery was at that time in Fort Regent (as I suppose there is always some such company). I had no acquaintance with the officers proper, but I had with some of the non-commissioned officers, a very intelligent and estimable set of men. At the same time, I became acquainted with James Thomson, the garrison schoolmaster, a quiet, amiable, somewhat melancholy gentleman. I had the pleasure of lending him Carlyle's *Sartor Resartus*, and a few other books. Presently, he much more than repaid my small courtesy by sending a few translations of Heine's shorter poems to the *Independent*. Years passed. I heard of a 'BV' publishing in Mr Bradlaugh's *National Reformer* a weird and remarkable poem, named *The City of Dreadful Night*. Subsequently, that with other poems appeared in a volume, with the real name of the author, James Thomson. Still it did not occur to me that the poet and my old friend of the Jersey garrison were one and the same person, until one day – another or more volumes having appeared – I, taking a look at the new poet's verse, among the books in the Boston Athenæum recently imported from England, I found certain translations from Heine which had appeared some years earlier in the *Jersey Independent*. Recently, rummaging among old letters and papers, I came upon the 'copy' of some of JT's translations, which had been returned to me from the printing office – the blue paper perhaps a little faded, but the writing, in very black ink, as perfect as when sent to the printer. Poor Thomson! His fate was a hard one. He came to be appreciated only when too late. That he had a fellow-feeling with the morbid side of Heine's character as poet was natural. Some of his translations will be found in ... *Poems selected from Heinrich Heine, by Kate Freiligrath Krocker.*

It is meet and pleasant that the daughter of one renowned German poet[322] should employ her talents in bringing home to the English people the works of another renowned poet whose birthplace was that of her father's fatherland. The translations of these selections are by various hands [and include] a translation by James Thomson of the poem entitled 'Where?'

> Where shall once the wanderer weary
> Meet his resting-place and shrine?
> Under palm-trees by the Ganges?
> Under lindens of the Rhine?

322 Ferdinand Freiligrath (1810-76).

Shall I somewhere in the desert
Owe my grave to stranger hands?
Or upon some lonely seashore
Rest at last beneath the sands?

'Tis no matter! God's wide heaven
Must surround me there as here;
And, as death-lamps o'er me swinging,
Night by night the stars burn clear.

I must confess I prefer Heine's prose to his poetry.[323] His verse is too monotonous, too much of harping on one string. I must confess, too, that the woes of poets singing of their cruel or lost loves do not deeply touch me, inasmuch as generally the grief-stricken bards managed to find a good deal of feminine compensation. According to Rosalind, 'men have died from time to time and worms have eaten them, but not for love'.[324] Too sweeping, that; but, in the main, true as regards poets. Heine's everlasting wailing over lost, real or imaginary, loves is unrelieved by the nobler strains embodied in 'Scots Wha Hae', and in Byron's apostrophes to Greece and Liberty. Though elsewhere savagely satirising German potentates and thick-headed despots, one seeks in vain in these selections for any outburst of song with the ring, or approaching to the ring, of the 'Marseillaise'. This is a want which – considering Heine's reputation – is a disappointment, and shows how merely superficial was his occasional lip-service before Freedom's altar. But I must not pursue this theme, on which much might be said. I conclude by warmly recommending this volume ... as affording the English reader unacquainted with German a fair and interesting knowledge of the life and writings of one of the most powerful, and in some respects the most extraordinary, of the chiefs of European literature in the nineteenth century.

3 September 1892

Review of James Thomson (BV), *Biographical and Critical Studies* (London: Bertram Dobell)

Few men have been more unfortunate in their lives than the author of the essays constituting this volume. Pity that he cannot now enjoy the consolation of knowing that the survivors among those who knew him in life honour his memory and are doing their best to atone for the world's

323 Heine was the contemporary poet most admired by Marx ...
324 Shakespeare, *As You Like It*, 4, i.

neglect whilst yet he had to struggle for bread and leave to live. Of these foremost men there foremost stands Mr Bertram Dobell, who a firm believer in Thomson's great qualities as a poet and a critic, is untiring in his efforts to place his deceased friend in his true light before the existing public.

In a brief and modest preface Mr Dobell says:

When publishing, last year, the first collected edition of the poems of James Thomson, I expressed a hope that it might soon be followed by a collection of his prose writings. I hoped then that there would have been a somewhat more general welcome accorded to the poems than has proved to be the case; for, though the zeal of Thomson's admirers leaves nothing to be desired, it must yet be confessed that their number is at present rather limited. It is, moreover, rather unfortunate that to the general public he is still known almost exclusively as the author of The City of Dreadful Night, so that it is difficult to gain a hearing for him except as a poet, notwithstanding the remarkable excellence of his prose writings. It is the desire, however, of his publishers to issue a collected edition of his prose works which shall comprise all that seems to be of permanent value in his remains. Such an edition, if carried out as intended, will extend to four volumes of original matter, and another containing his translations from Leopardi and Novalis. The book now issued is intended to form the first volume of the proposed edition. But it must be understood that it will depend upon the reception of the present volume whether the publication of the remainder is proceeded with.

Whether its sale be large or small, this volume cannot fail to enhance the reputation of James Thomson. It will enhance his reputation with readers familiar with The City of Dreadful Night, and others of his poems, inasmuch as they will see that, if Thomson was a poet, he was not less an able critic and an accomplished writer of the best English prose. But there are readers who have never met with Thomson's poetry, or who have essayed to read The City of Dreadful Night and broken down, repelled by the dreariness of the theme. The names in this volume – Rabelais, Ben Jonson, Shelley, Wilson,[325] Hogg, Browning, etc. – may attract such readers, and, reading, they can hardly fail to be captivated by Thomson's enthusiasm and the force and beauty of his language; and, perhaps, may be induced to seek or turn back to his poems.

No matter who may write, or what may be written about Rabelais, I suspect he will remain an enigma to the great mass of the English-speaking

---

325 That is, 'Christopher North'. See n304.

public. I have heard an auctioneer of books in Boston, US, Bohn's edition of Rabelais being at that moment under the hammer, express his astonishment that anyone cared for such a work. He had glanced at, if not read hundreds of books that had passed through his hands, and had come to be not very 'nice' as regarded the free and special qualities of a good many writers; but he looked upon Rabelais as well-nigh intolerable, and his much lauded work as a filthy extravaganza. For an Englishman or American to be able to appreciate Rabelais, he should be well-nigh as familiar with French as his own mother tongue; and should be fairly well versed in the history of the times in which Rabelais wrote, more especially their ecclesiastical aspect, and be able to understand why such men as Montaigne and Erasmus still held to the Papal Church, though fully alive to the corruption and atrocities of its rule. Considering it was to risk the penalty of death by burning that men dared to speak the truth, Rabelais' ribaldry and buffoonery were the mask and cloak necessary for his protection. In a more recent age, Swift, bent upon satirising European society and governments, and even mankind in general (the 'Yahoos'), had recourse to the fabulous conception of *Gulliver's Travels*, which in its original state is sufficiently Rabelaisian, justifying Pope's couplet:

> Whether thou choose Cervantes' serious air,
> Or laugh and shake in Rabelais' easy chair.

The vivid essay in this volume will do something towards imparting to English readers a clearer understanding and fuller appreciation of Rabelais than hitherto entertained. Saint-Amant,[326] as jolly as Rabelais, is even less known to English readers. Certain personal characteristics would make him as well as his poetry of special interest to Thomson; and hence the charming essay in this volume.

Thomson is the recognised high priest of the worship of Shelley, and even those readers who do not fully share may yet admire his enthusiasm, and wish there had been more anent the author of *Queen Mab* and *Prometheus Unbound*, even if less on one or two other topics. Thomson is to be numbered among Browning's admirers, and I should add interpreters – a much needed addition. I will limit myself to one remark: Where would Burns be today had he supplied his readers with such 'nettle-broth' poetry? A tender and appreciative estimate of William Blake, the mystical poet, will command sympathy. But I am at a loss to understand the space allotted to Garth Wilkinson. Great wits to madness nearly are allied, we know; and

---

326 Antoine Girard Saint-Amant (1594-1661), French poet.

probably the 'divine afflatus' of all poets comprises the insane, more or less. But the line must be drawn somewhere. It is my belief that if, within a circle of twenty miles from Charing Cross as a centre, Mr Dobell visited the several lunatic asylums, if known by the inmates as a publisher, he would be offered any quantity of verse, copyright and all, without fee – quite as good poetry as most of Garth Wilkinson's quoted in the essay on that abnormal genius. That on 'rare Ben Jonson' is almost an epitome of his works, and will afford rare pleasure to most readers. Perhaps the most enjoyable essays are those on Professor Wilson, the famous editor of *Blackwood's Magazine*, and on James Hogg, the Ettrick Shepherd – as wayward a son of the Muses as ever those fair divinities had to look after.

Mainly by his *City of Dreadful Night*, Thomson has earned for himself a title of which he is not likely to be divested. There have been other pessimistic poets, but 'BV' is the acknowledged 'poet of Pessimism'. Yet, reading this volume, and knowing nothing of *The City of Dreadful Night*, the reader might not unnaturally class him as an optimist, even a jolly, or at least joyous optimist. The volume should obtain all the circulation its editor could wish, enabling him to proceed with his desired great and generous undertaking of issuing a complete edition of the works of Thomson in prose, as in poetry.

9 May 1896

Truth in Fiction

According to Mr Walter Besant,[327] whose authority as a successful author and eminent novelist cannot be questioned, 'fiction is the machinery by which people learn everything nowadays'. Whether those who thus learn derive as much profit therefrom as those (or some of those) who 'run the machine', may be open to doubt. Does the intellectual and moral profit of the taught correspond to the pecuniary profit of the teachers? Says Mr Besant,

> When I stated that over fifty people in this country and in America were making more than a thousand a year by literature, my estimate was absolutely derided. We have since then ascertained that hundreds of people are making over a thousand a year by literature of various kinds; at least thirty in this country are making over two thousand, at least six or seven are making over three thousand, and I should say that at least one or two are making this year (1893) not less than four thousand!

327 Later Sir Walter Besant (1836-1901), bestselling novelist and historian.

What would William Cobbett, with his superb contempt for 'the race that write', have said to that? In his day that section was in numbers not more than a free corps company; now, from the captains to the rank-and-file, the whole must constitute an army – or at least sufficiently numerous to add three or four battalions to the national volunteers .... Mr Walter Besant is as large hearted as full brained, as testified by more of his works than *All Sorts and Conditions of Men*;[328] but it may be doubted whether, with all his love for his art, he really believes that the salvation of the world is to be wrought through literature. I suspect that the one, two, three, or four thousand is what the greater number of authors aim at, rather than the world's salvation. Whether from the ever-increasing stream of books, the flood of journals, or the inundations of printed concoctions of demoralising trash – scrappy and slanderous, false and foul – or as to the effect of the whole, I cannot say; but I see no evidence of any increase of solid intelligence and that practical knowledge without which freedom is a fraud and popular franchises only useful to the traders in politics and the traffickers in votes.

I am in no position to dispute Mr Walter Besant's dictum that 'fiction is the machinery by which people learn everything nowadays'. Indeed, I fear it is too nearly correct. If true, ''tis pity; and pity 'tis 'tis true'.[329] I admit the power of well-told fiction from the pen of a Defoe, a Fielding, a Scott, a Dickens, a Thackeray, a George Eliot, and a Charlotte Brontë; but with the great exceptions hinted at, rather than indicated, I must confess myself to be a bad novel reader .... As a rule, the novel does not interest me. Without ranking myself with the good bishop who gravely concluded that *Gulliver's Travels* was a 'pack o' lies', I must acknowledge I regard novel reading in general as an absurd waste of life – of that time which so rapidly leaves us never to return.

3 March 1894

I suppose I lose a great deal by not reading novels; but one thing I do not lose – my time in novel-reading. Noting the names of the authors in fiction whose works constitute one of the attractions – probably to many the chief attraction – of the *Weekly Chronicle*, I have tried two or three times to read chapters of their works in course of weekly publication; but I have soon broken down. I could not feel interested in fictitious joys and sorrows, triumphs and tragedies, when all the world of reality was before me. Yet I think there is nothing of the Gradgrind in my composition; and I fancy I

328 A novel published in 1882 in which an heiress sets up a self-governing co-operative workshop for dressmakers in Stepney.
329 Shakespeare, *Hamlet*, 2, ii.

could read again and revel in *Tom Jones*, *The Vicar of Wakefield*, a dozen of Walter Scott's stories, *Silas Marner*, perhaps half-a-dozen of Dickens's, and two or three of Thackeray's – a little of that author's cynicism going a long way. But with more modern, or, in present slang, 'up-to-date' novels, I have no acquaintance and no wish to have. I am content not to know. If I want tragedy, I can have it in verity and first hand without going far to seek it; and if I want comedy, I need not go to theatre or read novels. I have only to look on the amazing (not always amusing) follies of mankind. I have not a very profound respect or intense regard for Horace Walpole, but he deserves to be held in remembrance if only for his terse and striking view of the World as manifested by its inhabitants: – 'This World is a comedy to those who think, a tragedy to those who feel'. A reflecting man must both think and feel.

[Here intervenes the discussions of *The Little Minister*, by J.M. Barrie, and of Scottish Chartism extracted above.]

Although I do not like three volume, or even one volume, novels, the short story – the briefer, the better – is welcome. And I have no prejudice against Scottish stories, provided they are not more Scotch than Burns or Scott – who did so much toward making us all, from Cornwall to Caithness, one nation … My idea of model Scotch fiction is embodied in the famous and once widely-read stories known as *Wilson's Tales of the Borders*. Nothing sadder since the sorrows of Savage, than the early experiences of the originator of those excellent tales. John Mackay Wilson was born at Tweedmouth in 1804, and was apprenticed to a Berwick printer. Wilson having learnt his trade, was lured, like so many more have been, to the great metropolis in the hope of bettering his position as a working compositor. Alas! he found London in general very like 'stony-hearted' Oxford Street in particular. He failed to obtain work, was nearly starved, and 'homeless amidst a thousand (many thousands) homes' had to sleep as he best could in the open parks. Happily he had the character, the stability, the self-respect, which Savage's companion, Johnson, had, but in which Savage himself was so fatally wanting.[330] Years passed on, and Wilson, after many vicissitudes, slowly and painfully climbing the social ladder, became, in 1832, Editor of the *Berwick Advertiser*; and soon after, in 1834, commenced publishing the *Tales of the Borders*, the first number appearing on 8 November of that year. The *Tales* were issued in weekly numbers, and the last from the hand of Wilson was No.

330 Richard Savage (c.1696-1742), the Grub Street poet whose biography was written by his friend Samuel Johnson.

49. Probably early privations had sown the seeds of premature dissolution, for he died at the age of 31, in October 1835 – dying like Robert Nicoll,[331] all too soon. A death so lamentably premature was a loss to literature; and it is painful to reflect that Wilson was cut off at the moment he was beginning to taste the sweetness of bread which is secure, and to know that his talents were bringing him well-deserved popularity. He was a poet, the author of two dramas: 'The Gowrie Conspiracy', and 'Margaret of Anjou', also of *The Enthusiast and Other Poems.* But his poetical works I have not seen. The *Tales of the Borders* attained an astonishing popularity, and had an immense circulation ….

24 December 1892

SOME AUTOBIOGRAPHICAL FRAGMENTS

On Walter Scott and Bookshops

I consider it a duty, as it is a pleasure, to call attention to the new issue of Sir Walter Scott's works by Messrs Archibald Constable and Co, Westminster. Thousands who have borrowed these delightful books from libraries – the old 'circulating', still represented by the Smith and Mudie firms, and the present Free Public Libraries – must have felt more than a pang of regret that it was not in their power to become the possessors of such treasures. That regret may now be banished. This issue is a reproduction of the author's favourite editions in 48 volumes, with illustrations from the original plates and vignettes …. I can remember the time when – still a boy – I was in the habit of flattening my nose against booksellers' windows in Gracechurch Street and Bishopsgate, looking at the frontispieces and vignettes – here reproduced – laid open to attract purchasers, looking and longing in vain! It is said all things come to him who waits. Doubtful! But I have lived to see this charming edition of Scott's works, recalling days of more than 'sixty years since'. It is as cheap as admirable, and will be a boon to thousands who desire to possess as well as to read the works of the chief and sovereign of all the writers of prose fiction.

10 August 1895

---

331 Robert Nicoll (1814-37), Scottish poet, who died aged 23.

On Reading Robert Southey

It is more than sixty years since I read an early edition of Southey's *Life of Nelson*. Not a schoolbook; it was one of a small library, or collection of books, belonging to a certain school.[332] About two years subsequently the untimely recollections of that book brought me to grief – an incident on which I will say no more at present. My next acquaintance with Southey was through his revolutionary drama of *Wat Tyler*, which had been republished, to the author's deep disgust, by Hone, or Sherwin,[333] and later by Carlile and others. The drama of the Kentish rebel represented Southey's youthful effervescence; his *Life of Nelson* his matured powers. Turning over the leaves of [two] new editions, I find again the charm which fascinated me as a boy.

13 June 1891

On James Watson[334]

[James Watson was] a man of whom I had some knowledge, and for whom I feel much respect. I knew him in his shop in Finsbury, where I bought two of his books ... *Lectures by Frances Wright* and *Lectures or Essays by Robert Dale Owen*. I remember his informing, genial, simplicity of manner; and how instructive, pleasant, and encouraging was his conversation in reference to his books, his experiences, and the questions of the day.

17 April 1897

On Thomas Wakley

Between 1820 and 1860, Thomas Wakley, as medical reformer, founder of the *Lancet*, coroner for Middlesex, and MP for Finsbury, was one of the most famous men of the time. As one of the most advanced of the old-time Radicals, he enjoyed a wide popularity. I remember attending his first nomination on Islington Green.[335] To Thomas Wakley we mainly owe that great advance in civilisation – the abolition of naval and military flogging. He was one of the most genial as well as handsome of men ...

15 May 1897

332 The Royal Naval School, Greenwich.
333 In 1817 W.T. Sherwin had brought out a cheap, bestselling edition; a more expensive version published by William Hone followed with a preface by Hazlitt. Although written in 1794-5, the play had not previously been published.
334 James Watson (1799-1874), London bookseller and rationalist publisher. With Hetherington, Lovett and Cleave prominent in the National Union of the Working Classes and the London Working Men's Association but, unlike them, not a member of the First Chartist Convention.
335 In 1832.

On the War of the Unstamped

All who know Mr Abel Heywood, of Manchester, or who know him by reputation, will congratulate the worthy alderman on the honour recently conferred by the presentation of the city of Manchester....There was a time in Mr Heywood's personal history when the freedom of Manchester, meaning the freedom to be left alone to pursue a calling at once honourable and useful, would have been of practical value; but that freedom he was not permitted to enjoy. There was a public want to be satisfied, and he set himself to supply that want. It was not penny rolls he dealt in, but penny papers. He had just as much right to sell the one as the other. But, included in the reading matter supplied, were certain papers called 'The Unstamped', notably Hetherington's *Poor Man's Guardian*. That weekly being prosecuted for publishing 'news, events, and occurrences', without paying the stamp-tax of fourpence on every copy printed, all who sold it were liable to summary arrest and fine or imprisonment, the maximum being £20, or six months. It was said that some 500 vendors (shopkeepers and hawkers) were imprisoned for the *Guardian* alone, and that the total imprisonments for all the unstamped papers, amounted to as many as 750. Possibly some exaggeration, but that a large number of persons were imprisoned for various terms is unquestionable. Many individuals were imprisoned two, three, or more times, and so the number of convictions would considerably exceed the number of separate persons imprisoned. Subsequently, by the verdict of a special jury and the judgment of Lord Lyndhurst presiding in the Court of Exchequer, the *Poor Man's Guardian* was declared to be a strictly legal publication. Amongst the victims, as they were termed, was Mr Abel Heywood, then 22 years of age. He suffered four months' imprisonment ... I believe I am right in saying that, during his imprisonment, Mr Heywood's then small business was kept alive by the courageous service of enthusiastic volunteers, who, of course, ran the risk of also being imprisoned, among them my old comrade, John West, subsequently one of the brightest and ablest of the Chartist leaders .... To me this crowning incident in the life of Mr Heywood is of more interest than to most men outside of Manchester, for the reason that I have a lively remembrance of the stirring times when Mr Heywood suffered imprisonment. I, too, had the honour of sharing durance vile on account of the *Poor Man's Guardian*, and other unstamped papers, three times before I was twenty years of age; and though the first and second occasions were but brief terms of seclusion, the third exceeded Mr Heywood's by two months – quite long enough to test the pretty poetic sentiment, 'Stone walls do not a prison make, nor iron bars a cage', which is quite true when – you are outside of them. I have not heard that I am likely to receive the freedom of Richmond-cum-Sheen, or of that ancient and more likely locality, Hard Scrabble.[336] When I do hear of that, dear Mr Editor, I will let you know! Meanwhile I expect to find enough to do in guarding, defending, and exercising Freedom of Opinion in the columns of the *Newcastle Weekly Chronicle.*

19 December 1891

On Leaving the *Northern Star*

A correspondent 'who knew the (late) Mr Leno intimately' gives in last Saturday's *Weekly Chronicle* two or three stories as told by the deceased Chartist and Poet. One of these relates to some meeting at the John Street Institute in 1851, when, as is represented, 'the Jonesites and the Harneyites' mustered in opposition to Feargus O'Connor. Let me say I know nothing of 'Harneyites'. Of 'Jonesites' I have no authority to speak. It is not said that I was present, but the inference that I was would be but reasonable. I never heard of, and certainly I was not present at, any such a meeting. About that time I had parted from Mr O'Connor, on differences as to conducting the *Northern Star*, mainly arising out of my too pronounced sympathies with the European revolutionists. I was not so absurd as to seek Mr O'Connor's platform position. It is a pity but that the story had been told in our departed friend's lifetime; in that case, I dare say some simple explanation would have prevented any misunderstanding.

24 November 1894

On David Urquhart and the Foreign Affairs Committees

I had not the pleasure and advantage of personal knowledge of the late Mr David Rule, but from what I knew of him through the press in his representative character as a leading member of the Tyneside Foreign Affairs Committee, I ever esteemed him, and admired his manly, consistent, and unfailing patriotism. I happened to have been present at the inception of the idea of a Foreign Affairs Committee, and may claim to have had something to do with its baptismal name. After the discourse of the late David Urquhart, in the Lecture Room, a number of his listeners accompanied him to the room over Mr Barlow's shop, corner of Nelson Street. It was resolved to form a committee to obtain and circulate

336 An Americanism meaning 'barren or marginal farmland'.

information in subjects connected with the country or the Government's foreign policy, based more especially upon the blue books and national records. There necessarily arose the question of a name. Several names were proposed, but no one seemed to command general assent. A voice from the back seats suggested 'Foreign Affairs Committee', and it was at once adopted. That was my suggestion, but there my connection with the Foreign Affairs Committee ended. I was but a sojourner in Newcastle. Had I been a permanent resident, I would, doubtless, have been a member, though I could never have rivalled the late David Rule in his ardent pursuit of the special knowledge counselled by David Urquhart, nor in the great ability with which he presented incontestable, but not widely popular, conclusions in relation to foreign affairs. I could not follow David Urquhart in all his views, and, perhaps, could not always see eye to eye with his recently deceased disciple. But I honoured David Rule as a true patriot, an able writer and speaker, and an estimable man. I lament his death, but rejoice that his brother George is still with us to utter with voice or pen, when occasion demands, the good word for truth, freedom, and the safety of old England.

6 August 1892

On Editing the *Jersey Independent*

Mr Charlton is curious to know what opinion I had from the beginning of the Secession War. He twice presses me: Did I not, at some period, think the South would succeed? If I had so thought, or so feared, what then? But I have no recollection of any such thought or fear; most certainly I never said, or believed, that Jefferson Davis had made a nation. He says it would not have been any credit to me, or to anyone else living in the North at time, to believe without faltering in the success of the North. The sentence is obscure, but I guess his meaning.[337]

I will, if I can, satisfy Mr Charlton's curiosity. I did not go to the States until May 1863. Whilst still Buchanan was President, from the very inception of the Southern Conspiracy, and the beginning of the Secession War, I was editing the *Jersey Independent* (daily) until 29 November 1862, when I withdrew, because I did hold to one opinion on the side of the North, and found that I must abandon that opinion, or be silent, or withdraw. I chose the last. Twelve volumes of the *Jersey Independent* are in the British Museum; and anyone who chooses to search their columns will find what was my unfaltering course. I had not, I have not, need to make any apology, or get

337 Charlton was a Gladstonian and Gladstone had sympathised with the Confederate Secession.

any well-meaning, but, perhaps, injudicious, friend to suggest qualifications of anything I wrote during the Secession War. I have no wish to obtrude any recital of my own doings upon readers of the *Weekly Chronicle*; but to gratify Mr Charlton's curiosity, I will tell him that, whether defending Victor Hugo and his fellow exiles against the French and insular Imperialists, or urging the tempering of vengeance with mercy in subduing the Indian mutineers, or taking the side of the North against the slaveholders and their allies in this country, or protesting against the insane cry for war in consequence of the *Trent* affair,[338] or pleading for the Poles driven by systematic outrage and massacre into committing themselves to a hopeless struggle,[339] or, lastly, contesting the feudal exactions and oppressions ('Seigniorial Rights') of the Jersey Seigneurs upon their own dunghill – I have no reason to fear the most thorough searching of the record lodged in the British Museum.

12 December 1891

On the Temporary Loss of Use of his Right Hand

Under a cloud from the Valley of the Shadow of Death I lost my pen, or, what was worse, the use of the *penholder*. We have two hands, but with all but exceptional individuals the holding of the pen is limited to the right hand. Whether left-handed persons can also make use of the right in response to ordinary needs, writing included, I do not know. The distress consequent upon complete disablement of the right hand cannot be exaggerated. In taking food, and in all the ordinary everyday requirements, the left hand is but of little use, not of the slightest in writing. Had I been offered any sum on money on condition of inscribing my signature only, in fairly readable form, I could not have availed myself of the offer.

9 May 1891

On Not Writing an Autobiography

I might be charged with being wanting in ordinary courtesy if I refrained from noticing the kindly-intentioned letter of Mr G.A. Joyes in last Saturday's *Weekly Chronicle*. As to an 'Autobiography', I am afraid my reminiscences would be less interesting than my good friends suppose, inasmuch as I could not associate my name with the names of 'great men', whether in the political or the literary world. I never sought such acquaintance; rather I

338 The *Trent* was a British mail steamer boarded in Cuba in 1861 by two Confederate envoys to Europe. It was stopped by a Northern warship and the envoys captured.
339 There was a major Polish insurrection against Russian rule beginning in January 1863.

have shunned it; and so, of course, cannot complain of isolation, obscurity, and neglect. Concerning my private affairs, I am disposed to imitate the reticence of my deceased friend, Mr Samuel Kydd.

11 March 1893

A BIBLIOGRAPHICAL NOTE

The superb biography by A.R. Schoyen, *The Chartist Challenge: A Portrait of George Julian Harney* (London: Heinemann, 1958), continues to be one of the very few first-rate books about Chartism. It is a reduction of Schoyen's doctoral thesis, 'George Julian Harney' (London PhD, 1951), the loss of some footnotes being particularly regrettable.

Schoyen had not been able to trace the letters to Harney that remained in the possession of James Métivier's family and which were edited by his daughter and her husband, along with Harney's correspondence with Engels, as Frank Gees Black and Renee Métivier Black (eds), *The Harney Papers* (Assen: Van Gorcum, 1969). All letters to Harney owned by the family were donated to the British Library as late as 2006.

Over his long life Harney accumulated a substantial personal library of which almost 1,700 titles survive and split three ways over the years. On his death his widow presented 170 books and periodicals to Newcastle upon Tyne Central Library, which was to publish a catalogue of *The Harney Library: List of Books (Mainly Political) Presented by Mr and Mrs G.J. Harney, and Placed in the Reference Department* (1899). The bulk – of around 1,400 titles - found their way to Vanderbilt University, Nashville, Tennessee, as the 'Métivier Collection', described as the 'Gift of Prof. James Métivier, 1919'. The gift continues to be rather mysterious as there was certainly no connection between Harney and this major institution of the American South; but during the First World War Harney's stepson, James Métivier, had served in hospitals in Atlanta, Georgia, and Asheville, North Carolina, and come to know the Alumni Secretary at Vanderbilt. For the editor's preliminary report, see David Goodway, 'The Métivier Collection and the Books of George Julian Harney', *Bulletin of the Society for the Study of Labour History*, no. 49 (Autumn 1984). The Métivier Collection was then fully described in Margaret Hambrick, *A Chartist's Library* (London and New York: Mansell, 1986). The third section of Harney's library, totalling 239 titles and including volumes he had reviewed for the *Newcastle Weekly Chronicle*, frequently with clippings of his articles pasted inside the boards, remained in the family's hands until its donation in 2010-11 to the People's

History Museum, Manchester.

The *Democratic Review* and, as a two-volume set, the *Red Republican* and *Friend of the People* were reprinted in facsimile by Merlin Press in 1968 and 1966 respectively, the latter with a useful introduction by John Saville. Remarkably, neither edition sold out and both remain in print.

The editor's entry on Harney in Joyce M. Bellamy and John Saville (eds), *Dictionary of Labour Biography*, X (Basingstoke and London: Macmillan, 2000), pp. 81-92, has been shamelessly recycled for the bulk of the 'Introduction' to the present volume. It was Saville's commissioning of this article that led him to investigate Harney's *Weekly Chronicle* columns. He was astonished by their quality and has ever since wanted to edit a selection.

David Ryazanov, the great scholar of Marxism and founder-director of the Marx-Engels Institute, Moscow, was naturally aware of Harney's friendship with Engels but also that Harney and W.E. Adams were close; and in consequence the Adams Papers were acquired for the Institute in 1931. See David Saunders, 'The Papers of W.E. Adams (1832-1906)', *Historical Research*, LXXXII, 215 (February 2009).

Schoyen, *The Chartist Challenge*, chap. 11, provides an excellent discussion of Harney's journalism for the *Weekly Chronicle*.

INDEX

Also available from The Merlin Press

G Julian Harney, Editor
DEMOCRATIC REVIEW
A facsimile reprint of a Chartist journal, printed originally in 1849-1850. It provides commentary on contemporary politics in Britain, and on events in Europe after the revolutions of 1848. 222x144 mm. 632 pages
Hardback 978 0 85036 098 1 £30.00

RED REPUBLICAN & FRIEND OF THE PEOPLE
A facsimile Chartist reprint of two newspapers, originally published in 1850-1851, with news, letters and articles on poetry, politics, etc. Introduction by John Saville. 280x213mm. 470 pages
Two volumes in hardback 978 0 85036 096 7 £50.00

Ernest Jones, Editor
NOTES TO THE PEOPLE
A facsimile reprint of a Chartist journal, originally published in 1851-1852, containing fascinating articles on a variety of topics: colonies, historical notes, trade disputes, political polemic. 1032 pages
Two volumes in hardback 978 0 85036 097 4 £50.00

Joan Allen & Owen Ashton, Editors
PAPERS FOR THE PEOPLE:
A Study of the Chartist Press
An original study of the role of the Chartist Press in the campaign for democracy in Victorian Britain, and overseas, it includes a study of the press from 1838 to the late 1850s, it considers the press in England, Scotland, Wales, Ireland, Australia and New Zealand. Almost all of the contributors are well known specialists in the history of Chartism, they write from both innovative and revisionist perspectives. The editors provide set contributions in context and discuss how these essays expand our knowledge of Chartism. Contents: Editors' introduction- Prof Aled G Jones: Chartist Journalism and print culture in Britain 1830-1855, Dr Malcolm Chase: Building identity, building circulation: engraved portraiture and the Northern Star, Prof Owen R Ashton: The Western Vindicator and early Chartism, Prof. W Hamish Fraser: The Chartist Press in Scotland, Dr Glenn Airey: Feargus O'Connor, Ernest Jones and The Labourer, Dr Michael Huggins: Democracy or nationalism? The problems of the Chartist press in Ireland, Prof Edward Royle: The Cause of the People: the People's Charter Union and 'Moral Force' Chartism in 1848, Dr Joan Allen: 'Resurrecting Jerusalem': The late Chartist press in the North East of England, 1852-1859, Dr Paul A Pickering: 'Mercenary Scribblers' and 'Polluted Quills': the Chartist Press in Australia and New Zealand, Index. Eight contemporary engravings- b/w. 233x155 mm; 245 pages
Chartist Studies Series No. 7
Hb 978 0 85036 545 0 £45.00; Pb 978 0 85036 540 5 £15.95

Joan Allen

JOSEPH COWEN AND POPULAR RADICALISM ON TYNESIDE 1829-1900

This is the first full length study of Joseph Cowen, (1829-1900) a newspaper magnate, radical activist and Liberal MP who represented Newcastle from 1874 to 1886. During his political career he drew upon a coalition of support from working class associations, the Irish community and regional interest groups. At home and abroad he championed the cause of the underdog and enjoyed close friendships with Mazzini and Garibaldi, Kossuth of Hungary and the Irish Nationalists. This study breaks new ground by bringing together ethnic and urban studies, and considers the role of the press in building a radical power base. "this highly readable and innovative study makes an important contribution to understanding the dynamics and longevity of 19th century provincial Radicalism." Labour History

4 pages of b/w contemporary illustrations, 255 pages

Hardback 978 0 85036 583 2 £50.00 Paperback 978 0 85036 584 9 £15.95

Malcolm Chase

THE CHARTISTS: PERSPECTIVES AND LEGACIES

Malcolm Chase explores some of the maing channels and byways in the history of Chartism, both in the UK and in the wider world. In particular he considers the place of Chartism within the wider framework of Victorian politics; the Chartist Land Plan; the impact of Canada's 1837-8 rebellions on Chartism; Chartism's endurance in Wales beyond the 1839 Rising; the role of Children in Chartists campaigning; key questions in Chartist historiography; Chartism's impact on the mid-Victorian ethos of 'self-help'; and the workings of parliamentary democracy. *Chartist Studies Series No. 13*

260 pages

Paperback 978 0 85036 625 9 £15.99

www.merlinpress.co.uk

www.ingramcontent.com/pod-product-compliance
Lightning Source LLC
Chambersburg PA
CBHW072129020426
42334CB00018B/1730